MODULE, PROPORTION, SYMMETRY, RHYTHM

VISION + VALUE SERIES

MODULE
PROPORTION
SYMMETRY, RHYTHM

EDITED BY GYORGY KEPES

George Braziller, New York

A Review of Proportion by Rudolf Arnheim is reprinted from
THE JOURNAL OF AESTHETICS AND ART CRITICISM, XIV:1, 1955.

Duality and Synthesis in the Music of Béla Bartók by Ernö Lendvai
is reprinted from THE NEW HUNGARIAN QUARTERLY, III:7, 1962.

Patterns of Growth of Figures: Mathematical Aspects by Stanislaw Ulam
is reprinted from PROCEEDINGS OF SYMPOSIA IN APPLIED MATHEMATICS, XIV:
MATHEMATICAL PROBLEMS IN THE BIOLOGICAL SCIENCES, American Mathematical
Society, 1962.

CONTENTS

When Captain Gulliver visited the Grand Academy of Lagado, he saw "a frame . . . twenty foot square . . . in the middle of the room. The superficies was composed of several bits of wood about the bigness of a die . . . linked together by slender wires . . . covered on every square with paper . . . and on these papers were written all the words of their language . . . The pupils . . . took each of them hold on an iron handle . . . and giving them a sudden turn the whole disposition of the words was entirely changed. . . . The professor showed me several volumes in large folio already collected, of broken sentences . . . and out of those rich materials [he intended] to give the world a complete body of all arts and sciences . . ."

The paradox is old enough. The ridicule is plain, and yet that ambitious professor of Lagado was logically without flaw. More than that, the extension of his method has convinced us today that, just as all our prose might indeed appear from his mindless but modular frame, so our pictures, fabrics, devices, formulae—all knowledge—share the modular nature. The whole even of our world—radiant energy and protean matter, crystals and cells, stars and atoms—all is built of modules, whose identity and simplicity belie the unmatched diversity of the works of man and nature. The world is atomic, which is to say modular; our knowledge is modular as well. All can be counted and listed; our very analysis implies atoms of knowing, as the material itself is atomic. The prodigality of the world is only a prodigality of combination, a richness beyond human grasp contained in the interacting multiplicity of a few modules, but modules which nature has made in very hosts.

The explosive growth of sheer number out of the apparent poverty of combination is hard to grasp. Here is the seat of the paradox. School algebra will quickly show that the letter-frame would probably display one meaningful three-letter word in English—if not Lagadoan—for every few-score randomly-selected squares of wood. Yet to expect to find any single meaningful sentence of the length, say, of the proverb "a stitch in time saves nine" would require not a mere folio or two of the professor's, but a library of folios, well-printed, stored in shelves filling a large university building like the great libraries of Harvard or Berkeley. And the land masses of the earth would have to be covered with such buildings cheek by jowl before you would be sure—barely sure—of reading this one particular sentence. Of course you would find all shorter statements, Himalayas of chaff and gibberish for each pithy $E=mc^2$. Everything would be there, everything brief enough. A vast desert of meaninglessness would surround the oasis of a sentence or two of sense, while a very few longer remarks would be found, in all the languages of Babel. You could not reasonably hope for a meaningful paragraph. The lottery of meaning is an unfair game.

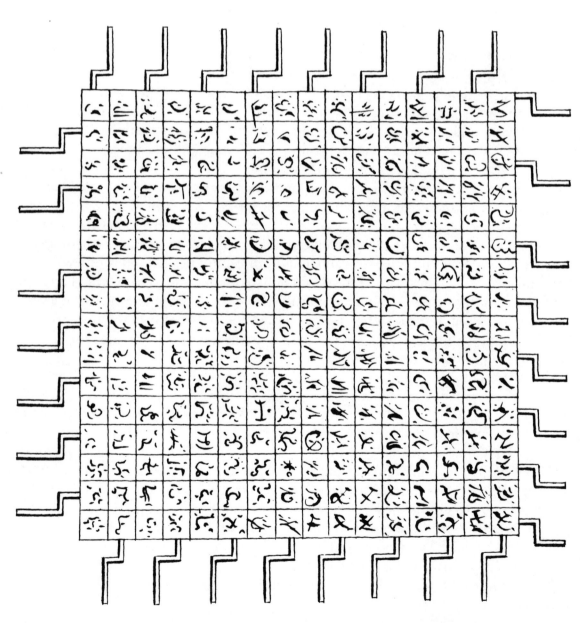

Fig. 1. The book-writing frame of the Grand Academy of Lagado, in the shadow of the flying island of Laputa. Random throws of the cranks would rearrange the characters of this exotic language and allow the logical hope of eventually spelling out all knowledge. (From Jonathan Swift, *Gulliver's Travels*, 1726.)

The philosopher Gottfried Wilhelm von Leibnitz himself, before Swift, gave up atoms and modularity. Even he could not believe the computations he knew how to make. For he argued against Newton's corpuscles that if indeed the world were modular, some repetition must logically occur, and no one—not even a diligent friend of his who searched a whole afternoon over the lawn of a German princess—had ever found two blades of grass which were absolutely identical. He was logically correct, but absurd before the combinatorial facts. The palace lawn was worlds too small. The storyteller Jorge Luis Borges alone among imaginative writers has fully grasped the paradox in his *Library of Babylon*, a universe filled to the ends of space with random books, which house men still lost for want of meaning. The parable is as keen for us as was Lagado for the Royal Society, but it is more soundly reasoned. The world is modular, yet it never repeats, nor does it supply meaning randomly. The possibility of the typewriting apes and the script of *Hamlet* is no more than an arithmetical joke, a game with logic.

為難此圖美：皆向左番風之夕
浦前呈爛爆晴烟低葉紛婀娜縈
柔初觀駛目若零影諦視凝神還
衣磬薄裸但覺書紙如書空惟知
變化縱橫無不可他人之弍已云
雖不能知蘭之飯亦頗二載觀品
氣嚴人肌骨寒手必不置行與坐

Fig. 2. A Chinese text of the calligrapher Chu I-Tsun. Even these diverse characters are in the end built out of strokes of the brush and hence are modular. (In the collection of Cathay Publishers, Shanghai. Reproduced from Chiang Yee, *Chinese Calligraphy,* Cambridge, Mass., Harvard University Press, 1954.)

Our Latin alphabet, and the construction of every expressed meaning out of its few dozen modular bits is the most natural of introductions to the atomic world. For the claim is made that modular atoms build all of matter. But is this enough? Can we extend that claim to all languages, to all knowledge? The Chinese calligrapher might appear to defeat the analysis. His characters do not much repeat; he spins a book, perhaps out of many thousands of distinct characters. The atomic model, the modular device, arises much less readily out of such a literary tradition. Indeed, there has not been a lack of bold speculators to base, on this difference in our alphabets, the strength of atomic ideas in the West, in contrast with the vitality of an organic wholeness in Chinese thought. But the matter is not so simple. The Chinese scholar himself consults a dictionary of radicals, arranged by the number of strokes in the character. The strokes are his alphabet. The objection still persists, for the variety of placement and turn of the stroke of the brush far exceeds the number of letters in the richest alphabet. Yet it is limited. A few widths of stroke, a few turns at the ends, a few lengths of stroke, and the rest is placement. But placement itself is limited. In principle, one imagines there is an infinite choice for where to begin or to slant the stroke within the imaginary square that bounds each character. Of course this is not so; choice among a dozen positions vertically or horizontally will more than suffice. The tiny variations which lie between such a rough net of possibilities represent changes, not in meaning, but in calligraphic style. Our handwriting, too, presents letter variability. So in fact even the character is modular, though the strokes of which it is built, and the pictorial composition they enter, are far more complex than our letters. Chinese text can be rendered in English, or paraphrased by using a numbered list of characters, or redrawn by a division into small squares which remain blank or become blackened, as one copies a map. No, Chinese cannot escape the analysis of the frame, no more than does our Western cursive manuscript hand.

5

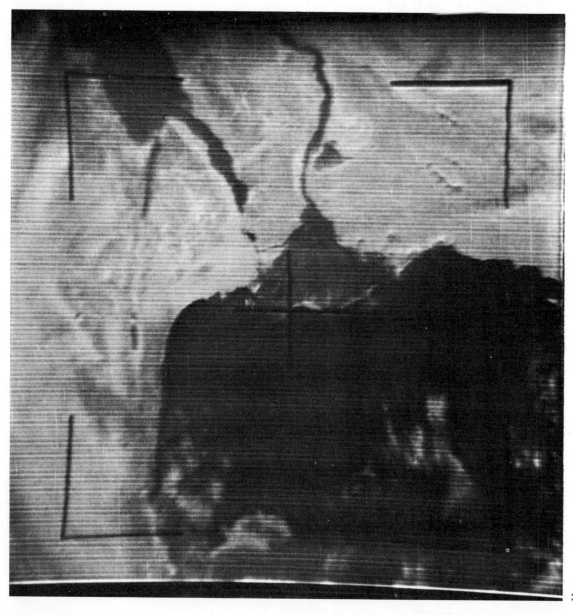

3a

Fig. 3a. On September 22, 1962, a camera flying in orbit in the weather satellite TIROS 5, about seven hundred kilometers above the surface of the eastern Mediterranean, and a hundred kilometers northwest of Alexandria, took this photograph. Some time later the electronic translation of the image was flashed to the ground at Point Mugu, California. This illustration shows the face of a TV screen bearing the result. One can see dark croplands of the Nile delta, the irrigated course of the Nile, the oasis of El Faiyûm, the Suez Canal, and the Dead Sea. The south direction is uppermost in this illustration.

Fig. 3b. This illustration shows the printed output of the computer which spells out exactly the picture seen in Fig. 3a, now translated into numbers and letters. The digits and letters represent thirty-six levels of grayness at each point of the array which forms the picture, 0, 1, 2, . . . A, B, . . . Z, with 0 the darkest and Z the brightest level reproduced. Actually only the upper right quarter of Fig. 3a is reproduced here. The dark Nile can be found flowing numerically onto the print about the seventeenth line from the left. (Photos courtesy Dr. Albert Arking, of the Institute of Space Studies, NASA Goddard Space Flight Center, N.Y.)

```
FEEDDDOEDDDDCDDDCDDDDDCC DDDDDD"DDCCDCDCCDDDDDDEFFEDEDEEEEEFFEEDDDDDDEDDDDDEGEEGFFFFGGGGHHHHHHIIMHJIJKLMNOMJX20
EDGEDEDEDEDDDDCCDDCDDDDDEDD"DDDDCDDDDDCCCDEDEEDEDEDDDDDDFEDEEFFFEFGGGGGHGGGHHHIIIIKIKKMMMIQJO
EBAEDDDDDDDEEDDDCCDDCDCCCDDD"DDDDCCCDDDCCCDDDDDDEDDDDDDDDDCDDDCDDDDDDEEEEEEEEFEFFGFGGHHHIIJKKLMLINJO
DCFEDDEDDEEDDEDDDDDCDCCDCD"DDDDCDCCDDDDDDEDEEEEEEDDDDEDDCDDDDDCEDEEFEEEDDEEFFFGFGGHHHHIIJJKKMLHV70
DFHDDDEFEDEDEDFDFDEDDDCDCCDD"DCDDCDCDDCDDDDDCDDEEEDEDFEFFEEDDDDDDDEDDDEDEEDFEGEEFEEGGGGHHIIIJJKKMNJNOO
EDEDDEEEFFEEDEEEEDDDCDDDCCCCN"DDDDCDDDDCDCDDDCDCDEEEDDEFEEGEFDFEEEEEDFFFEEEEEEEDDDEEEEEFGGGGHGHHIIJJKKLMLHTEO
EFDDDEEEFEEDDFEDEDDDDCDDDCDC"EDDDDDDEDDEDEDDDDDDDDDDDDDEFFCFFFEEDDDEEEEFFEEDDEEEDEDEDEEEFEGFFFGGGGHHIJKLNMJRJO
EFDDEEEFEEEFEEDDFEDDDDDDDDDDD"EDDCDDDDDEDDDDDEDDDDCDDDDEDDGFEEGFEFEEEDFDFFFGEEDDEDEEEEEFEGFFFGGGHIJHJKLMNIPMC
EEEEFGFFEEFFEEFFFFEEDDEDDDDD"DEDDEEEEEEEEEEEEEDEEEEEEEFGFFFFEEEEFGGGEEFFEEFFFFFFGGGGIHIIJJKLMOLHY20
DDDDCFEEDEEFFEFLFDDDDDDCDDD"DDEEEDDDDDDDDDDCDDDCDDDDDDDFEEEFFEFGFGFGEEEEEEEEFFEFEFEEGGGHIIJKLLNLJVAO
EDDEFEFGFFFFFFFFFDDEDDED"DDEEEGGFEDEDEEEFEEDDDLFFFEFEEEEEEGEEFFEFEEFEEEEFFFGFGFHFHHHIIJJMLLOMIW5C
EEEEFFEFFGFFFFFFFFDDEDDDE"EEEEDEFFGGGHOFEEFFFFEFEEEFFFFFGEEEEEEEEEDDFEGGGGGGGFFFFFGFGFGFGGHHGIHIIJKKLLOLIZ2C
FFEFFFFFFGFGHFFFLFFFFFFEEEEE"EEEFEEFFGFEGEFLFFEFEFFFGEEFLFEEEFEEFFGGHHHHHHIIIIIJJKKLMONJS8C
FEFEEFEEGFGHGGFGEGFFGEFEEEE"GGIJHGHGGHFEEEDFFEEFFFGEEEFEEEFFEEDDEEEEEEFFEEFFGGGHHHHFFFFGGGGGHHIIJJLKMONJX70
FEFEEEFFFGGHGHFGFFGGHFFEEEEDE"EDEFEFFGFFEGGCFGFGEGEEFEEEFEEFEEFFFFFFGGGGGFGGGGGGGGFFFGGGGGGGGGHIIIJJLLMPNJY6C
FEEFEEEEEFFEGEFFEFFFGFGFEEDDE"DDDDEEFFFFGFFGFIGEEGEEEEEEEFEEFFFEEFFFFFFGFFFGGGGFGGHFFGGHGHIIIJIKLLOMIUAC
DEEFEFFEEFFGGGGFGGFFFFFLEEE"EEEDDDEEEEEFFFGFGFEEEEFFGFFFFFEEFFGGGFGFHGGHFGGGGGGGGGHHHIIIJJLLNLHY5O
DEDFEFEEEEEFFFFFFEEDFFFEEEC"CCCDCDDDDEDGEFFEEEEFEDDDDDEEEFEFEFEDEEFFFFEEEEEFGFFFFFGFGGGHHHIIIIKKNLIT9C
EGEGEEEFGGGGHFHHFGFUGGGGHFGGF"EEDEEEEEEFFGFGFFEEEEEFEEDFFGFGFGGFGEEEEFFFGGGHGFGGFGFHHGGGGFGGFGGFGGHIIIIJJJJLLMMLVN4C
EFFEEDEEGFFFHFFFFGGGGGGHHGFFF"EEEEEDEEEEFFFFGFFGFEEDEEFFEGGGEEDFEEEEEFFFFIHHIIIIIIJKJKKKKLLMNKIXOC
DEEDDDDEEEFGFGFGFGGGGGGGHFFF"EEEEEDEEFFDFFEEEEEDDDEDDEGGFFFEEEGFFMGHGFGGGGFGGGGGGGHHHIIIIIIJJKKKLMMKIUQ3C
CEGEEEEDEEGFFIHHHGHGGGHHIG"GGGGEEFEEEFFFEEEEDDEDDEEFHGGGGFGEEFFHGNHGMHHHHHGFFFGGGGGGHHHIIIJJJJLKKJJJJJKMHX6C
9CFFFEDDDDEEFEGHHHHGGGGHIM"GEFFFFGFEGEE GEFGEFEDBEDDEDDEGFFFOFFFGFGGHGGFFFFGFGGGFFFGGGGGGFGGHHHHIIIIHJJJJKKKLMMIPKC
9CFGFGEEDDDEEEGFFGFGGHHHH"HGGGGFHGGEFFEEEEEDDDCDDDDEEGGGGFFFFFFFFFFFFFFGGGGFFEGFHFHGGIGHHHHJJKKKKKLMLIPKC
RFGFGGEDDDEEEEEDDDDEGHHGGF"MHHGHGGFGGGHGFFEEECDCDDDDCDEEFGGFFEFGFGFEFEFFFFFGFGGGHGGGGGGHHHIIA6IKJIIIIIIJJKJJJJKKMLGB8C
CFFFGGDDDCDEEEEEDEEDDDFHHHH"HGGGGFGFGGFGFFEEEEDFEFFGFFGFGFHHFFGFFGGGHHHHIIIIKKLLILMMIIIKKLMLHU3C
9FGGFEEDDDHDDDDEEEDDDFGHGG"MGGGGGGFFEEFDCDDDDDDDDDDEGGGFFGFEEFFFEEEFEEFEEMHHINGHGHHHHIHIJJJJJXLMML4Z0C
8DFFFEEDDDCDDDEEFEDEDEEFGH"QGGGFFFFEEFFFHGJIJIIJIIIIIHIHIJIJJKKKJJJJJ9BLKJJJIJJIHHJJJLKLMNKIXOC
6BFGFFDDECEDDEDDDEEFEFEEDDEEF"FHGFFEEEEFFEEDCDDEEEQFFEGHMHFFFEEEEEEEEEEFEEEEFFIIHHIIIJJIJKKJJKKKLMMLIU3OC
68DGGFFFEDEEDDDDDEEFGGGHGGGHHIG"GGGGEKFEEFEEFFFFEEEEDDEDDDEFHGGGGGGGGGGGGHIHJJIIIJKMDKKIIJKIHIJKKKKLKMMNPNISDO
768FGGFFEEEDDDDDDEFEGHHGHGEEEE"IH88T55555443434233444434343343333333334333330TGJIJJJIKLLKJJJJKMKHX4C
858CEFFDECDDCDCDDDDDEFEDDDE"FA44545444445455555555563656565655656056567666666637HIIHIHHIJJKIHHJJKMKHV1C
C66AEEFEEDDEDCDDDDLDEFFDDDD"N"EFEEEEEEFEGEEEEEEEEEFFGFFFFFEFGFFFFFEFGGGGGHHHIA6IKJIIIIIJJKJJJJJKKMLGB8C
875 9DEFEEEDDDDEEEEDEEDDEEE"EFFCKMMKMMKKJJJHIJLMMNMMOONNNONMLMNMOODPPOQNDONMMA6LKJJJIIJJKJJKLKLMLGR6C
C764DEEFEEEDEDDDDDDEDEDEFFEDD"NDEGJIKKIJHHHIHGFHHIIIJKKLLKKLKIJJKJLLLLKKLKKK96LKJJJJIJKKJJKLLLMNLHU4C
EA57CFGFEEFEEEEDEDEOEEEFFEE"DEGGGJIIHHHIHHHGFFFHGJIJIIJIIIIIHIHIJIJJKKKJJJJJ9BLKJJJIJJIHHJJJLKLMMOLHU1C
ED77BEHFEFGEEDEEEDEDEEGEE"EEFGHFIIJIHIJHIGGHGGGIHMGHGIFHIHHFHGGHHHHIJKKIJJJKC6LKIJKIIIHHGHJKMLMNNPMHY7O
EC668FGGFFEEEFFEDEDEEEFFFF"EEEGFHIIJJHJHHHHHHGGHGGGMHGGGGGGHIHJJJJJJKKDBKKIIJIIHIJKKKKLKMMNPNIISDO
D868BFGHGGFEEEFFEEEEEEFF"GF"EEEFFFGHHIHMJJHGIIIIHHHHHGGFGFGFHFHGFFGGGHIIIIJKJLLLKKKIJKIKJLKLKJLLMMNOM4U6C
456A8FFHGFFFEFEEEEFFEEEEFEE"FFEFEDEDEGHHHGGHHIHHHHIGHGFEGEFGGFGGGFGGGHHHIHIJJKA7LKJKKKKLKKKKLMMMNNNMSU5C
7668DGHIHGEFFEEEEEEEEFEEE"EEEEFEE0FFHGGHHMGGFIHIHHGFFEFFGHHGFHGHHHHHIIMH6BKJJJLKJKJJLLLMLMLMLLGIF2C
7779EGFHGGGEEEEDDDEEEDEFEE"EDEEDEDEDDEGGGFGHHHGFIJGGEEGGFEFFGGFHGGGGHHHIIIHGB8JJJIJJJKJJLLLJJLLMJHJJFY20
878 4FGHIIFFFGEEEEEEDEFEFEEE"EEDEEEEDDDDEFFIGHHGFJJJGFFDEFFGFFGGHFHGHIHIJJJGTBKKKIJIJJKKLMLLIKJLLJ4Q0C
9779DGGHIIFFFGHHFGFFGFEEFFFFF"EEDEEFEDFDEDEEEEGFFEEFGGGFDDEDGFFHGFHGHGNIJJIJB6LKIIIIIIIIIKKJJKLMLFR7C
777AEHHHIHHGHGIJIHHFGEFFEEE"DEDEELEDDDDDEDDDEEDDEBADFEFFEGEFGFFGGHHGHIIJHA9JIHGGFFFPGHIIIIJJLMKFS1C
889BEHGIJJJIJKKJHHIHHFEEEE"DEEEEEDEEEEEEEDDEEDEEEEGFFEDEGEGFFFFTHEHHMFHGGGGFFHIBEGEEEGEEGGLJEN8C
678DGHHJJJKKKKKJHHHIGFEEEEFE"EDEGHKHHFEEEEDEDGEGGFFFFFHESGGGFFFHI98JHMGFFFFE6FEFFGHHKIEP5O
67CFHGHHHIJFJKJJGJHHHHGDFEE"EEDFEDEDEDDEDEEEEEEEGFGEEGECBEFEEEFFDDFEFFGGEFHHID6IIHGGFGFEEFEEEGGKJFMFC
59EHHHHHGIIJIJHGIHIGGMFFEE"E*EEEEEEDDEEEEEEEEEDDCDEEEFGEEEFFEGGGHIIJB7KJIHHFEEEEEDEEGGLJEN8C
69DGGHFHGFIJHGGHHIHFGGFEEE"EEEEFEEDEDDEDULEFLD8DEDEE8EFHGGBDDEEEEFEFFFFFFHB8KJJHHGEFEFGHGFFGGKKEFP8C
5AFGFHGHHNHHEEIIJGGIIGEEE"EEFEEEEEEDEDDDDDDEEEEFFEEDEDEFEEEEEEFFFFFGGGA7IJIIHGGGFGHHNILKEM8C
78FFGGFHGHHHIHIJIHHGIIEEEEE"E*EDEDEEREDEEEEEEEEEDDDDDDDEEEEFFEEEEEEEEEEFFGGA6JIHJIHHHIGGGHGHIJMQLEM7C
8CFGIHGGHIGGHHJIHHGHGGEEEEED"DEEEEEEEEEEFEEEEDEEEEEEEDEEEEEEEEEEEDDEEFFGFFFFFEEFGGGB5GGHHIIJJIHIIIJLLNOMGIHO
```

3b

We have reached the stronghold of the position. All written knowledge can be modularly expressed. Consider now the image made by the painter or the photographer. In a land of the TV set, who does not know that somehow an image too can be read off in the simplicity of electrical pulses? The illustrations shown here display the process in detail. A picture—to be sure, a rather coarse dramatic image—is spelled out in ordinary letters and digits. In orbit TIROS flashed to the ground by radio what its cameras saw. The spelled-out picture is recombined into an image. To improve the images by adding the subtlest of visual detail, to represent the most delicate of palettes as well, to present not merely a flat image, but a sculpture in the round, are all merely to demand a numerically greater list of letters from our machine. Since every letter is translatable into a choice of one among a few dozen options, and since a few dozen options can be described in a handful of true-false, on-off, or yes-no choices, it is not hard to prove that every image and piece of knowledge is expressible via the intermediation of a tediously long, bland series of mere on-off decisions. This is the basis of the theory of information on which a point of view towards knowledge more unifying than any other mode of analysis has in the last decades been built. Knowledge itself, and science of course within it, is seen to be modular at base.

How close this is to the structure of eye and brain, the material foundation of sight and of insight, is not yet clear. Certainly the tangled knot of the brain and its ravelling out into hand and eye are woven out of a numerous skein of rather similar neurons. But their complex geometry and their subtle function are still a good deal beyond contemporary understanding. The general view of the information theorist predisposes one to the conviction that not even in the brain, the most complex of known physical systems, will the fundamental simplicity of nature be found wanting. It has been known for years that the behavior of simpler beings, say of the army ant which has a complex enough way of life, is in fact woven again out of a simple modular set of cliché responses, whose "words" are combined of the exigencies of the environment and the stereotyped alphabet of the insect's response. A troop of such ants set moving on a smooth floor can sometimes be caused to form a circle, each ant following the scent of his predecessors in line. The circle will move aimlessly in fatal procession toward nowhere until exhaustion. The situation spells *march;* in the natural environment, the external world varies the command enough, by blurring the signals between ants, to allow a message of behavior more serviceable than a suicidal marathon.

The work of men too has many obvious modularities. The masonry wall and the woven fabric are two of the oldest. How varied are the world's masonry buildings, how diverse the patterns of woven stuffs! yet in each case the modular idea gave the craftsman a small alphabet from which he chose and chose again to yield the mosaic pillars of Erech or the rich, figured cloth of the Peruvian coast. Here it is not knowledge but a material structure which has been synthesized from simple recombining parts. Illustrated on the following pages is a modern and beautiful example of the same idea, far from the craftsmanship of the past, yet remaining in its full debt. This up-to-date example is a style of building computers themselves just adopted by the largest manufacturer of such devices. By its designers, the machine is "written" as a book might be. For letters, they use the individual circuit elements of the electronics trade, transistors, resistors, capacitors, and the like. A major distinction from the literary metaphor is that, unlike our letters, the electronic "letters" have not reached a stable standardization. They are, on the contrary, very much in the process of change, for after all they function for the fast-evolving machine, while the printer's letters must appeal to human eyes, which remain constant. These evolving small components are placed onto the receptive surfaces of small ceramic chips or cards with connections printed in conducting inks to form the words of the text. These cards, of which a large and growing font exists in the factory, are then themselves chosen to be set into racks, in an order and choice which parallels the assembly of sentences. The complete statement of many related sentences is the finished computer.

Shown on the following pages in Figs. 4a–4e is the modular assembly of electronic circuits which yield computing machinery of evolving complexity. All illustrations refer to the IBM System/360 computers. These pictures are best described in analogical terms, comparing the elements shown to elements of the familiar written, or better, printed language. (Photos courtesy International Business Machines Corporation.)

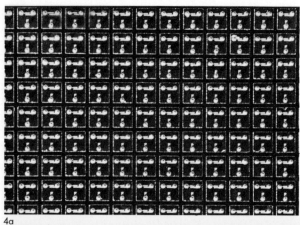

4a. Here is a set of the building blocks, individual identical transistors, in the course of their manufacture. They are not used as a block pattern, but rather one by one. In metaphor, this is the type-founder's shop producing a block of lead type, all one single letter. Each square transistor is about the width of a typewritten period.

4b

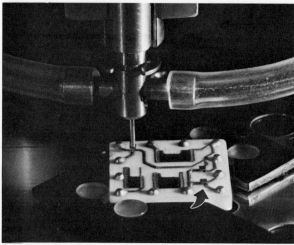

4c

4b. A collection of "letters" broken apart and ready for use. This is like a font of "a's" of a typesetter. An ordinary transistor, like many found in the familiar portable radio, is shown for comparison beside a thimbleful of the miniature modules.

4c. The assembly of "letters" into a meaningful "word." The ceramic tile, about one half inch square, is receiving the proper transistors from an automatic machine. It already bears a screen-printed copper-and-solder circuit pattern. The small thickish square indicated by an arrow is a transistor; the larger dark rectangles are printed resistance elements.

4d. A "word" is sealed into a metal shell, labeled, and inserted into a functional "sentence." The modules are meaningfully interconnected behind the circuit card. Other cards bear six, twelve, twenty-four . . . modules.

4e. The sentences are arranged into a statement of power. The circuit cards are plugged into a connection board to provide the logical operations for a computer's arithmetic processing unit, its memory, or an input-output translating device.

4d

4e

Such a computer spins much sense, mathematical and verbal, out of pulses which forever flow in its modules of small parts. This has seemed strange to many persons, who have only now in seeing it happen come to realize how great a change in quality can stem from a sufficient quantity of intrinsically elementary decisions. It is still passing strange to watch the computer output so well approximate some forms of thought. But the idea that a mere machine could embody repeated meaningful choice is very old, arising not first in the more abstract modes, but in fact in the weaving of cloth, which not merely in metaphor is based on the self-same analytical idea. The next illustration serves as a reminder that the weaver and maker of fabrics was the artificer who first stored information, structure, to be read, not by humans, but by a machine. The simple pattern of cross-stitch instructions suitable for a human embroiderer to read is worth presentation; it seems likely that older versions of such instructions, pricked out on squared paper for the operator of a draw loom making figured cloth, were the direct ancestral strain of the familiar punched card machine-language. Its line of descent runs from the human reader to card-reading looms of the eighteenth-century French silk textile industry, to the very successful Jacquard figure-weaving machine of about 1800, to Babbage's difference engine, to the Hollerith card machines of the United States Census of 1890. It was always easiest for machines to finger and not to gaze at the messages sent them; they still read mainly Braille, for machines were until very lately blind. (The machine which reads the strange figures on your bank check has a magnetic sense of touch, more subtle than that of the machines which read punched cards only; it recognizes the digits by detecting the iron content in the special inks that form them.)

So for artifact, machine and wall, cloth and picture, book and drawing, all the expression of human hand and mind, the modular idea proves itself both as the ground plan of much of our product —of everything expressed graphically—and as an irresistible analytic scheme, capable of measuring knowledge itself as the sum of simpler choices. This point of view, this power of analysis is not more than a generation old. It arose out of an even bolder analysis, now perhaps as old as the century: the quantum physics. Built upon the modular idea, it has won sway over the whole of the universe of physics, save only gravitation.

Let us enter it step by step. Jean-Baptiste Fourier, great mathematical physicist of a hundred and fifty years ago, felt it plausible to found his whole treatise on an axiom, that the infinitely repeated subdivision of a pure substance, say of water, would not change its intrinsic properties. This is of course the perceptual continuity we see and touch and taste in this world in which we live. Exactly as Leibnitz

Fig. 5. Instructions for the making of cross-stitch embroidery, to be followed by a human craftsman.

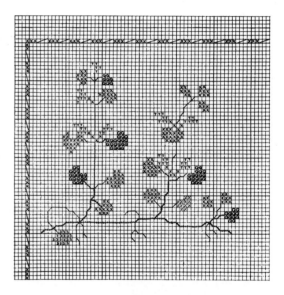

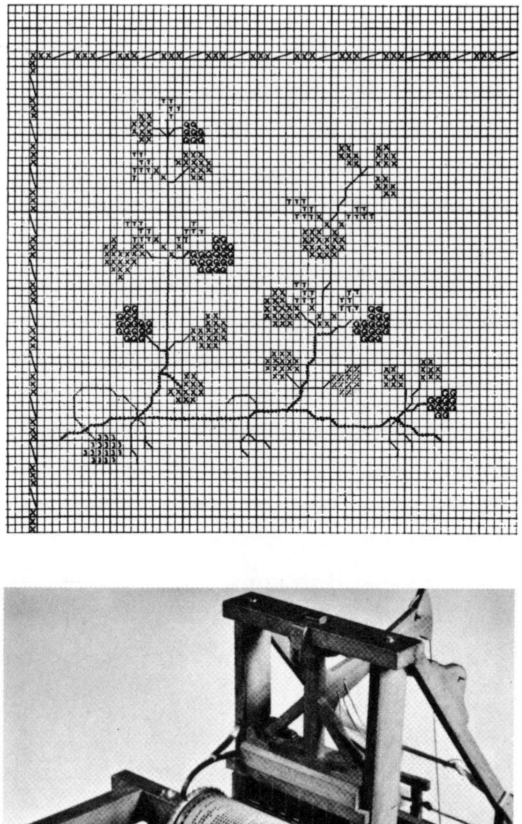

Fig. 6. A loom of the silk-weaving industry, Vaucanson, 1750. (Conservatoire des Arts de Métiers, Paris.)
The tactile instructions for the weave were read by the machine from the perforated cylinder seen in the center.

is refuted by mere number, so is Fourier. His was the error of size. There are *atoms,* but they are so small that we cannot expect our senses to reveal them; to our coarse inborn instrumentation, water remains watery to the tiniest drop. But in fact the history of the study of matter is largely a history of the refutation of that percept by reasoning from the properties of matter to the existence of atoms, and supporting the inference by even more powerful means of perception. Today the battle is well won; atoms are as real as chairs, and rather better understood. No one would argue that woven cloth, for example, would retain its properties in squares one millimeter on an edge. The thread is easily seen, and indeed the weaver will testify that the properties of his yarn are not the properties of the fruit of his loom, though the yarn may foreshadow some of them. Nowadays we can very nearly weave materials from atoms, and we observe the same results: matter has properties which depend on the assembly of many modular constituents, tediously repeated, in a small alphabet of relationships, but spelling out in the end new and unexpected messages. Cloth is more than yarn, and yet it is only yarn modularly repeated.

The first lexicon of matter was the roster of chemical elements, the next, the modularity of crystals, then the color patterns of visible light which are the spectra. By now the chain of argument is so intricate and so complete, and yet still so fruitful, that it is an unsuitable task to try to sketch it here. Rather look at two examples which display the modules to our eyes, mediated to be sure through complicated apparatus, but with results so rich in connotation and detail that we can bury skepticism, recalling only that every photograph can reveal its object only in some single light; yet every real object contains more than one image for photography.

Reproduced here is a small bit of a remarkable crystal. It is very plainly assembled out of identical, rather simple modules, near-spheres by this light. They are piled in a regular and repetitive three-dimensional display, which is the crystal. But these modules are by no means atoms. Each one is a proto-organism, a virus particle, capable of inducing in a suitable living host, the tobacco plant, a characteristic disease, leaf necrosis. (The pathology is inessential to the argument, and reflects only the investigator's stake in choosing this particular virus for study.) What turns out to happen is that each of the modules is capable of entering a particular host cell, and once within, of subverting the metabolic machinery of the cell to turn out replicates of the module, at the expense of the normal growth and function of the leaf cell. Hence the disease. In this illustration one sees a photograph made by using the geometrical principles of the microscope, with lenses not shaped of glass to bend light, but rather made of well-shaped magnetic fields to guide rays of electrons to form the photographic image. The

Fig. 7. An electron micrograph showing a crystalline heap of tiny identical modules. The whole heap is about one-tenth the diameter of a hair. Each module is a particle of tobacco leaf necrosis virus, containing five or ten millions of atoms. Such modules—tiny for us, giant for atoms—are typical of the fine structure of living beings. (Photo courtesy Dr. Ralph Wyckoff.)

whole crystal fragment shown is about one-tenth the diameter of a human hair. These modules hold some five or ten *million* atoms. The existence of these intermediate structures, modular, but far greater than atomic size, is one of the hallmarks of life. No metal or mineral shows such great modules in its assembly to crystalline form. The domain of these modules—can we call them giant molecules?—is the domain of life. How cunningly they are marshalled to lend life its mobility, to allow it growth, to endow it with heredity, are stories told in another place. Suffice it here to say that modularity, on a scale below the microscope but far above the atom, is the scheme of life. The intimacy of relationship between the metaphors of computers, with the theory of modular information on the one hand, and modern genetics and developmental embryology on the other is the burden of the most dazzling scientific tale of the last twenty years. We must pass it by.

Not only the biological giant molecules, but even individual atomic modules can be displayed. We can see them in the illustration on the opposite page. This is a photograph of a fluorescent screen of a vacuum tube like that of a TV tube, with an image painted out of it, not this time by electrons, but by the heavier charged particles called ions of helium. These ions were made out of the gas of the tube, produced very close to a tiny metal tip, which is a perfectly smooth near-hemispherical crystal of platinum. They are electrically repelled by the voltage on the tip, shoot out, strike the screen, and set it aglow. They image the atomic arrangement of the crystal; nearly a thousand facets of the complex surface of intersection between the regular hexagonal crystal lattice and the over-all hemispherical shape of the tip appear. A near-ideal regularity is displayed, usually by small groups of atoms blurring into a single image, once in a while even by individual atoms. Some central facets appear blank because their atomic surfaces are too flat; the ion formation favors those locations where individual atoms tend to protrude beyond their neighbors, because they lie at edges or corners of the atomic latticework. The whole pictured tip is about one five-hundredth part of a hair's breadth.

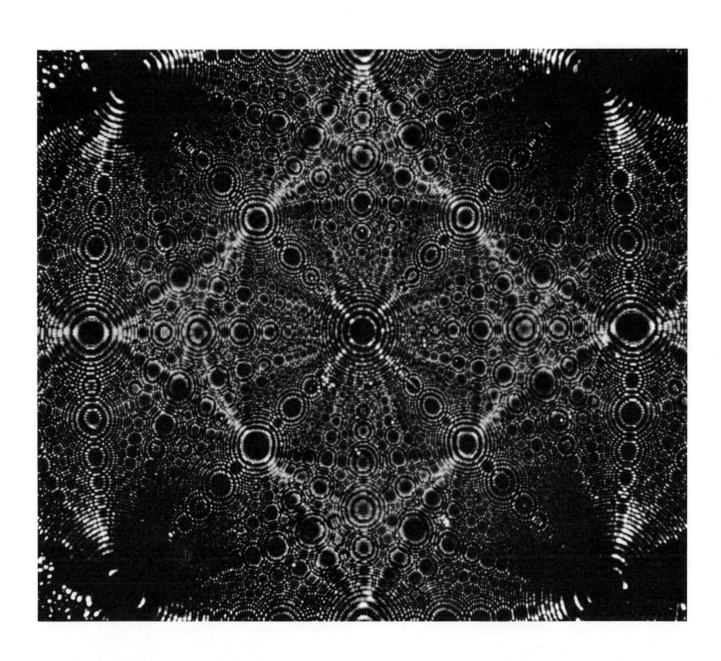

One impression cannot escape us; whatever else we may see, the modular construction of the metal crystal is plain. No continuity, no smooth ground stuff of malleable metal appears to our eyes; our most powerful, almost magical magnification has yielded the discrete muster of atomic parts, multiplied in a pattern austere and elegant. Hidden within the luster of metal worked by hammer and roll, there always lie the patterns of the snowflake or of the Alhambra's tiled walls, patterns conforming in most details to the severe mathematical canons for the uniform assembly of identical modules. Exactly this did the crystallographers long ago infer from the well-developed forms of crystals; it has remained for our time to display the arrays of atoms themselves.

What is most striking of all is the absolute identity of all the hordes of atoms, members of one species. Indeed, we now have criteria for identity so stringent as to imply that no surprises can arise which will cause us to subdivide certain classes whose members we have recognized as one and the same! The atom is not the uncuttable, as the Greeks would have it. Far from it; we part atoms in each match flame, or in rubbing lucite against wool. Even the core of the atom, the nucleus, a million-fold more refractory than the outer atomic shell, we part easily enough, if more dramatically. But what is in essence atomic is identity. The variety of our world which lies so richly at hand is a modular variety; matter is modular. Its modules fulfill the most precise of stereotypes, free from the interesting variations of the craftsman's hand or the furnace heat. Their number alone, and the motions and interactions of those myriads, weaves the intricacies of reality.

Those uncuttable particles, the atoms of the philosophers, could well be identical. They were made so, it was put forward, in the dawn of time. But how can objects with structure, with subsystems like electrons and nuclei, sensitive to environment under by no means unrealizable circumstances, hold their immutable identity of form? This is the puzzle whose solution is the theory of the quantum. For it turns out that motion, too, the kind of orbit traced out by a planetary electron in the solar system of the atom, is modular. The concept of freely assigned orbit, as in the familiar mechanics of our human scale or larger, turns out to fall into contradiction before the theory of the mechanics of the quantum. Only certain states of motion are possible, modules of energy or momentum, if you wish, and a system has a set of modules which define its nature. True, systems of many atoms may combine these so deftly that they approximate the smoothly continuous motions of Newton and of common experience. They do this much in the manner that the modular atomic lattices allow the sculptor to make any shape he chooses by the rough judgment of the eye, though in reality his materials on the atomic scale lie in rigidly controlled pattern.

If such abstract measures of material motion as energy are affected with the brick-like modularity which is the natural order, it may not come as wholly strange that radiation, the light we see, shares the same quality. Indeed, we nowadays regard all the world as built out of certain subatomic fundamental modules, or particles, whose classes we are still enumerating. Why they are precisely identical by classes we know not. They seem to occur in families, as the tiles of a mosaic, grouped not by color but by sets of other intrinsic properties. They interact with each other in ways which are complex, but which themselves reflect a complex set of essentially discrete rules. Out of all this tangled skein time has woven the fabric of the world. Continuity, and its strange child, the randomness of chaos and formless motion, are present only in the gaseous state and in the gravitational orbits which hold the planets and the stars in their courses. In time and space we still see no modularity; these categories are less real to us still, more tinged with metaphysics, than the matter which they somehow contain, the matter which somehow lends them features. But here we grope at the edge of knowledge.

The world is both richly strange and deeply simple. That is the truth spelled out in the graininess of reality; that is the consequence of modularity. Neither gods nor men mold clay freely; rather they form bricks. If it were not so, order and diversity would be no allies, but eternally at war.

C. H. WADDINGTON

THE MODULAR PRINCIPLE AND BIOLOGICAL FORM

The term "module" is not commonly used in biology, and a biologist who undertakes to discuss the application of the modular principle to biological forms should, perhaps, begin by stating what he takes that principle to be. As I understand it, the idea of the module covers two related notions: firstly, using some standard unit of length or volume as the basis for a whole design; and secondly, adopting throughout the design a single definite series of proportional relations. I am taking Le Corbusier's Modulor as a classical formulation of the principles, allowing, however, that the set of proportions that he worked out in his book, *The Modulor,* are only one particular example, and that many other schemes of proportion would agree equally well with the general principle.

Now the first point to be made—if only to get it registered, since it will lie in the background even when it is not in the foreground of all the following discussion—is that, in the most profound sense, biological forms can never be modular in the sense in which an architectural or pictorial design may be. It is of the essence of biological structures that they are involved in processes of growth and development. Even when we can, for some purposes, identify a basic unit, fundamentally it is not constant but changes (usually increases) as time passes. Similarly, as we shall see, the system of proportions usually alters as development proceeds. The only reason why it is not completely beside the point to discuss modular theory in connection with biological forms is that in many organisms, including

the one the artists are most interested in, man himself, there is an extensive period in life—adulthood—during which developmental changes are relatively slight. They can therefore be neglected, if we are willing to remain at a level of discussion which is humanistically important even if it is biologically superficial. However, one must always be ready to find that, in a particular context, such neglect ceases to be justified if we wish to make comparisons which are really illuminating and not merely rhetorical.

With this point in the open, let us begin by considering the application to biology of the simplest aspect of modular theory, the use of a basic unit. At first sight one might think that biological forms are definitely modular in this sense, since they are built of elementary units, namely cells. However, it is only in very simple and small organisms that the cells play the part of a modular unit. Usually they are far too small in proportion to the total size; their relation to the whole form is more like that of the bricks in a skyscraper than of the units of the design. Moreover, in the small organisms in which the cells are few enough to function as the module, it is only exceptionally that the design is based on arrangements of an unmodified module. Usually, even in groups of only a few cells, there is some differentiation of these units into slightly different kinds, and the form is achieved by an orderly arrangement of these different units. A few examples of such simple few-celled organisms can be seen in Fig. 1.

Fig. 1. Few-celled organisms: species of pediastrum.

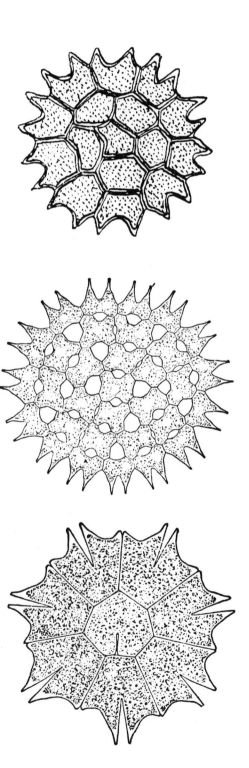
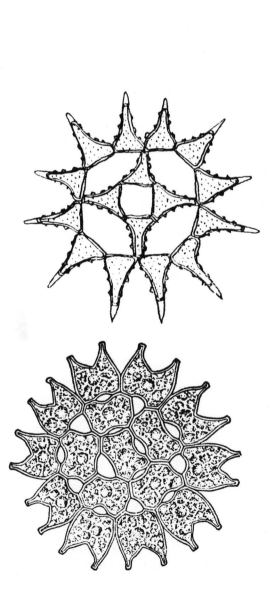

There are, of course, also many biological forms which are built up of units, in which these units are much larger than cells, being in fact composed of large numbers of cells just as the modular unit in a building may be constructed of numerous bricks. How far can modular principles be said to apply to these more complex biological structures? There is—and this is one of the main points to be made about biological forms in general—a whole range of different situations. At one extreme there are structures in which the units are very similar to one another and are arranged into quite regular patterns. The best known example is perhaps the honeycomb, in which the symmetry is so pronounced as to be nearer to the crystalline than the modular. Fig. 2 shows another form, a lump of coral, which is similar in that it is also made of a number of tubular elements assembled into a compact mass; but here the tubules are further apart and their arrangement is less regular, although there is still a hint of the formation of ordered rows. Fig. 3 shows the bony plates covering part of the back of an armadillo. Its pattern is considerably more orderly than that of the coral, although still far from the perfect regularity of the honeycomb. For one thing, it includes elements of at least two main orders of size: one small and squarish, the other larger and rectangular. Also, there is an orderly increase from the top to the bottom area in the length of the rectangular units. Finally, neither these elements themselves nor their arrangement is precisely geometrical.

2

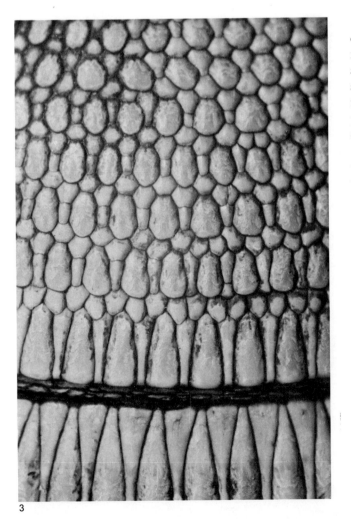

These two examples show rather well one of the characteristic features of those biological forms which involve the repetition of a basic unit. Both the patterns are rhythmical, the coral more loosely, the armadillo's skin in a more definite way. By a rhythm I mean, roughly speaking, something which is almost a regular periodicity but not quite. As Alfred North Whitehead defined it in the *Principles of Natural Knowledge:* "The essence of rhythm is the fusion of sameness and novelty; so that the whole never loses the essential unity of the pattern, while the parts exhibit the contrast arising from the novelty of their detail. A mere recurrence kills rhythm as surely as does a mere confusion of differences. A crystal lacks rhythm from excessive pattern, while a fog is unrhythmic in that it exhibits a patternless confusion of detail." Whitehead held that rhythms were characteristic of life in some ultimate philosophical sense. Without attempting to follow him into such deep water, I think that there is no doubt that rhythms are very characteristic of many of the objects made by living things.

Fig. 2. A lump of coral.

Fig. 3. Bony plates of the back of an armadillo.

3

It is instructive to compare these rhythmic biological structures with other patterns in which rhythm is absent or very weak. Figs. 4 and 5 are two other examples of patterns based on the repetition of circular elements. Fig. 4 is a biological specimen, a pattern formed on the upper surface of a cowrie shell. Here the arrangement of the dark-colored rings is too irregular to exhibit much rhythm, although there is some in the disposition of the large irregularly shaped black patches. Fig. 5 is not biological, but is an unsophisticated human pattern, a Nigerian dyed cotton cloth. Here again we are not dealing with a precise periodicity, yet I have the feeling that the divergences from precision are of a kind which do not engender a feeling of well-marked rhythm. Possibly this is because all the elements of the pattern seem to be out of place by about the same absolute amount. The divergence of the main straight lines from perfect straightness is not much greater than aberrations of the smaller circles from perfect circularness. In a rhythmic pattern the differences from perfect periodicity are more closely related to the magnitude of periodicity in question.

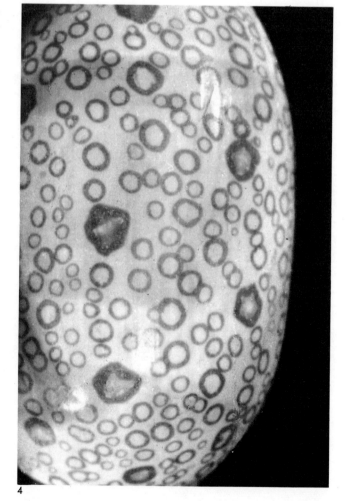

4

Fig. 4. Pattern on the upper surface of a cowrie shell.

Fig. 5. Nigerian dyed cotton cloth.

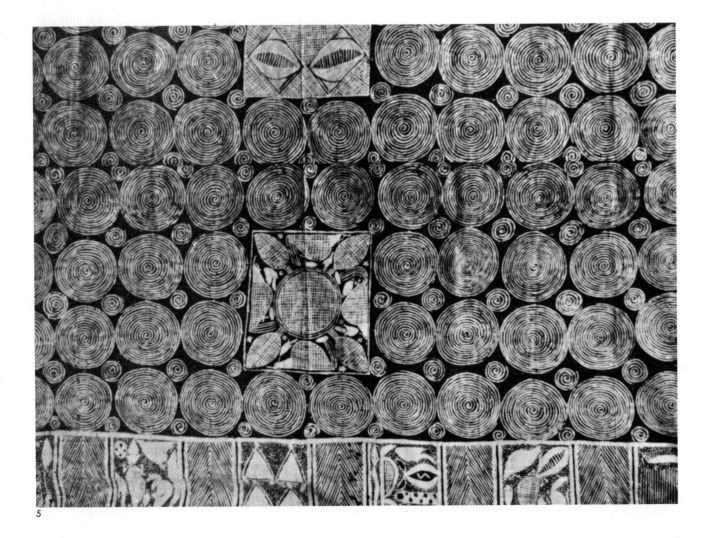

5

To compare with these non-rhythms, we provide the following four typical biological examples. The mouth of the cowrie (Fig. 6) shows on its lips two examples of linear rhythms. The solitary coral (Fig. 7) is an example of a basically radial symmetry somewhat affected by bilaterality. The pattern on another type of cowrie shell (Fig. 8) and the skeleton of a type of coral known as "sea-fan" or gorgonian (Fig. 9) are instances of all-over patterns. All of these examples are typical of the degree to which biological repetitive patterns are modular. It is a rather slight degree; in general the repeated units vary more or less considerably, and their arrangement is usually quite far from a regular geometrical pattern.

6

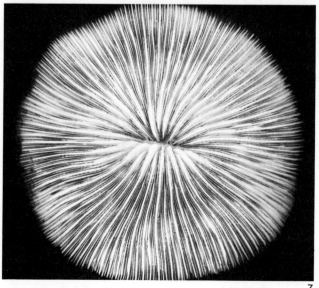

Fig. 6. The lips of a cowrie shell.

Fig. 7. A solitary coral.

7

26

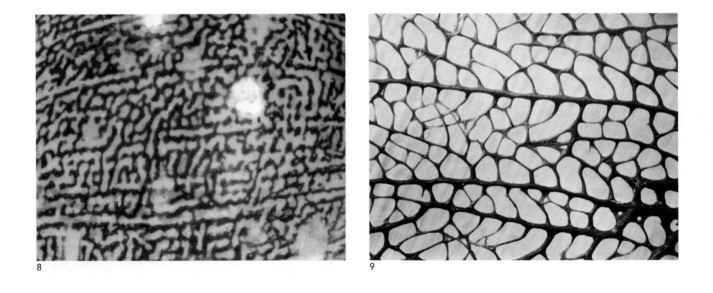

Fig. 8. Pattern on another type of cowrie shell.   Fig. 9. Skeleton of a type of coral ("sea-fan" or gorgonian).

In many biological patterns the variation of the units is not random, but follows regular rules. One example of this has been shown in the armadillo's skin, but the other patterns have been selected so that this factor had little importance in them. It raises another aspect of the modular principles, that of proportion. In this connection also we can find a vast range of different conditions among biological entities, just as we did in connection with patterns depending on the repetition of units. But probably the dominant characteristic of biological proportions is that any given form usually exhibits the simultaneous operation of several rules of proportion, rather than of only one. And in discussing these proportions it becomes extremely superficial to omit the time factor, since in the great majority of instances the proportions of a biological form change as it grows and develops. This is not quite always the case. For instance, Fig. 10 shows a shell which owes its beauty to the regularity of its shape, which arises from the constancy of the proportions of the spiral tube and of the angle at which it is coiled. Many snails, however, are not so modest, and their shells, even when based on a spiral of regular proportions, are ornamented with all sorts of excrescences, giving rise to forms which vary from the flowingly rhythmic (Fig. 13) to the baroque or the rococo (Figs. 11, 12).

10

11

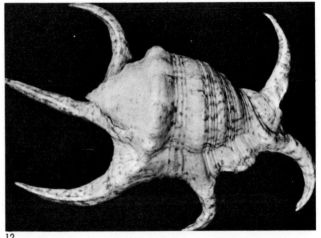

12

13

Change of proportions during growth is, however, the more usual situation. It is, of course, characteristic of man's own body. In the cold eye of science the proportions of the average human figure, from before birth to maturity, appear as shown here in this diagram from P. B. Medawar, *Essays on Growth and Form* (Oxford University Press, 1945):

Fig. 14. Lucas Cranach, the elder. *Venus and Amor.* Kröller-Müller Museum, Otterlo, Holland.

Fig. 15. Female figure from doorway of the Buddhist temple at Karli, near Bombay, India.

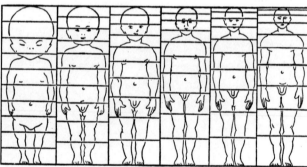

There is, clearly enough, a tendency for the head to become proportionately smaller, and the limbs proportionately longer, as growth proceeds. And these diagrams show only the general average. In particular individuals there may be variation in the relative rates at which the lengthening of the limbs or the slowing-up of head growth proceeds; and some individuals may go further along the general path than others.

As a reminder of the variability of biological proportions within one and the same species, it is amusing to compare a nude by Cranach (Fig. 14), exaggeratedly "adult" in its proportion of limb to body, with the more succulent but equally life-like version of the same form produced by an Indian sculptor on a Buddhist temple. (Fig. 15).

30

14

15

Although the most famous exposition of modular theory, in Le Corbusier's book, *The Modulor,* is plentifully illustrated with a little drawing of a man, with the implication that the system of proportion worked out there is based on relations within the human body, it is actually clear that man's frame contributed nothing to the system except a general order of magnitude. The basic module has a length based on a man standing with his arm raised an arbitrary height above his head, but the division of this length into segments, which gives rise to the whole modular system of proportions, is arrived at by a peculiar mathematical procedure which has nothing to do with any sort of biology, human or other.

The change of proportions of a biological organism during its development is brought about by differences in the growth rates of the various parts, some of which grow faster than others. There is very often a simple relation between the growth rates of well-defined parts, such as the limbs, head, and so on. This relation—which is certainly not universal, but is very common—is a simple constant proportionality, which exists not between the sizes of the parts, but between their rates of growth. In mathematical terms, if x and y are two parts of an animal (*e.g.,* x the head and y the rest of the body, or the arms) then the relation is that the rate of increase of x is a constant multiple of the rate of change of y: *i.e.,* $dx/dt = a\ dy/dt$. From this one can deduce the relation between the sizes of the two parts at any particular time of development. It will be of the form $x = b\ y^a$. It is clear from this that if the constant a is larger than 1, then x will be increasing faster than y; for instance, if the y in the formula is

the size of the main part of the body, then as the body gets larger, any organ x for which a is greater than 1 gets bigger in proportion, while if a is less than 1, the organ appears proportionately smaller as the total size of the body increases. This type of relationship is spoken of as "allometry" (or "allometric growth"); instances in which a is greater than 1 are referred to as positive allometry, the opposite situation as negative allometry. In the growth of man, the legs show positive allometry, the head negative, in relation to the body as a whole.

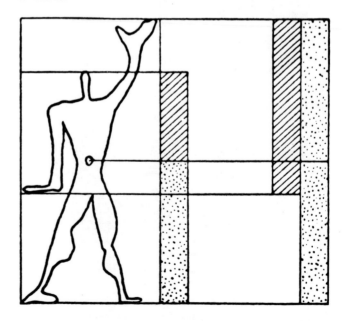

From Le Corbusier, *The Modulor,* Cambridge, Mass., Harvard University Press, 1954.

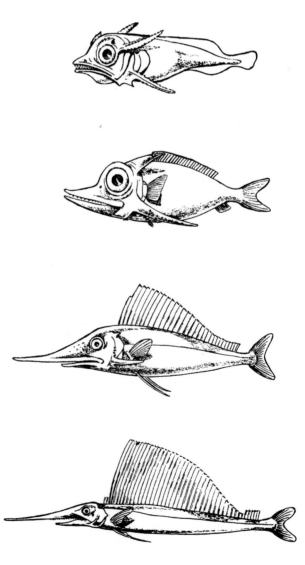

In many animals, the laws of allometric growth are adhered to with remarkable precision for long periods of development. Sometimes there are sudden changes in the values of the constants for particular organs, for instance, in connection with changes in growth rate connected with sexual maturity or other alterations in the general physiological conditions. The exact mechanisms underlying this whole system of growth regulations is still very obscure, and of great interest to biologists, but the causal analysis of the phenomenon is not the point at issue in the present context. Here it is more important to note some further examples of the kind of visual images which arise from this type of growth. A very simple example is seen in Fig. 16, which compares the growth of the beak in two species of birds, the black-tailed godwit (upper) and the lapwing (lower). In the godwit there is strong positive allometry of the beak, and it is obvious that the proportions change enormously as the bird grows up. Fig. 17 shows a similar situation in a sailfish during growth. There can be no standard modular proportion in such forms.

33

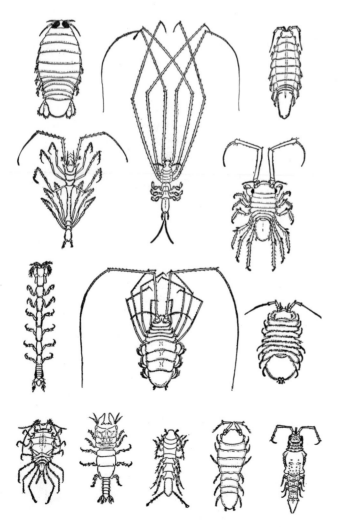

More complex alterations in proportions are brought about when growth of an allometric type occurs in biological forms consisting of many segments. Fig. 18 shows outline drawings of a number of species of marine isopods, *i.e.,* animals whose basic type is best known to most people in the form of a woodlouse. In the woodlouse, all the segments have grown at more or less equal rates, and even in the adult they are all of approximately the same size. The drawings in Fig. 18 are not growth stages of any one species, but illustrate the different types of adult which have been evolved from the woodlouse type. Their evolution has involved alterations in the growth rates of the various segments, some of which now show strong positive allometry, *e.g.,* the eight anterior ones in the third drawing from the top at left or the four posterior ones in the second from the top at center. Similarly, if one looks at the legs, it is clear that three pairs toward the front end of the animal top-center have been growing enormously faster than the rest of the body; and so on and on in all the variety of forms that have been produced. Very clearly, there is no standard system of proportions, but instead the proportions of the various regions and organs of the body can be varied almost arbitrarily.

Fig. 18. Animals related to the woodlouse.
From Bernard Rensch, *Evolution above the Species Level,* New York, Columbia University Press, 1960.

But a closer looks shows that the variations are not really arbitrary. There is an interesting type of orderliness, and one very typical of biological forms. The growth constants of neighboring segments, whether of the main body or of the legs, are nearly always closely related to each other. It is very rare to find a very long segment next to a very short one, more usually there are gradual changes in growth constants as one passes from one segment to the next. For instance, in the second animal from the top at center they increase fairly steadily from front to back, with perhaps rather a steep rise near the middle, while in the third from the top at left they remain small in the most posterior segment, then there is a considerable rise followed by a slower gradual increase with a final tailing off again in the most anterior parts. If one were to plot the growth constants along the length of the body or along the legs, they would fall on some relatively simple continuous curve instead of being scattered about in a quite arbitrary way. Such curves are known as growth gradients, and they express a type of orderliness which is very characteristic of biological form. It results in there nearly always being some recognizable relation between the neighboring parts of a biological system. For instance, a child's leg is not only shorter than an adult's in proportion to the body, but also has a different internal system of proportions between the thigh, knee, calf, ankle, etc. But both in the child and the adult the lengths of the segments form a *system* of proportions, and the legs do not give the impression of a mere assemblage of unrelated sections.

This kind of organization of the form is so important in biological organisms that it is worth looking at some further examples. The illustrations on the following pages show a situation in which not only the proportions of the elements, but also the number of elements has been varied. The hands and feet of all mammals are built on plans which are derived from a design with five digits—fingers or toes. Man retains this primitive pattern, but evolution has produced many types of animals —horses, pigs, deer, cows, and more exotic creatures—in which the numbers have been reduced, and the proportions of the various bones in a finger or toe altered. The drawings in Fig. 19 show a sample of these variations. In all of them, the "relationship of neighbors" is apparent in two ways: between the different digits, and between the bones within any one digit. The relationships may be quite different in different cases. In Myrmecophaga, for example, the central digit is enlarged and there is a gradual falling away toward the sides, whereas in Macrorhinus we see that it is the two outer digits that are largest. But whatever form the modifications have taken, whether symmetrical or asymmetrical, they always give the appearance of an over-all alteration in a general system, never of a set of changes in a number of isolated and unrelated items. Even when the elements in the pattern have no very obvious functional dependence on one another, such as the bones of a limb must have, they usually show a relatedness in form when different modifications of the pattern are compared. For instance, look at the spines and knobs on the snails illustrated earlier.

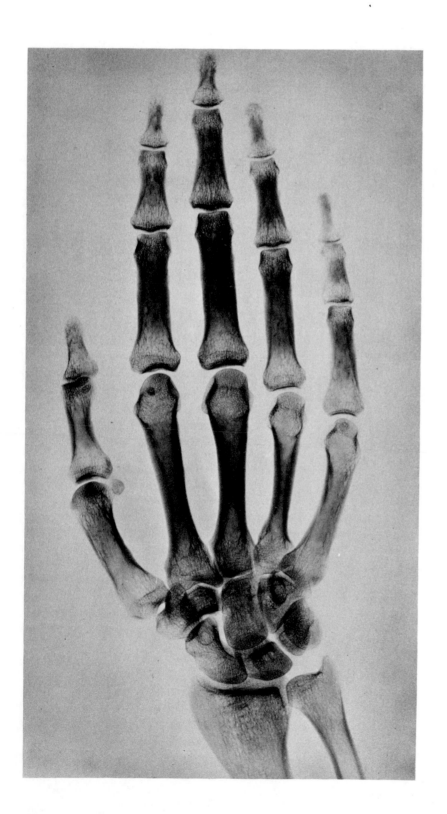

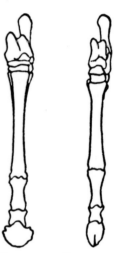

Equus   Thoatherium

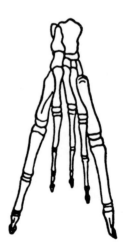

Macrorhinus

Fig. 19. Hands and feet of various mammals.
Drawings from P. Tschumi, *Revue Suisse Zoologique*, 1953.

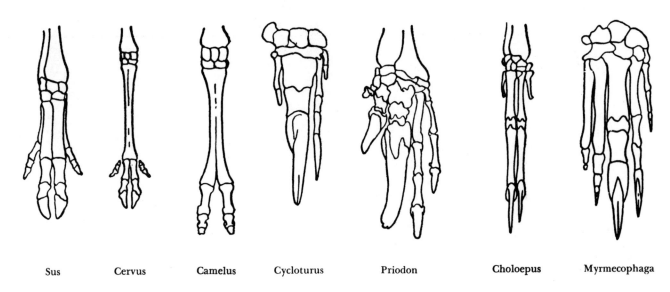

| Sus | Cervus | Camelus | Cycloturus | Priodon | Choloepus | Myrmecophaga |

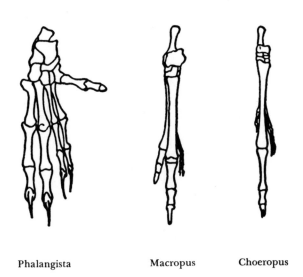

| Phalangista | Macropus | Choeropus |

It is, in my opinion, this relatedness of contiguous parts which is particularly characteristic of biological structures. They are certainly not usually modular in the sense of being assembled by the arrangement of one or a few kinds of constant elementary units. Nor, as we have just seen, do they often employ a standard system of proportions. The Golden Mean is not an idea of a biological type. How could there be such a thing in a form which is altering the relative proportions of its parts as it grows up? On the other hand, biological forms are certainly not chaotic or arbitrary in the mutual relations of their parts, but nearly always convey a strong impression of order and organization. There are, I believe, principles which apply to the forms of the individual parts or organs of which an animal is built. These have not been discussed in this article, which is concerned with the question of the arrangement of units and with proportion, that are the province of modular theory. Within this province, I have argued that the biological rules are not those of the module, but rather of a kind which one might summarize by the phrase, "the relatedness of neighbors."

ARTHUR L. LOEB

THE ARCHITECTURE OF CRYSTALS

The snowflake is the beauty queen of the Solid State (Fig. 1). She reveals herself in an abundance of different shapes and appearances. She is cited for her fickleness as well as for her constancy, for although she never appears twice in exactly the same configuration, her symmetry is invariably hexagonal; when any snowflake is turned 60° around an axis perpendicular to its plane, its original appearance is reproduced. The reason for its constancy lies in the arrangement of the atoms in the crystals, while the variety in external shapes is caused by environmental conditions governing the growth of the crystals.

Consider now beauty and the beast among crystals: diamond and graphite. Both are made up of carbon atoms only. In diamond each carbon atom is surrounded by four equidistant carbon atoms at the corners of a regular tetrahedron (Fig. 2a); in graphite each carbon atom is surrounded by only three equidistant carbon atoms at the corners of an equilateral triangle (Fig. 2b). In diamond a three-dimensional network of carbon atoms is formed, the properties of which are brilliance, hardness, and high electrical resistance. In graphite the two-dimensional networks form planes; the lubricating power of graphite is due to the ease with which such planes slide along each other. Graphite is, in contrast to diamond, a good electrical conductor. We have in this case a spectacular example of the interrelation between the microstructure of solids and their macroscopic properties.

In investigating the nature and properties of the world around us, we tend to alternate between the collection of data and the organization of the results of experiments. This alternation is very important in the progress of science; the organization process would be futile without experiment. The alternation of these two methods motivates further investigations and reveals universal principles linking very distinct physical phenomena. Abilities of scientists vary: some are ingenious in the design of experiments, while others are adept at discovery of patterns and relationships. The discovery of order is thus quite subjective, and the structure of matter as it is known to us is partly of our own making; we tend to structure our perceptions and to create frames of reference suitable for relating various observations to each other.

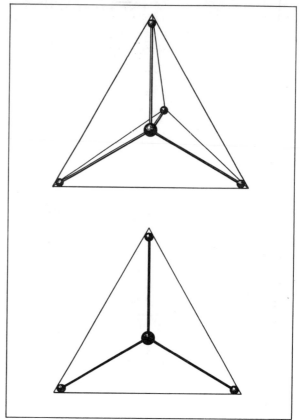

Fig. 1. Snowflake.
Fig. 2a. Arrangement of carbon atoms in diamond.
Fig. 2b. Arrangement of carbon atoms in graphite.

PATTERNS AND SIMPLICITY

The search for order and structural regularity in the world around us has been a powerful motivation in human evolution. Pythagoras' discovery of the simple ratios in the frequencies of musical notes, Leonardo da Vinci's *sectio aurea* in architecture and design, Johannes Kepler's *Harmonica Mundi,* and Mendeleev's Periodic Table of the Elements have all eventually had a strong effect in guiding fundamental research and eventually on our daily lives. (Pythagoras' discovery was ultimately traced to the modes of vibration of air in pipes or of strings under tension; Mendeleev's order of the elements was explained on the basis of the orderly structure of electrons inside the atom.) Occasionally these attempts have led to occultism and cabalism, and even some of Kepler's statements represent unwarranted extrapolations into mysticism. Notable among recent discoveries of hidden regularities in man-made creations was M. van Crevel's analysis of Jacob Obrecht's *Missa Sub Tuum Praesiduum.*[1] Using a new system of transcribing the music of this fifteenth-century Mass into modern notation, making the space occupied by each note proportional to its duration, Dr. van Crevel discovered simple relations between the durations of the various portions of the Mass, and between the pitch and duration of the individual notes.

It is notable that some of the greatest masterpieces of art possess a simplicity and regularity of structure. This regularity may be at once obvious, or hidden, as it was in Obrecht's Mass. Equally notable is the fact that the structures required or generated by the laws of physics are also generally simple, with the result that we often find such structures pleasing. This makes us wonder whether simplicity is a subjective norm, or whether simplicity can be evaluated quantitatively.

Consider first the mirror designed by Archimedes for focusing the beams of the sun on the enemy off Sicily. The laws of optics require such a mirror to be parabolic in shape (Fig. 3). Such a curve is described mathematically by relating the distance of any point P on the curve to the axis, y, to the distance of that same point from a line tangent to the parabola at its apex, x:

$$y^2 = 4fx \qquad (1)$$

The symbol f is called a parameter of the parabola; it represents the focal length of the mirror: beams incident on a parabolic mirror parallel to its axis are all reflected by the mirror to the same point, which is called the focus of the mirror. Whereas a parabola may not be easy to construct with ruler and compass, it is nevertheless a simple figure, being completely described by Equation (1) and the numerical value of the parameter f.

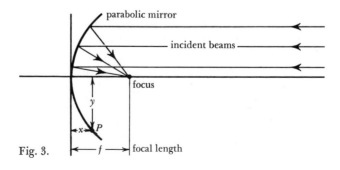

Fig. 3.

An example of a simple curve occurring in nature is the shell of the nautilus (Fig. 4).[2] The mathematical expression for this shell is a logarithmic spiral, not because the nautilus is magically expert in the use of logarithms, but because the rate of growth of the shell of the nautilus obeys physical laws that happen to generate a logarithmic spiral. The growth of the spiral is mathematically similar to the growth of capital by interest compounded continuously: whenever an entity grows at a rate proportional to its own size, this same growth law occurs. The time needed to double capital by continuously compounding interest is proportional to the logarithm of 2; that needed to triple the capital is proportional to the logarithm of 3. The time required to increase capital a hundredfold in this fashion is only twice as long as that needed to increase the same capital tenfold. The logarithmic spiral is completely defined by two parameters: its initial value and its growth rate. It is therefore a simple curve.

Another curve famous for its architectural beauty is the catenary. As its name implies, it is the curve formed by a chain suspended freely between two fixed points (Fig. 5). The mathematical expression of this curve consists of the so-called hyperbolic cosine function, and the numerical values of two parameters; for instance, the horizontal distance between the suspension points and the vertical distance between the highest and the lowest point on the curve. Again we have encountered a curve generated by physical forces, in this case those of gravity and of tension, which is aesthetically attractive.

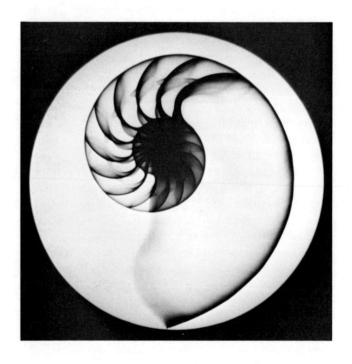

Fig. 4. X-ray photo of a nautilus shell.

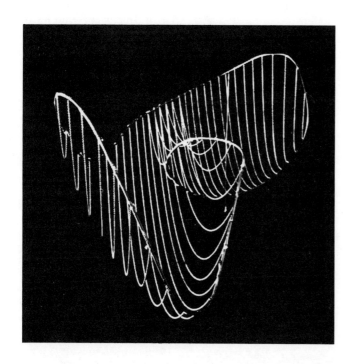

Fig. 5. Chains in curved frame. Structure study by Frei Otto and collaborating team members.

Personal experience led me to an interesting encounter with spheroids.[3] A spheroid is generated by rotating an ellipse around one of its axes: when rotated around its major axis, the ellipse generates a prolate spheroid; when rotated around its minor axis, it generates an oblate spheroid. I was asked to assist in the design of an apparatus for measuring the thermal conductivity of a ceramic material. To this purpose a cylindrical shell of the ceramic was fitted snugly around a heating cylinder, and in turn wrapped with an insulating cylindrical mantle. By measuring the temperature drop along the direction of heat flow, one can find the thermal conductivity of the ceramic. The big problem was that of finding the direction of heat flow. If the cylinder could be made sufficiently long, then one can safely assume that sufficiently far from the ends the heat flows radically outward. Unfortunately, the cylinder could not be made sufficiently long to warrant this assumption. Thus I was asked to design hemispherical guards to prevent axial heat flow through the end surfaces of the cylinder. The complete mathematical description of this apparatus would have involved two equations (one for the cylinder, the other for the sphere), and the following parameters: radius of the cylinder heating core, outer radius of the cylindrical ceramic shell, outer radius of the insulating mantle, length of the cylinder, and the three radii of the respective spherical heating core, ceramic sphere, and spherical mantle, making seven parameters total. In analyzing this apparatus, I was able to show that the heat flow could never be exactly controlled with this geometry, because of the discontinuity of curvature at the junctures of cylinder and hemispheres. I subsequently designed another apparatus which consisted of confocal spheroids (confocal spheroids have different major and minor axis-lengths, but the same foci) separating heating core, ceramic shell, and insulating mantle (Figs. 6a, 6b). In such apparatus all the heat flows out along hyperbolic paths perpendicular to the spheroids; the mathematical description requires one equation (of a spheroid), and the following parameters: distance between foci, and the major axes of three spheroids, four in all. It is important to note that the apparatus requiring two equations and seven parameters did not conform to the laws of natural heat flow, whereas the simpler apparatus requiring only one equation and four parameters did conform to those laws. Physically the laws of heat flow favor the simpler structure, which is also aesthetically more pleasing.

Summarizing, then, we maintain that simplicity of structure can be expressed quantitatively, and that both present-day aesthetic judgment and physical laws favor simplicity. This simplicity is not always obvious, and requires the choice of a proper frame of reference. Dr. van Crevel's discovery in Obrecht's Mass illustrates a simplicity of structure of which the listener might have been instinctively aware, but its technical design remained hidden for centuries. The simplicity of structure derived from physical laws is related to the fact that the differential equations relating forces and motion in physics are seldom of an order higher than two, so that the number of parameters describing this motion is usually small. Only when complex obstacles of human design are placed in the lines of flow are geometrical complexities created in the flow lines. It is this realization that has led to the streamlining of fast-moving objects, affecting in turn the representation of motion in art.

Fig. 6a.

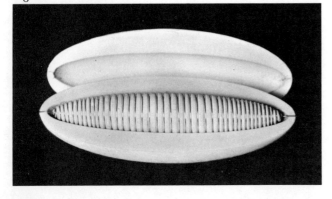

Fig. 6b.

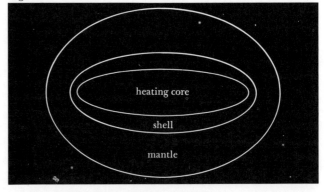

MODULES AND GENERATING FUNCTIONS

Let us return now to the structures of graphite and diamond, and let us see how much information is necessary for a complete description of these structures. In graphite *each* carbon atom is at the center of an equilateral triangle whose corners contain carbon atoms (Fig. 7a). According to this requirement each carbon atom at the corners of the triangle is itself at the center of such a triangle, of which the original carbon atom is a corner (Fig. 7b). If the original carbon be at the center of an "upright" triangle (solid lines), then its three nearest neighbors are at the centers of "inverted" triangles (broken lines). When we continue to surround each carbon atom by a triangle of carbon atoms, an infinite array is generated, of which a portion is shown in Fig. 7c. Half the carbon atoms are at centers of upright triangles, the other half at the centers of inverted triangles.

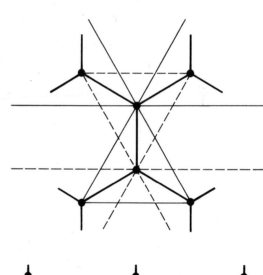

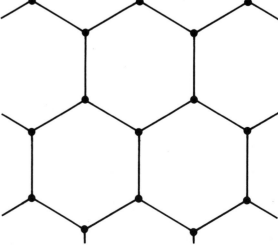

Fig. 7a. Arrangement of carbon atoms in graphite.
Fig. 7b. Small portion of sheet of carbon atoms in graphite.
Fig. 7c. Sheet of carbon atoms in graphite.

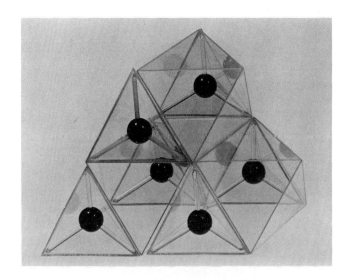

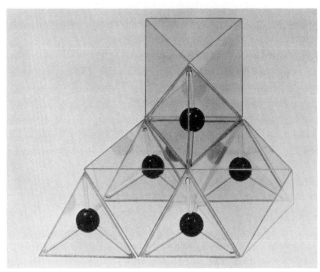

The three-dimensional diamond structure is generated similarly: half the carbon atoms are at centers of upright tetrahedra whose corners contain carbon atoms, each of which is at the center of an inverted tetrahedron. The generating rule for both graphite and diamond is that each carbon atom has identical environment, except possibly for orientation. In graphite each carbon atom has three, in diamond four, nearest neighbors; this difference in nearest neighbors accounts for all the differences between graphite and diamond!

An interesting modification of the diamond structure is that obtained by replacing all carbon atoms at the centers of upright tetrahedra by zinc ions, and all carbon atoms at the centers of inverted tetrahedra by sulphur ions. The resulting structure is that of the mineral sphalerite, in which each zinc ion is surrounded by four sulphur ions at the corners of an upright tetrahedron, and each sulphur ion is surrounded by zinc ions at the corners of an inverted tetrahedron. We shall see later that there is another mineral, wurtzite, that also answers to that description, so that a complete description of nearest neighbors does not necessarily provide sufficient information for uniquely generating a structure. Sphalerite and wurtzite are represented respectively in Figs. 8 and 9, where the spheres represent zinc ions, the corners of the tetrahedra sulphur ions.

In these examples, infinite patterns were generated by using a building block or "module" (triangle for graphite, tetrahedron for diamond), and the condition that all identical atoms have identical environment.

Fig. 8. Model of sphalerite.

Fig. 9. Model of wurtzite.

44

Fig. 10a.   Fig. 10b.

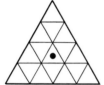 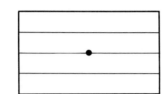

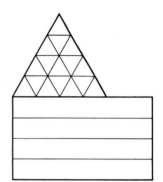

The rule determining the environment of each atom is
called a "generating function."   Fig. 11a.

Fascinating planar patterns can be generated in this
manner. Take, for instance, an equilateral triangle and
a rectangle (Fig. 10a), placed in juxtaposition (Fig. 10b).
The triangle and the rectangle are both symmetrical figures. If we place a pin at the center of the triangle, perpendicular to its plane, then rotation of the triangle
through 120° around the pin appears to reproduce the
original triangle. A complete rotation around the pin
produces the same pattern three times; the direction of
the pin is therefore called an *axis of threefold symmetry*. A line perpendicularly bisecting both diagonals
of the rectangle is an *axis of twofold symmetry*.

Whereas Fig. 10b has no symmetry at all, if a second
triangle identical to the first one is placed in the position shown in Fig. 11a, then the twofold symmetry of   Fig. 11b.
the rectangle is restored, and now applies to the whole
pattern. To restore the symmetry of the triangle, three
rectangles would have to be placed around it (Fig. 11b).
Continuing with the rule that each rectangle contains a
twofold axis, and each triangle a threefold axis, an infinite pattern is generated, of which a portion is shown
in Fig. 11c. It is notable that in Fig. 11c additional
symmetry has emerged, namely axes of sixfold symmetry in the space between the triangles and rectangles.

In Fig. 12a we show two distinct triangles·in juxtaposition. The generating rule is that each triangle contains
a threefold axis: Fig. 12b emerges. In Fig. 12b a third
type of triangle appears between the first two types,
which also contains a threefold axis.

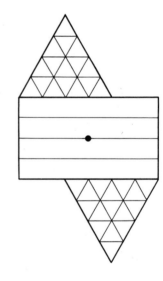

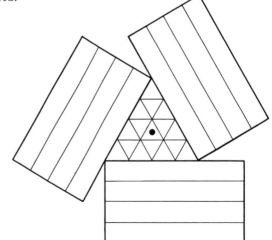

45

Fig. 11c.

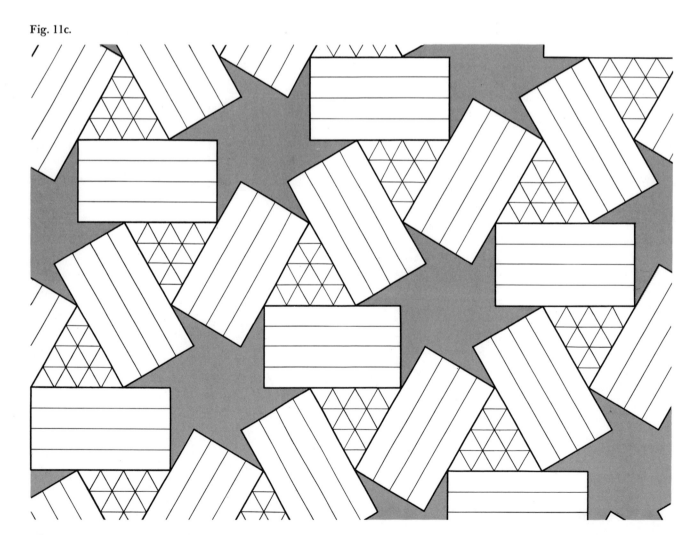

Fig. 12a.

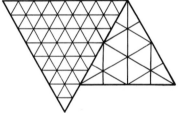

Fig. 12b.

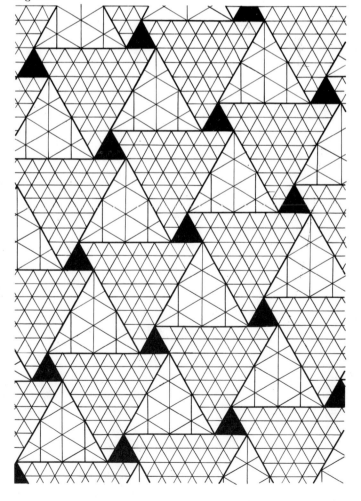

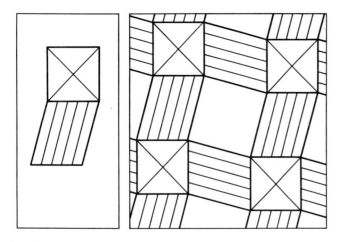

Figs. 13a, 13b.

In Fig. 13a we show a square (fourfold axis) in juxtaposition with a parallelogram (twofold axis). The generating rule that each of these polygons maintain its symmetry axis generates Fig. 13b, which contains in addition a second set of fourfold axes.

Le Corbeiller and Loeb have shown[4] that in general a k-fold and an l-fold axis placed parallel to each other imply an m-fold axis as well, where k, l, and m are positive integers satisfying the equation:

$$\frac{1}{k} + \frac{1}{l} + \frac{1}{m} = 1 \tag{2}$$

The reader may amuse himself by plugging in values for k, l, and m; the patterns of Figs. 11c, 12b, and 13b are observed to fit Equation (2). When a square and a triangle are placed in juxtaposition, the generating rule that the square maintain its fourfold and the triangle its threefold symmetry fails to generate a pattern: experiments to produce such a pattern always run into interference between the squares and the triangles. If we set $k = 3$, $l = 4$ in Equation (2), then we find $m = 12/5$, which is not an integer!

In the pictorial and musical arts there are nowadays many experiments with modules and generating functions. Sometimes the module is subjected to very rigorous generating functions, whereas some artists allow chance to generate aural and visual patterns from the module. In neither case does the creation of the pattern from the module constitute in itself a creative act, for creativity necessarily involves decisions by the artist.

Figs. 11, 12, and 13 were created mechanically from the module, but the dimensions of the module, colors and texture are to be freely chosen. It is important to recognize that these patterns produce a framework for endless variations to be chosen by the artist. Although generated from very simple modules by simple generating functions, these patterns are sufficiently complex that they might not have occurred to the artist by the use of free imagination only. They appear complex to the eye because of their unfamiliar framework, but because of their small number of parameters and generating functions they should really be considered quite simple. Rules such as Equation (2) can assist the artist by telling him in general what combinations not to attempt. (Forbidden are, beside the triangle-square combination, two distinct types of sixfold axes, combinations with fivefold axes, and any combinations of axes of symmetry with a value greater than six.)

As an illustration of a very simple, rectangular framework on which the artist has superimposed his own imagination, we have chosen a tableau of seventeenth-century Delft tiles (Fig. 14). A more unusual frame of reference is represented in Fig. 15, by the contemporary Dutch graphic artist, M. C. Escher, who chose a very fanciful module and rigorously applied the generating function to it.

Thus in art the module and the generating function have a function in synthesis. We shall see presently that in science they have an analytic function, namely to assist in the recognition of patterns occurring in nature and the interrelationships of these patterns.

Fig. 14.

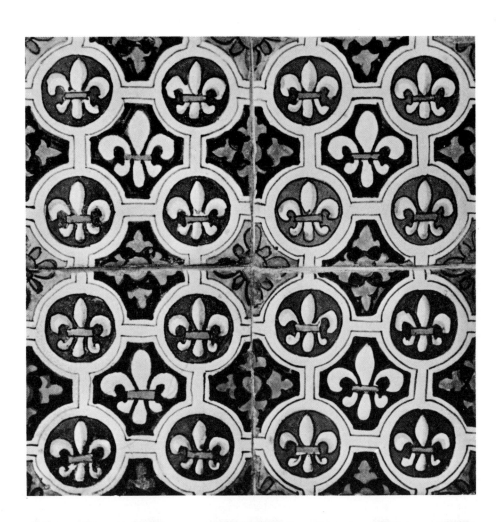

Fig. 15.

THE STRUCTURE OF CRYSTALS AND EFFICIENT PACKING

Not all crystals have configurations as simple as those of diamond and graphite. In Fig. 16 we show a model of the mineral spinel, which contains the elements oxygen, aluminum, and magnesium.. In this model the balls indicate the centers of the different ions. The radii of the balls have no particular significance; the ball-and-rod models have the advantage that they are open, and hence allow one to see inside. Actually, the ions all have different sizes; for our purpose we can assume that each type of ion is characterized by a rigid sphere of a given radius (the length of the rod in the model thus represents the sum of the radii of the ions joined by the rod), and that these ions arrange themselves in an efficient manner, *i.e.*, such that the interstitial volume between them is minimized.

The model shown represents a so-called unit cell of a crystal: when ten million identical unit cells are placed side-by-side in a row, and ten million of such rows are placed next to each other, and when finally ten million of the resulting layers are stacked on top of each other, then a model of a crystal of spinel is obtained, scaled by a linear factor of at least one hundred million. This model, which would be a cube two thousand miles on each side, would represent the atomic architecture of one cubic centimeter of crystal. That ten million times ten million times ten million completely identical unit cells of such complexity as shown in Fig. 16 should exist in one cubic centimeter of matter is cause for wonder. To one convinced of the ultimate structural simplicity of physics, it is even cause for skepticism! However, we are about to find a simplicity and regularity of pattern analogous to that discovered by van Crevel in the works of Obrecht: always present, but well disguised. To do so, we shall find the most efficient way of packing together spheres, first spheres of uniform size, then spheres of different radii.

As a simple example of efficient packing, consider a number of identical circular disks on a table top. When these disks are in a square array (Fig. 17a), 79% of the total area of the table top is covered by the disks, while 21% is left exposed. On the other hand, in the triangular array (Fig. 17b) as much as 91% is covered by the disks, with only 9% of the table top exposed. The triangular array represents the most efficient way of packing the disks: here each disk touches six neighboring disks, whereas in the square array it only touches four neighbors. The triangular array is accordingly called a "closest packed" array.

The geometrics of close packing produce some interesting physical patterns. Imagine a group of bees, each constructing a cylinder of wax around himself. If each bee produces a cylinder with the same radius, then the most efficient use of space will be made if the bees locate themselves in a triangular array. When the cylinders just touch, they form a closest packed array. Since the wax is soft, the cylinders will from here on flow together to form the familiar hexagonal honeycomb pattern (Figs. 18, 19). That this pattern, the result of a simple biological growth law, is generally considered attractive, is illustrated here by its use in textile design (Fig. 20).

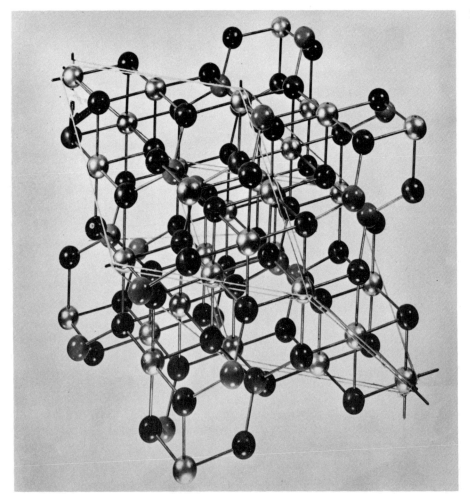

Fig. 16.

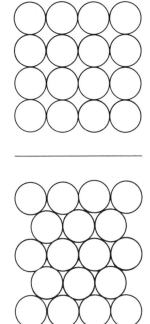

Figs. 17a, 17b.

Fig. 18. Artificial honeycomb. Courtesy Hexel Products.

Fig. 19. Natural honeycomb.
Courtesy American Honey Institute.

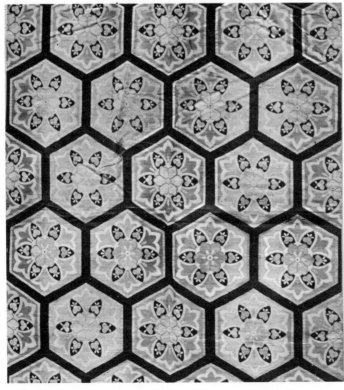

Fig. 20. Japanese silk, late 18th or early 19th century.
The Metropolitan Museum of Art, New York.

53

In a metal, all crystal elements are identical: the crystalline structure of most metals is primarily determined by the closest packing of identical spheres. The centers of the metal atoms, like the bees, arrange themselves at the corners of triangles (Fig. 21). A single layer of spheres would, however, constitute only a two-dimensional crystal; therefore we shall now extend the notions of close packing to three dimensions.

In order to stack two closest packed layers of spheres on top of each other, all the spheres in one layer must be directly above or below the centers of the spaces between the spheres in the other layer (Fig. 22). Let us denote the location of the centers of a single layer of closest packed spheres by the symbol D. When these centers are joined by straight lines, a triangular net is formed (Fig. 23); the points where these lines meet (at the centers of the spheres) are called the "nodes" of the net. The triangles are called "meshes." Half of the meshes in the triangular net point to the top of the page; the other half, pointing to the bottom of the page. These are labeled respectively E and F. This array of symbols, D, E, and F, provides the blueprint for much of our crystal architecture (Fig. 24).

Suppose a pin were stuck into one of the nodes of the triangular net, perpendicular to the plane of the net. If the entire net is rotated 60° around the pin, then all the D-nodes would still be D-nodes. However, the E-meshes and F-meshes would now have changed places.

When a second close-packed layer is placed on top of the first, the spheres in the second layer can be *either* over the E-meshes *or* over the F-meshes in the first layer. It should be noted that the distance between adjacent E and F sites is less than the diameter of the spheres, so that no adjacent E and F sites may be simultaneously occupied. We have just seen, however, that a rotation interchanges the positions of E- and F-meshes, so that there is no essential difference in the two resulting double-layer structures.

In a close-packed double layer of spheres each sphere touches six neighbors in its own plane, and three more in the adjacent plane. All nine neighbors are equidistant. When the center of each sphere is joined to the centers of its nine immediate neighbors, a three-dimensional net results (Fig. 25). In this three-dimensional net the triangular meshes arrange themselves as the faces of tetrahedra. Half of these tetrahedra point upward, the other half downward.

Although one can cover the entire area of a plane with equilateral triangles, half pointing upward, the other half downward, one cannot fill all of space with tetrahedra alone. As shown in Fig. 26, both octahedra and tetrahedra are needed for filling space. Half of the tetrahedra point upward; the other half are inverted. The cells between the meshes of the three-dimensional net are called "interstices." The number of close-packed spheres, of upright tetrahedral interstices, of inverted tetrahedral interstices, and of octahedral interstices are all equal to each other.

There is only one way of closest packing a double layer of identical spheres: the spheres in the second layer

Fig. 21.

Fig. 22.

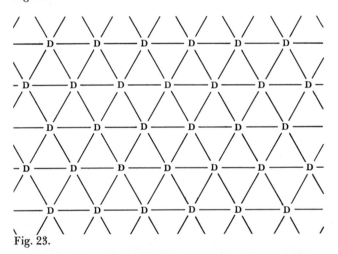

Fig. 23.

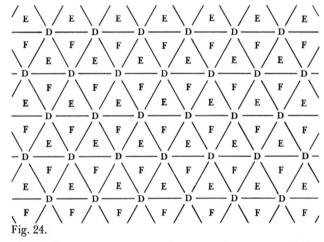

Fig. 24.

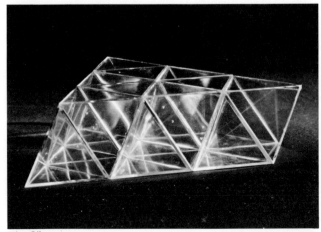

Fig. 25.

Fig. 26.

lie above *either* the E- or the F-meshes in the first layer; we have seen that the structures resulting from the two choices are related to each other by a rotation.

When a third layer is to be placed on the second one, a choice is again to be made, and this time the choice is not a trivial one. Referring to Fig. 24, let us suppose that the first layer of spheres lies above the D-positions, and the second above the E-positions. The meshes in the second layer are centered above the F- and the D-positions; it is here that the spheres in the third layer will be located. If the D-meshes are selected, then the third layer is directly above the first layer (Fig. 27). If the F-meshes

are selected, on the other hand, then no two layers are directly above each other (Fig. 28). The two resulting structures are now quite distinct; the one characterized by DED stacking is called "hexagonally close packed," the one characterized by DEF stacking is called "cubically close packed." Usually the stacking of successive layers continues the pattern set by the first three layers: hexagonally close-packed structures are characterized by DEDED. . . (or DFDFD. . .), cubically close packed by DEFDEF. . . (or DFEDFE. . .). Occasionally mixed modes of stacking occur, for instance, in the mineral carborundum.

Fig. 27.

Fig. 28.

OCCUPANCY OF INTERSTICES: CRYSTAL BUILDING BLOCKS

Fig. 29.

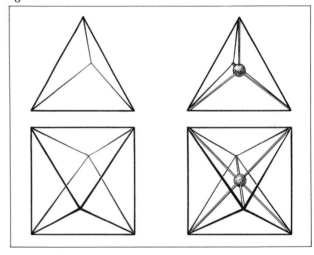

Most metals can be represented by closely packed spheres: copper, silver, gold, and platinum are cubically close packed, while magnesium and zinc are hexagonal. Cobalt, nickel, and lanthanum exist in either form. Nonmetallic crystals usually contain several different elements, each represented by a sphere of characteristic radius. Such is the case for the spinel, which contains oxygen, aluminum, and magnesium. We have now an important clue in tracking down the system underlying the apparently complex spinel structure: ignore the unit cell, but look for closely packed ions. Furthermore, look for smaller ions in the octahedral and tetrahedral interstices between the closely packed ones.

We have seen that the net formed by joining the centers of closely packed spheres divides space into tetrahedral and octahedral cells or interstices. It should therefore be possible to represent crystals by tetrahedral and octahedral modules (Fig. 29), empty when the interstices are not occupied by small ions, containing a sphere when a small ion occupies the interstice.

The volume ratio of the octahedral and tetrahedral modules is found conveniently as shown in Fig. 30. An octahedron is surrounded by four tetrahedra to form a large tetrahedron, the linear dimension of which is twice that of the smaller tetrahedra. Since geometrically similar figures whose linear dimensions are in the ratio $2 : 1$ have volumes in the ratio $(2)^3 : (1)^3$, *i.e.,* $8 : 1$, the large tetrahedron has the same volume as do eight small tetrahedra.[5] When four small tetrahedra are removed from the large one, the octahedron remains, which therefore has the same volume as do four small tetrahedra. The volume ratio of a regular octahedron and a regular tetrahedron of the same edgelength is therefore $4 : 1$.

Fig. 30.

Fig. 31.

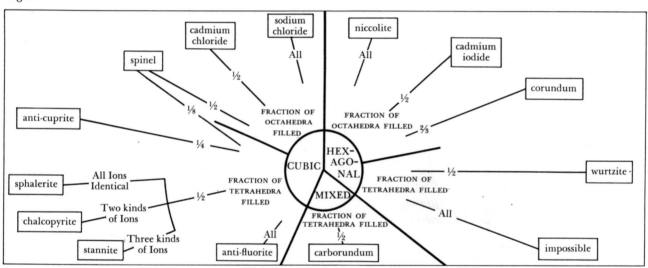

We can assemble these modules in various permutations and combinations to synthesize models of existing or impossible crystal structures; the systematic relationship between these structures is given in Fig. 31.

One of the simplest and most familiar of crystals is rock salt; it contains equal numbers of sodium and chloride ions. The large chloride ions are closely packed, and the sodium ions occupy all octahedral interstices, as seen here in the moduledra model of rock salt (Fig. 32).

Structures in which all tetrahedral interstices are occupied are also quite common; since there are twice as many tetrahedral interstices as there are closely packed ions, the chemical formula for these crystals has the form A_2X, where X represents the close-packed ions, A the ions in tetrahedral interstices. Examples are potassium oxide (K_2O) and the mineral fluorite (F_2Ca).

Both rock salt and potassium oxide are cubic; here the tetrahedra of any double layer are adjacent to the octahedra of the next double layer. In hexagonal packing all octahedra of one double layer are adjacent to the octahedra in the next double layer, the tetrahedra next to tetrahedra. When all octahedra in a hexagonal structure are occupied, the hexagonal analog of the cubic rock salt is produced: this is the structure of the mineral niccolite (NiAs). It is curious that the hexagonal analog of potassium oxide has never been found. The reason is easily understood when this hypothetical structure is synthesized from the modules: the ions occupying adjacent tetrahedra exert such a strong repulsion on each other that the structure would be unstable. In the cubic form of potassium oxide the filled tetrahedra are always next to empty octahedra, so that the repulsions are minimized.

Fig. 32.

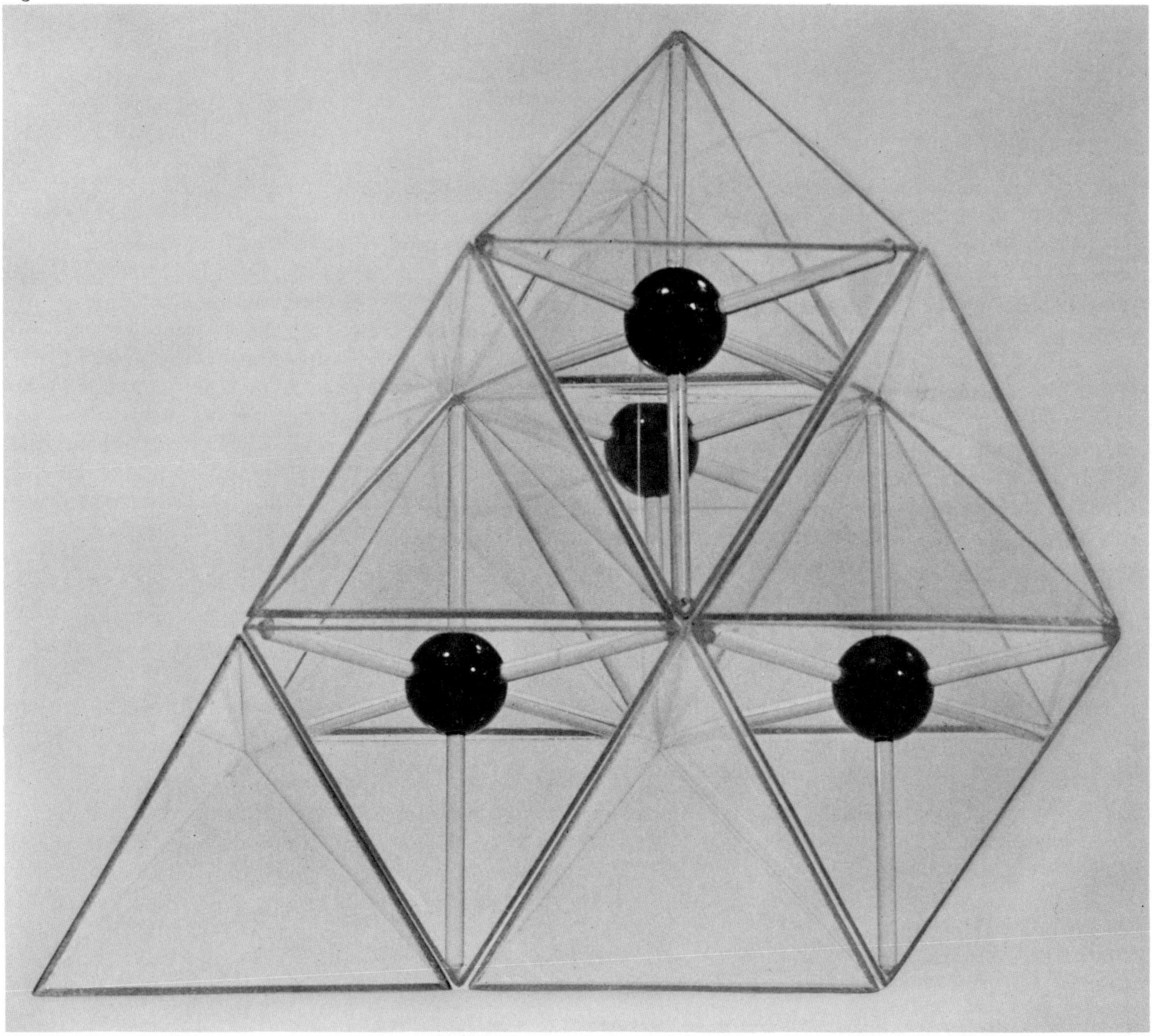

Rock salt, niccolite, and potassium oxide exemplify structures in which the number of interstitially located ions just equals the number of appropriate interstices available. In such structures as zinc cyanide, sphalerite, wurtzite, corundum, and spinel, however, there are more available interstices than there are ions to occupy them, so that we must find a way of describing the distribution of ions over sites.

It should be noted that the centers of the interstices form triangular nets just as do the centers of the close-packed spheres. Thus we encounter in the close-packed structures the following stacked nets and their relative positions (the following table covers two layers of modules, *i.e.,* three layers of closely packed spheres):

Content of Net	Relative Position	
Top of Stack	*Hexagonal*	*Cubic*
Close-packed ions	D	F
Tetrahedra pointing down	E	E
Octahedra	F	D
Tetrahedra pointing up	D	F
Close-packed ions	E	E
Tetrahedra pointing down	D	D
Octahedra	F	F
Tetrahedra pointing up	E	E
Close-packed ions	D	D
Bottom of stack		

The repulsion between identical ions occupying some nodes of a triangular net is minimized when the ions are uniformly distributed. The nodes of the triangular net must therefore be subdivided into different classes, each of which forms itself a triangular net (Figs. 33a, 33b). The number of such classes cannot be arbitrarily chosen, but must be expressible in the form $(k^2 + kl + l^2)$, where k and l are positive or negative integers.[6] For instance, when $k = -l = 2$, the net is subdivided into four classes (Fig. 33b); when $k = l = 1$, into three classes (Fig. 33a). It is *not* possible to subdivide the triangular net uniformly into two or into eight classes. On the basis of this rule the various structures of Fig. 31 can be assembled. For example, in the cuprite structure, the copper ions are closely packed, while the oxygen ions occupy one quarter of all tetrahedral interstices ($k = 2$, $l = 0$; Fig. 33b). Corundum, with chemical formula Al_2O_3, has closely packed oxygen ions; two thirds of all octahedral interstices are occupied by aluminum ions. The distribution of aluminum ions is found by setting $k = 1$ and $l = 1$. We thus arrive at a subdivision of the triangular net into three classes, of which one is empty, and two are filled (Fig. 33a).

The observation that the triangular net cannot be uniformly subdivided into two or eight classes provides the final clue to the mystery of spinel. First, let us return to sphalerite, that derivative of diamond. Its chemical formula is ZnS; the sulphur ions are closely packed. We have already seen that each zinc ion is tetrahedrally surrounded by sulphurs; we now know that per sulphur ion there are two tetrahedral interstices available. Thus one half of all tetrahedral interstices in sphalerite is occupied by zinc. Since the triangular nets cannot be uniformly subdivided into two equivalent halves, the logical solution open to Nature was to fill all of the upright tetrahedra, and to leave all the inverted ones empty! This distribution of ions gives sphalerite a peculiar and very useful electrical polarity.

It should be recalled that we cited another mineral, wurtzite, in which all zinc ions are surrounded tetrahedrally by sulphur ions, and all sulphur ions tetrahedrally by zinc ions, but which is different from sphalerite. A glance back to Fig. 31 now reveals that wurtzite is the hexagonal analog of the cubic sphalerite!

Spinel has the chemical formula $MgAl_2O_4$; the oxide ions are cubically close packed, the magnesium ions occupy some of the tetrahedral interstices, while the aluminum ions occupy octahedral sites. We recall that there are as many octahedral interstices as there are close-packed ions. Also, we note that the number of aluminum ions equals one half the number of oxide ions. Therefore the aluminum ions occupy one half of all octahedral sites. Unfortunately, as we have seen, it is not possible to subdivide the triangular net into two equivalent triangular nets, as would be desirable in order to minimize the repulsion between the aluminum ions. The actual arrangement of aluminum ions very ingeniously sidesteps this problem, for in spinel the aluminum ions occupy alternately one quarter and three quarters of successive nets of octahedral interstices. Of

Fig. 34.

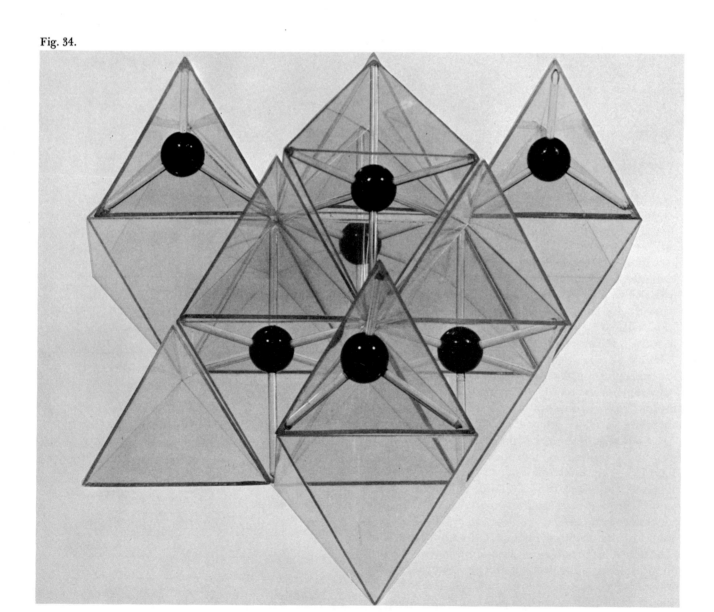

tetrahedral sites there are eight per formula unit $MgAl_2O_4$; since there is only one magnesium ion per formula unit, one eighth of all tetrahedral sites is occupied by magnesium ions. These magnesium ions occupy one quarter of each of the two tetrahedral nets adjacent to the one-quarter filled octahedral nets. The tetrahedral nets adjacent to the three-quarters filled octahedral nets remain empty (Fig. 34). The occupancy of interstices by ions in the spinel structure is therefore logically summarized as here below (in the following table + indicates tetrahedra pointing upward and − indicates tetrahedra pointing downward):

Empty net of − tetrahedral interstices	
Three-quarters occupied net of octahedral interstices	(Al_3)
Empty net of + tetrahedral interstices	
Close-packed oxygen net	(O_4)
One-quarter occupied net of − tetrahedral interstices	(Mg)
One-quarter occupied net of octahedral interstices	(Al)
One-quarter occupied net of + tetrahedral interstices	(Mg)
Close-packed oxygen net	(O_4)
Total:	$2MgAl_2O_4$

By following through several steps in the unraveling of the complexities of the spinel structure we have uncovered simple patterns in this and other crystal structures. Fig. 34 contains all the information necessary for a model of spinel; the frame of reference dictated by the closest packing of spheres has led to a great simplification over Fig. 16, a model of the same mineral, but in a clumsy frame of reference.

The crystal structures discussed here by no means cover the vast variety of naturally occurring minerals and man-made crystals. Yet they represent a large fraction of these crystals, and the analysis of the spinel problem does not essentially differ from the analysis being performed on yet more complex structures. The important conclusion in the present context is that the natural design turned out on proper analysis to be simpler than had been originally imagined. And the simpler the design, the fewer parameters are needed for a description of the structure. In turn this facilitates the communication of information regarding the structure among scientists themselves as well as between scientists and automatic information storage, processing, and retrieval systems. Most importantly, the recognition of the design simplicity leads to the discovery of universal interrelationships between vastly different materials.

1. M. van Crevel, "Structuurgeheimen bÿ Obrecht," in *Tÿdschrift der Vereniging voor Nederlandse Muziekgeschiedenis*, vol. XIX (1960–1961), p. 87.
2. See, for instance, Hermann Weyl, *Symmetry*, Princeton, N.J. (1952), p. 70.
3. M. Adams and A. L. Loeb, "Thermal Conductivity: II, Development of a Thermal Conductivity Expression for the Special Case of Prolate Spheroids," in *Journal of the American Ceramic Society*, vol. 37 (1954), pp. 73–74.
4. P. Le Corbeiller and A. L. Loeb, "Symmetrical Subdivision of the Euclidean Plane," in *Ledgemont Laboratory, Kennecott Copper Corporation Technical Report TR-47.*
5. A. L. Loeb, "Remarks on Some Elementary Volume Relations between Familiar Solids," in *The Mathematics Teacher*, vol. LVIII (1965), pp. 417–420.
6. A. L. Loeb, "The Subdivision of the Hexagonal Net and the Systematic Generation of Crystal Structures," in *Acta Crystallographica*, vol. 17 (1964), p. 179.

STANISLAW ULAM

PATTERNS OF GROWTH OF FIGURES: MATHEMATICAL ASPECTS

This paper will contain a brief discussion of certain properties of figures in two- or three-dimensional space which are obtained by rather simple recursion relations. Starting from an initial configuration, one defines in successive "generations" additions to the existing figure, representing, as it were, a growth of the initial pattern, in discrete units of time. The basic thing will be a fixed division of the plane (or space) into regular elementary figures. For example, the plane may be divided into squares or else into equilateral triangles (the space into cubes, etc.). An initial configuration will be a finite number of elements of such a subdivision and our induction rule will define successive accretions to the starting configuration.

The simplest patterns observed, for example, in crystals, are periodic and the properties of such have been very extensively studied mathematically. The rules which we shall employ will lead to much more complicated and in general nonperiodic structures, whose properties are more difficult to establish, despite the relative simplicity of our recursion relations. The objects defined in that way seem to be, so to say, intermediate in complexity between inorganic patterns like those of crystals and the more varied intricacies of organic molecules and structures. In fact, one of the aims of the present note is to show, by admittedly somewhat artificial examples, an enormous variety of objects which may be obtained by means of rather simple inductive definitions and to throw a sidelight on the question of how much "information" is necessary to describe the seemingly enormously elaborate structures of living objects.

Much of the work described below was performed in collaboration with J. C. Holladay and R. G. Schrandt (*Notices of the American Mathematical Society*, 7, 1960, p. 234 ff. and p. 642 ff.). We have used electronic computing machines at the Los Alamos Scientific Laboratory to produce a great number of such patterns and to survey certain properties of their morphology, both in time and space. Most of the results are empirical in nature, and so far there are very few general properties which can be obtained theoretically.

I. In the simplest case we have the subdivision of the infinite plane into squares. We start, in the first genera-

tion, with a finite number of squares and define now a rule of growth as follows: given a number of squares in the nth generation, the squares of the $(n + 1)$th generation will be all those which are adjacent to the existing ones but with the following proviso: the squares which are adjacent to more than one square of the nth generation will *not* be taken. For example, starting with one square in the first generation, one obtains, after five generations, the configuration shown below. It is obvious that with this rule of growth the figure will continue increasing indefinitely. It will have the original symmetry of the initial configuration (one square) and on the four perpendicular axes all the squares will be present—these are the "stems," from which side branches of variable lengths will grow.

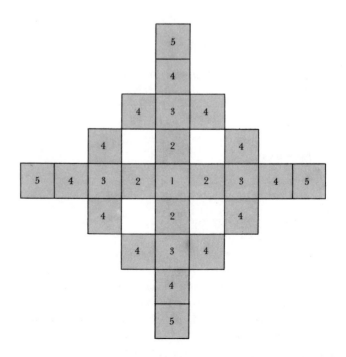

We can consider right away a slightly modified rule of growth. Starting again with a single square and defining the $(n + 1)$th generation as before to be squares adjacent to the squares of the nth generation, we modify our exclusion proviso as follows: we will not put into existence any square for the $(n + 1)$th generation if another prospective candidate for it would as much as touch at one point the square under consideration. With this second rule we obtain after five generations the figure shown here below. With this rule we will again notice immediately that the "stem" will continue indefinitely, but now the density of the growing squares will be less than in the previous case. In this case again one can calculate which squares will appear in the plane and which will remain vacant.

A general property of systems growing under the rules (and even somewhat more general ones) is given by a theorem due to J. C. Holladay. At generations whose index number n is of the form $n = 2^k$, the growth *is cut off* everywhere except on the "stems," *i.e.*, the straight lines issuing from the original point.

The old side branches will terminate and the only new branches will start growing from the continuation of the stems.

One of the most interesting situations arises when the plane is divided into equilateral triangles and starting from one initial triangle we construct new ones, generation by generation. We can again have the analogue of the first rule, *i.e.*, for the $(n + 1)$th generation we consider all triangles adjacent to a triangle of the nth generation. As before we shall not construct those which have two different parents in the nth generation. The system which will grow will have the sixfold symmetry of the original figure. There will appear a rather dense collection of triangles in the plane. The second way is to take the analogue of the second rule of "conflict," *i.e.*, do not construct a triangle in the $(n + 1)$th generation if it would so much as touch at one point another prospective child of some other element in the nth generation. (We of course allow two prospective children to touch on their base from two adjacent parents.) This rule will lead to a pattern which has fewer elements and a smaller density in the plane than the one constructed under the first conflict definition.

One can prove easily that the initial hexagonal symmetry will persist and that the growth will continue indefinitely with the "stems" increasing in each generation by one element, *i.e.*, forming continuous lines. The side branches have variable lengths and get "choked off" at variable times (generations). The author did not manage to prove that there will exist infinitely long side branches. It is possible to demonstrate that there will be arbitrarily long ones. Example 5 at the end of this paper shows a segment of the growing pattern. It represents one half of a 60° section. The other half is obtained by a mirror image. The other sections are obtained by rotation.

For the construction with triangles under the first rule, Holladay's cut-off property holds for generations with index of the form 2^k. Under the second rule it was not even possible to prove the value or indeed the existence of a limiting density of the triangles obtained by the construction (relative to all the triangles in the whole plane).

In the division of the plane into regular hexagons and starting with, say, again one element, one can obtain the analogues of the two patterns. Again the analogue of the more liberal construction has the cut-off property. For the more stringent rule it was, so far, impossible to predict the asymptotic properties.

II. The construction of the elements of the $(n + 1)$th generation is through a single parentage: each element attempts to generate one new one in the next generation. In the division of the plane into squares, triangles, hexagons, etc., one could adopt a different point of view: in the case of, say, triangles, one can consider instead of the areas of the triangles, their vertices only and imagine that each pair of vertices produces a new vertex— namely, the one forming the triangle with the two given vertices as their sides. Actually, the origin of the above constructions is due to the following point of view:

In a paper, "Quadratic Transformations" (Los Alamos Laboratory Report LA-2305, 1959), P. R. Stein and the writer have considered problems of "binary" reaction systems. Mathematically, these involve the following situation: a great number of elements is given, each element being one of, say, three types. These elements combine in pairs and produce, in the next generation, another pair of elements whose types are unique functions of the types of the two parents. The problem is to determine the properties of the composition of the population, as time goes on. If x, y, z denote the proportions of elements of the three types in the nth generation, then the expected value of the numbers of particles of each type in the new generation will be given by a quadratic transformation. For example, the rule could be that an x type and a y type particle together produce an x type, the $(x + x)$ a z type, $(x + z)$ a y type, $(y + y)$ an x type, $(y + z)$ a z type and $(z + z)$ a y type. (Actually there are more than ninety possible and different such rules—we assume, however, that once a rule is chosen it is valid for all time.) The rule above would lead to the new proportions x', y', z' given, as follows:

$$x' = 2xy + y^2,$$
$$y' = z^2 + 2xz,$$
$$z' = y^2 + 2yz.$$

This is a transformation of a part of the plane into itself. We have three variables, but $x + y + z = 1 = x' + y' + z'$. By iterating this transformation one obtains the expected values of the numbers of elements of each type in the subsequent generations. In the above-mentioned study some properties of the iterates of the transformation were established. In particular, in some cases there may be convergence to a stable distribution, in others there is a convergence to an oscillating behavior, etc.

These studies concerned a random mating (or collisions) between pairs of elements. The question arose as to the behavior of such systems if the binary production were not a random one but instead subject to some constraints, say, due to geometry. A most stringent one seemed to be to imagine, for example, that the elements form the vertices of a division of a plane into regular triangles, each vertex being of one of the three possible "colors." Then consider an initial configuration as given and assume the production of new elements by pairs of vertices forming sides of the triangular division. In the simplest case one can start with one triangle whose three vertices are all different in type. The next generation will be formed then by the three pairs as parents and each side of the given triangle will produce a new vertex whose color is a function of the two colors of the parents. We shall obtain then a second generation and continue in this fashion. It is immediately found, however, that the construction cannot be uniquely continued. After a small number of generations it will appear that two pairs of vertices forming two sides of the configuration will have a single vertex as completing the two triangles to be constructed. Which color to assign to the new vertex? It may be that the two sets of parents will give a conflicting recipe for the color of the new point.

One way out of this dilemma would be not to consider a point for which a conflicting determination of color may be given and leave its position vacant. This recipe extended to points which are doubly determined by two sides of previously constructed triangles gave rise to the study mentioned in the previous paragraphs. Actually the patterns mentioned above could be considered as consisting of points which are of three different kinds (imagining, for example, that the new ones arise in a "molecule" as a result of a double bond, etc.). As it is, R. G. Schrandt and the writer have considered also other recipes for determining the color of points which were given conflicting determinations by the two pairs of parents. One rule (Rule No. 1) was to choose the type not involved in the conflicting determination: since there are three types, if the two determinations for the new points differ, one may choose the third one. Another rule (Rule No. 2) was also considered: to decide, at random with equal probability, which of the two contrasting determinations should be chosen. Still another rule (Rule No. 3) was to choose, in case of such a conflict, a fourth color whose proportion will be denoted by w and such that an x type $+ w$ type produces x; $y + w$ produces y and $z + w$ produces z and $w + w$ produces w in subsequent combinations. This could have an interpretation of representing a molecule of a type which cannot propagate except in combination with itself. We have studied experimentally, on a computing machine, the propagation of such systems. The Rule No. 2 in particular involves sometimes a random determination of points somewhat similar to the study in the Los Alamos Laboratory Report LA-2305 mentioned above on random mating. Under all these rules, there seems to be a convergence of the number of particles of different types to a steady distribution (in contrast to the behavior given by iteration of the quadratic transformations where in many cases there is an oscillatory limit or even more irregular ergodic asymptotic behavior). In some cases the convergence seems to take place to a fixed point (*i.e.,* a definite value of x, y, z), and under Rule No. 2 to values, numerically not too different from the fixed point of the corresponding quadratic transformation. It has not been possible to *prove* the existence of a limiting distribution but the numerical work strongly indicates it. It should be noted that all the initial configurations were of the simplest possible type, *e.g.,* consisted of one triplet of points. A detailed description of this work will appear in a report by R. G. Schrandt.

III. We return now to our discussion of growing patterns where we do not label the new elements by different colors but merely consider, as in part I of this paper, the geometry of the growing figure. The problem arose of considering the properties of growth of such figures with a rule of erasure or "death" of old elements: suppose we fix an integer k arbitrarily and to our recursive definition of construction of new elements add the rule that we erase from the pattern all elements which are

k generations old. In particular, suppose $k = 3$ and consider the growth from squares, as in the first rule in part I of this paper, with the additional proviso that after constructing the $(n + 1)$th generation, we shall erase all points of the $(n - 1)$th generation. (The construction allows the configuration to grow back into points of a previous generation of index l where l is less than $n - 1$.) In this construction, starting, say, with two squares to begin with, one will observe a growth of patterns, then a splitting (due to erasures) and then later recombinations of the pattern. A search was undertaken for initial patterns which in future generations split into figures similar or identical with previous ones, *i.e.,* a reproduction, at least for certain values, of the index of generation. It was not possible, in general, even in the cases where a growth pattern without erasure could be predicted, to describe the appearance of the apparently moving figures which in general exhibit a very chaotic behavior. In one starting configuration, however, one could predict the future behavior. This configuration consists of two squares touching each other at one point and located diagonally. Under our Rule No. 1 with erasure of the third oldest generation, this pattern is reproduced as four copies of itself in every 2^pth generation ($p = 1, 2, 3 \ldots$), displaced by 2^p units from the original pattern. The same behavior holds for starting patterns of, say, four squares located diagonally, or eight points or sixteen points, etc.

In case of a triangular subdivision the behavior of growth with a rule of erasure for old elements was also experimentally investigated. The process of growth was considered as follows: given a finite collection of vertices of the triangular subdivision of the plane—some labeled with the index $n - 1$ and others with n—one constructs the points of the $(n + 1)$th generation by adding vertices of the triangles whose sides are labeled either with $n - 1$ and n or n and n—again, however, not putting in points which are *doubly* determined. One then erases all points with the index $n - 1$. In case of squares our rules of growth enable the pattern to exist indefinitely, starting with any nontrivial initial condition. This is not always the case for triangles. In particular, a starting pattern of two vertices with the same generation terminates after ten generations—that is to say, all possible points of growth are conflicting ones and these are not allowed by our rule of construction.

One has to point out here that in the case of the "death" rule, which operates by erasure of all elements that are *k* generations *old,* the initial configuration has to specify which elements are of the first and which of the second generation. Two vertices, one labeled first and the other second generation, will give rise to a viable pattern.

IV. In three-dimensional space a similar experimental study was made of growth of patterns on a cubical lattice. The rules of growth can be considered in a similar way to the recipes used in two dimensions. Starting with one cube one may construct new ones which are adjacent to it (have a face in common). Again one will not put in new cubes if they have a face in common with more than one cube of the previous generation. The analogue of the first rule gives a system whose density in space tends to 0. This is in contrast to the situation in the plane where a finite density was obtained for this case.

R. G. Schrandt has investigated on a computer the growth of system with a rule for erasure of old elements. The case of erasure of elements three generations old was followed. The patterns which appear seem to be characterized by bunches of cubes forming flat groups. These groups are connected by thin threads. Description of these patterns and a few general statements one can make about them will also be contained in Schrandt's report.

These heuristic studies, already in two dimensions, show that the variety of patterns is too great to allow simple characterizations. The writer has attempted to make corresponding definitions in one dimension with the hope that some general properties of sequences defined by analogous recursive rules would be gleaned from them. Suppose we define a sequence of integers as follows: starting with the integers 1, 2 we construct new ones in sequence by considering sums of two previously defined integers but not including in our collection those integers which can be obtained as a sum of previous ones in more than one way. We never add an integer to itself. The sequence which starts with 1 and 2 will continue as follows: 1, 2, 3, 4, 6, 8, 11, 13, 16, 18, 26, 28, ... The integer 5 is not in it because it is a sum of two previous ones in two different ways. The next integer which is expressed in one and only one way of the sum of previous ones is 6; 7 has a double representation

but 8 is uniquely determined; 11 is the next and so on. Starting with 1 and 3 one obtains the following sequence: 1, 3, 4, 5, 6, 8, 10, 12, 17, 21, ... Unfortunately, it appears to the writer that even here it is not easy to establish properties of these "unique sum sequences." For example, the question of whether there will be infinitely many twins, *i.e.,* integers in succession differing by two, seems difficult to answer. Even a good estimate of density of these sequences relative to the set of all integers is not easily made.

The aim in presenting these disconnected empirical studies was to point out problems attending the combinatorics of systems which, in an extremely simplified and schematic way, show a growth of figures subject to simple geometrical constraints. It seems obvious that, before one can obtain some general properties in "auxology," a great deal of experimental data have to be surveyed. It was possible to study the effect of many variations in our rules on the computing machines. A scope attached to the machine allows one to survey the resulting patterns visually—their computation takes only a very short time. This work is continuing and perhaps some more general properties of their morphology will be demonstrable.

Example 1. Starting with the black square as the first generation, each successive generation consists of those squares that are adjacent to one and only one square of previous generations. In most of these illustrations, only cells in certain directions were drawn. Growth in other directions is the same because of symmetry conditions.

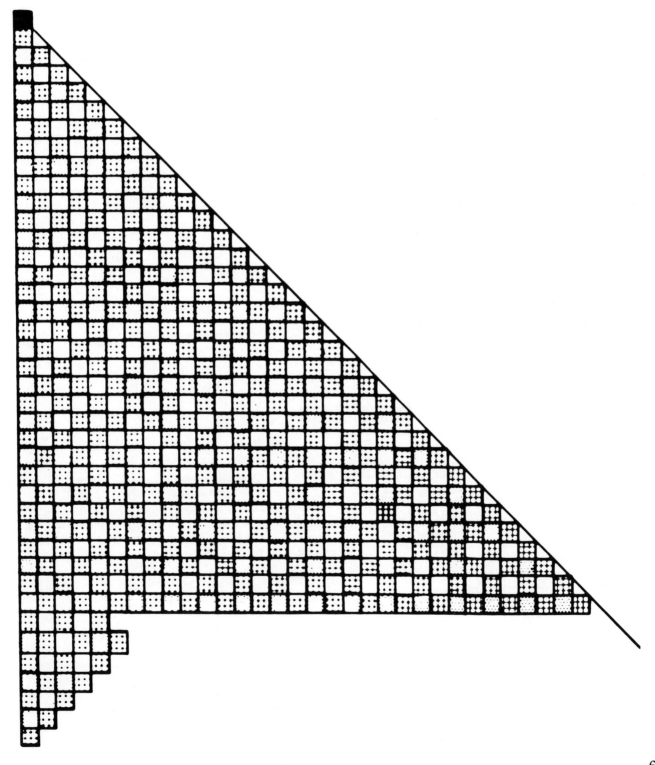

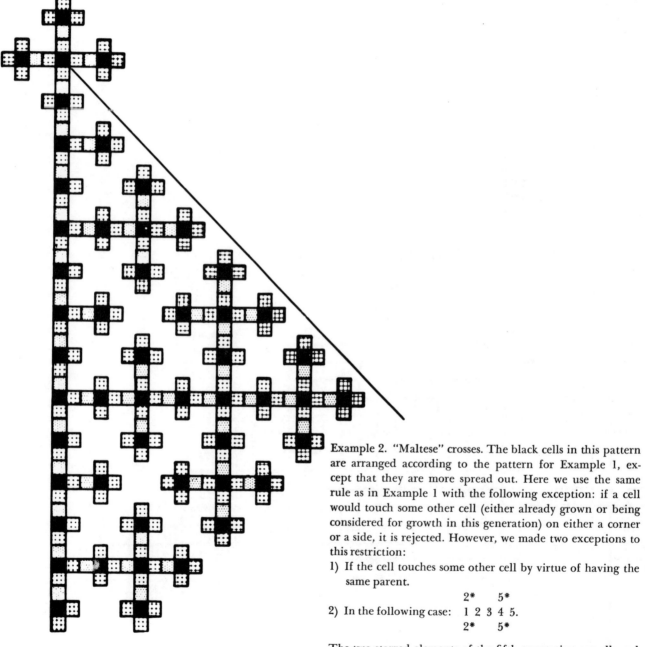

Example 2. "Maltese" crosses. The black cells in this pattern are arranged according to the pattern for Example 1, except that they are more spread out. Here we use the same rule as in Example 1 with the following exception: if a cell would touch some other cell (either already grown or being considered for growth in this generation) on either a corner or a side, it is rejected. However, we made two exceptions to this restriction:

1) If the cell touches some other cell by virtue of having the same parent.

2) In the following case:
$$\begin{array}{cccccc} & 2^* & & 5^* & \\ 1 & 2 & 3 & 4 & 5. \\ & 2^* & & 5^* & \end{array}$$

The two starred elements of the fifth generation are allowed to touch potential, though previously rejected, children of the third generation. This has to be allowed to enable the growth to turn corners. Note that the children of the third generation were rejected only because of the potential children of the starred members of the second generation.

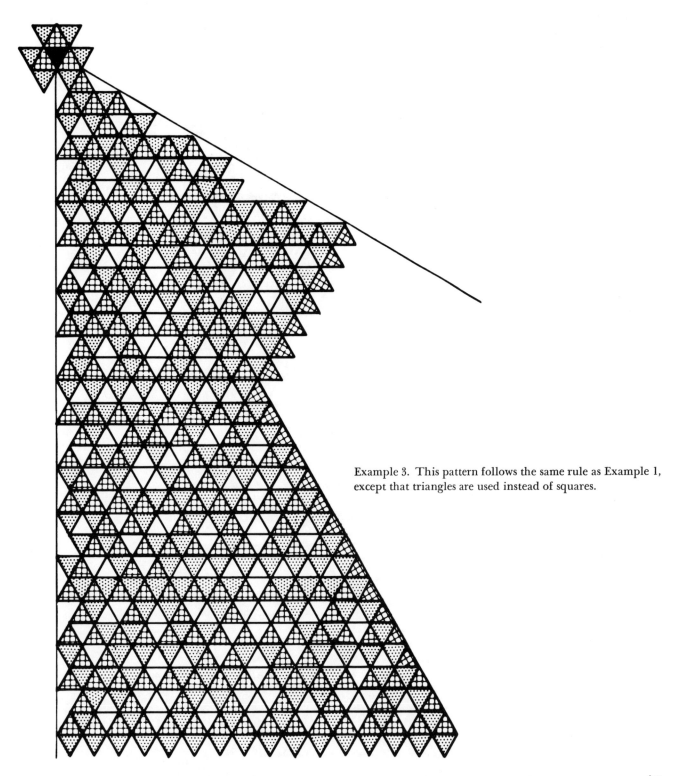

Example 3. This pattern follows the same rule as Example 1, except that triangles are used instead of squares.

Example 4. This pattern follows the same rule as Example 3 with one exception: if a new cell would touch the corner of some old cell (other than a parent), it is rejected.

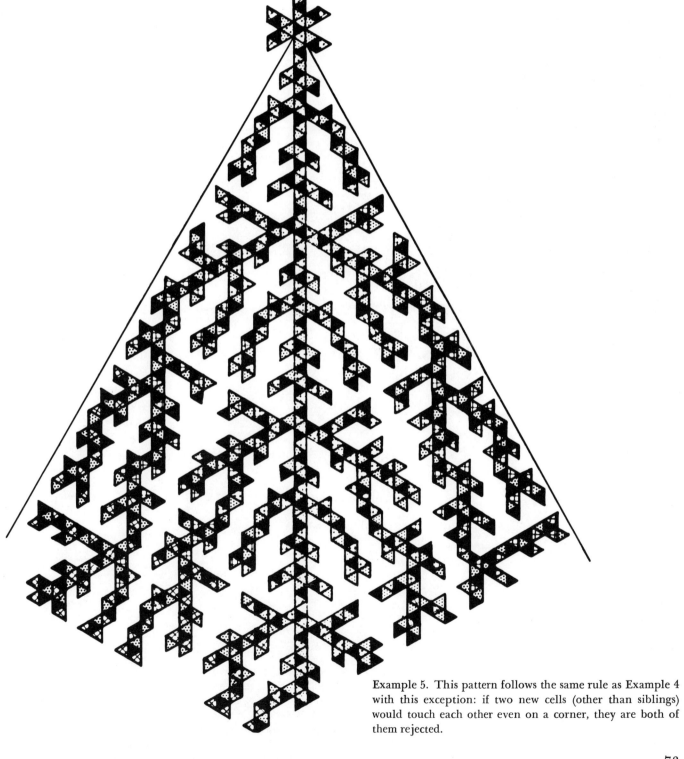

Example 5. This pattern follows the same rule as Example 4 with this exception: if two new cells (other than siblings) would touch each other even on a corner, they are both of them rejected.

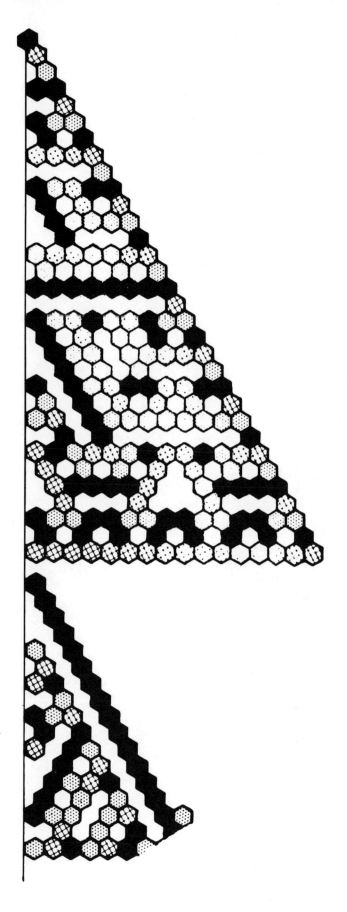

Example 6. This pattern follows the same rule as Example 1, except that hexagons are used instead of squares. The reason it is disconnected is that a triangle of cells is left out. This triangle is the same as that formed in the first few generations for what is drawn plus a mirror image of it.

Sculpture by S. Filipowski, 1964.

MODULAR IDEAS IN
SCIENCE AND IN ART:
VISUAL DOCUMENTS

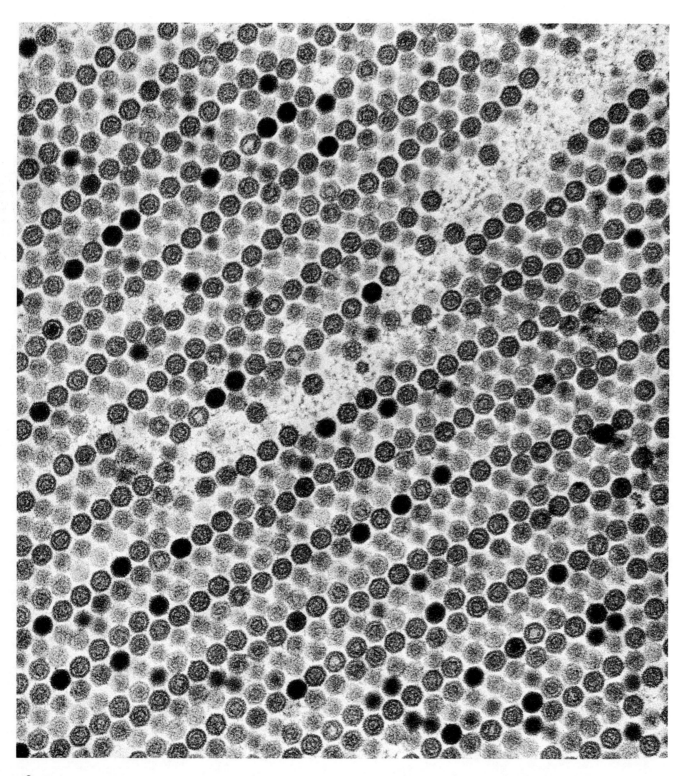

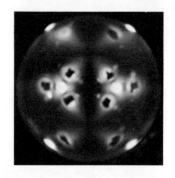

Below: Sordaria fimicola.
Photo micrograph by Arif S. El-Ani.
New York State Department of Health.

At right: Uranium oxide on tungsten.
Molecule structure recorded by field
emission microscope. Courtesy Professor
Erwin W. Müller.

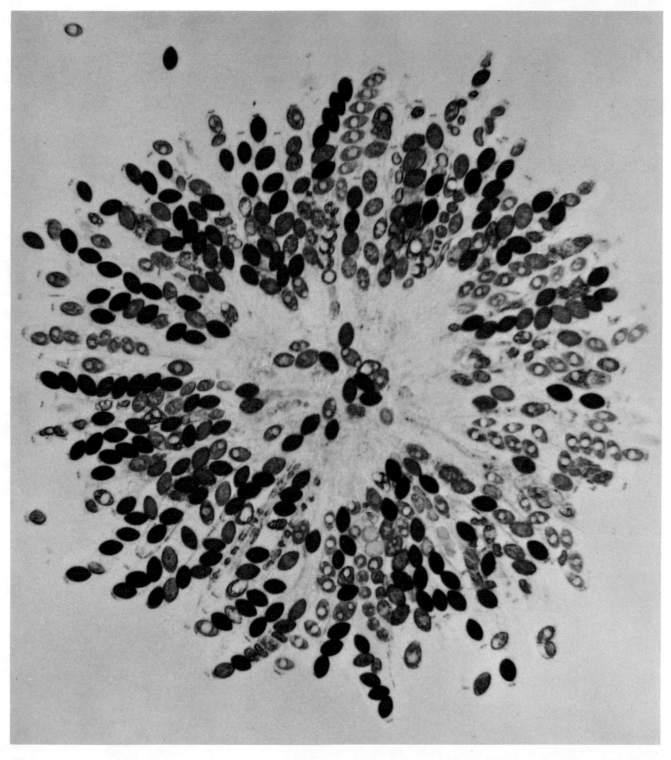

Floor mosaic of the thirteenth century.
Church of St. John the Evangelist,
Ravenna. Photo Gyorgy Kepes.

Sunflower seeds. Photo Tet A. von Borsig.

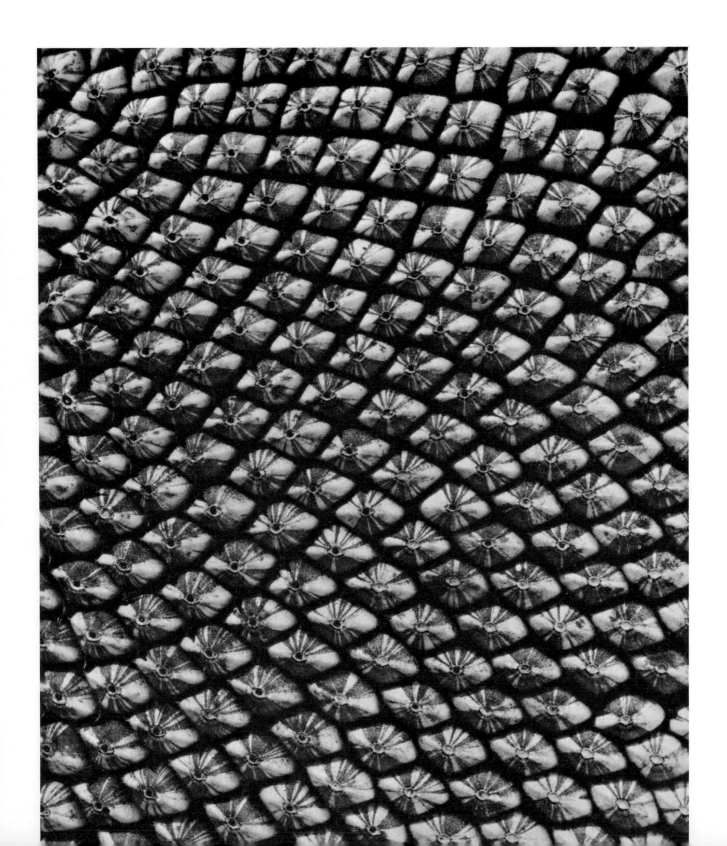

a

a. Snowflake.

b. Crystal of virus. Magnification: 44,000 X.
Electron micrograph. Courtesy Dr. C. Morgan,
Department of Microbiology, Columbia University.

c. Pattern from Hokusai's *Shingata Komontcho*
of 1824, a book for the textile trade.

d. R. Buckminster Fuller. Structure Study.

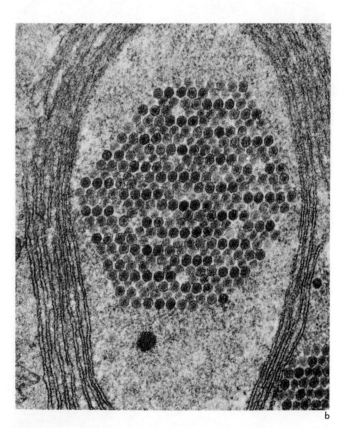
b

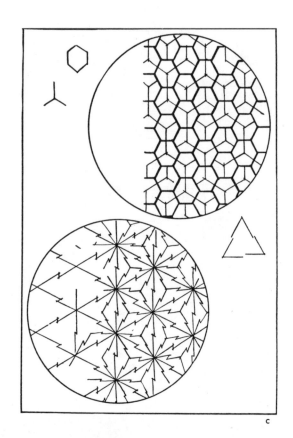
c

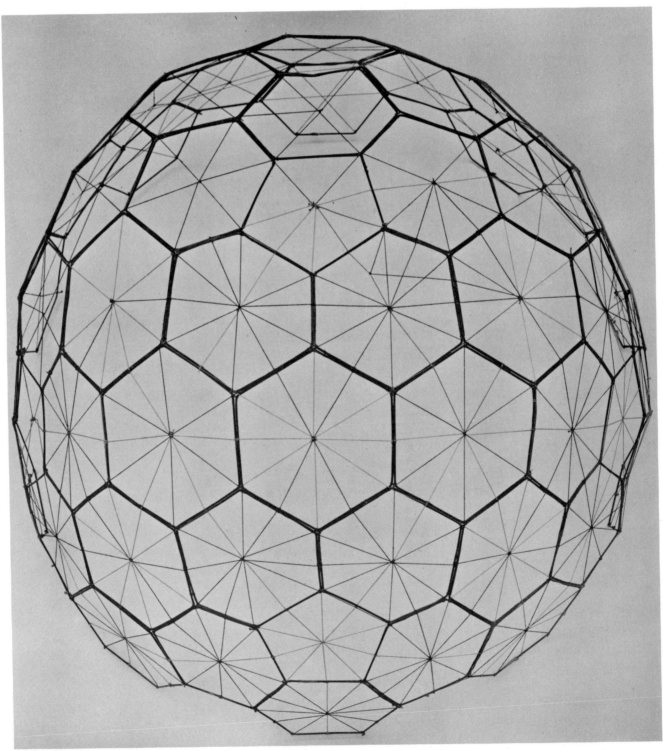

d

Flower. Photo Tet A. von Borsig.

Regular bodies drawn by
Leonardo da Vinci for
the *Divina proportione*
of Luca Pacioli, 1509.

Bruno Munari. *Tetracono,*
1965. Photo Ugo Mulas.

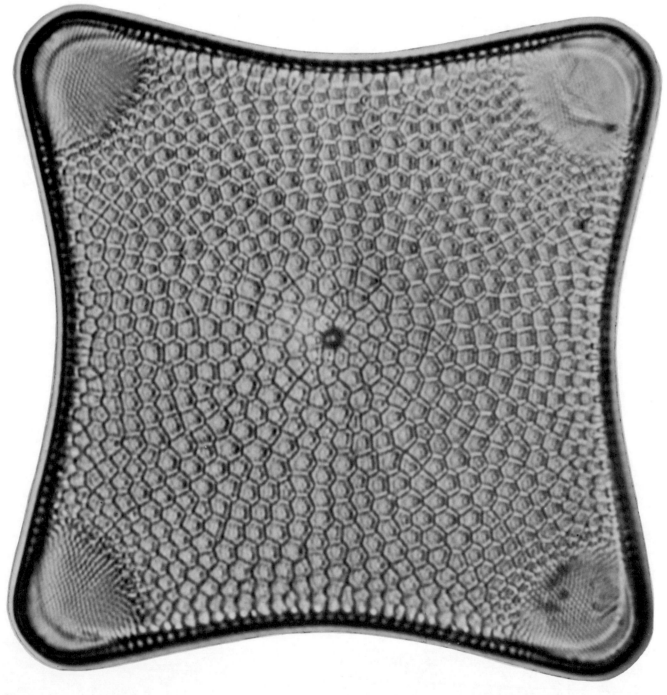

R. Buckminster Fuller.
Geodesic dome.

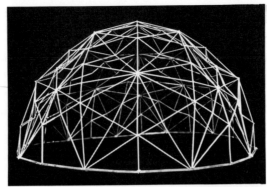

Below: Radiolaria.

At left: Rose window of the 15th century, Sainte-Chapelle, Paris.
Above: Rose window of the 12th century, Cathedral of San Ruffino, Assisi.

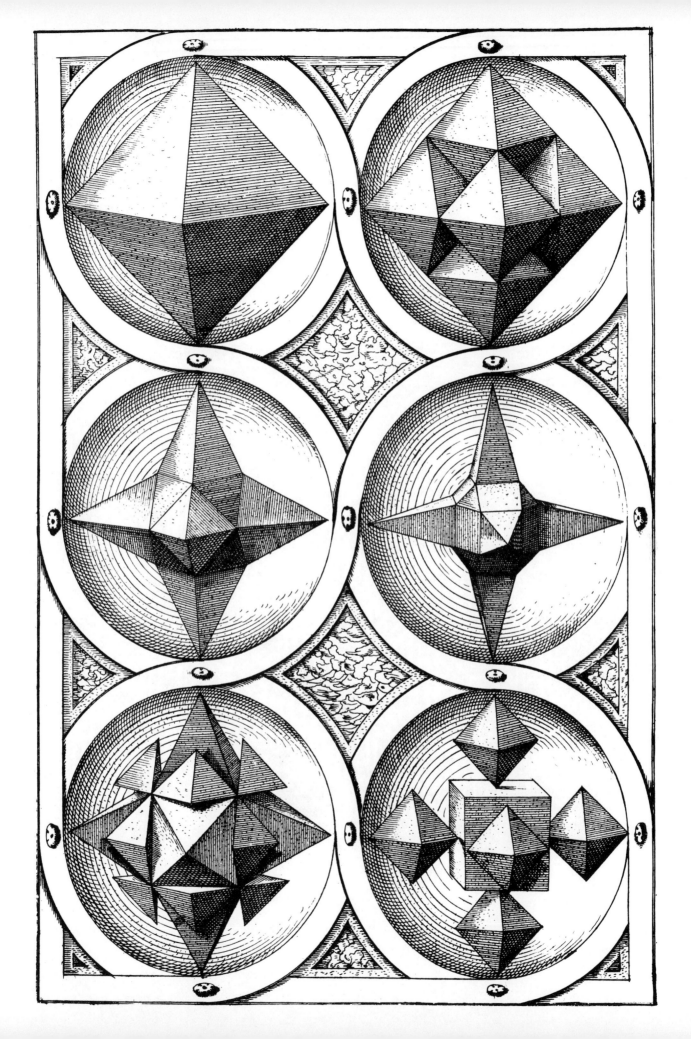

Rubbing from New Guinea.

Modular sunscreen.

Exterior wall panels of precast Schokbeton concrete.
Torrington Manufacturing Plant, 1963–1964, Nivelles, Belgium.
Architects: Marcel Breuer and Hamilton Smith.

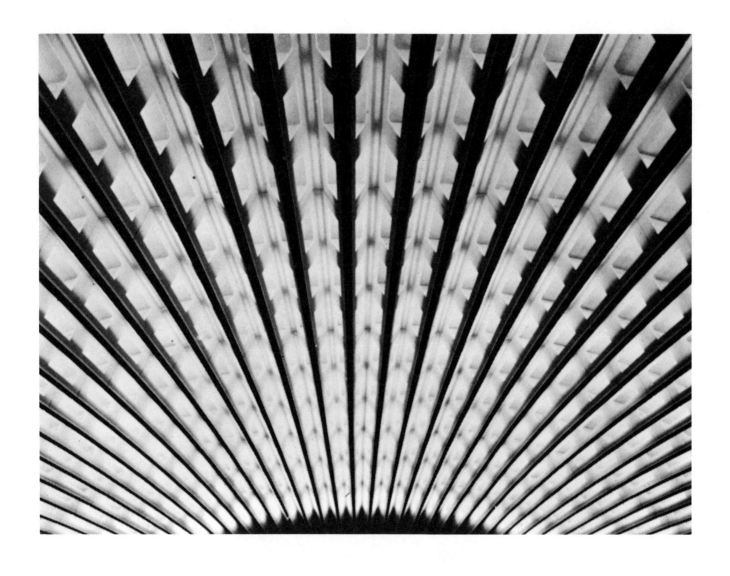

Ceiling ribs of prefabricated units of Ferro-cemento.
Palazzo dello Sport, 1958–1959, Rome.
Architect: Pier Luigi Nervi.

Light animated modular surface.
Getulio Alviani. *LL 360 14/14 INV*,
aluminum relief, 1964.

Modular pattern animated by illumination.
Design by Gyorgy Kepes.

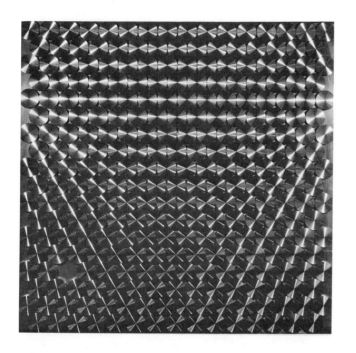

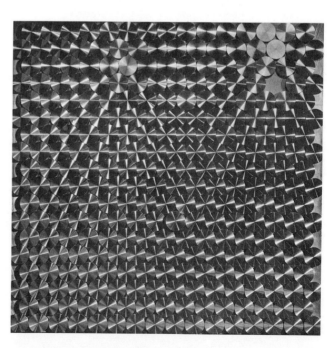

Rhythmic animation of a surface through the
illumination of modular units placed in
different combinatory relationships.
Student work, Massachusetts Institute of
Technology. Courtesy Professor R. Preusser.

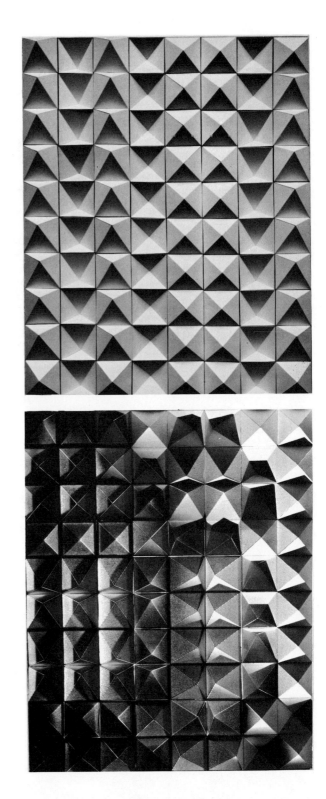

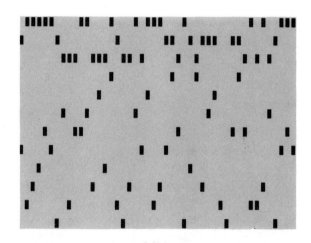

Below: Rhythmic surface created by superimposition of equidistant concentric circles and parallel lines. Herman Baravalle, *Pictorial Mathematics.*

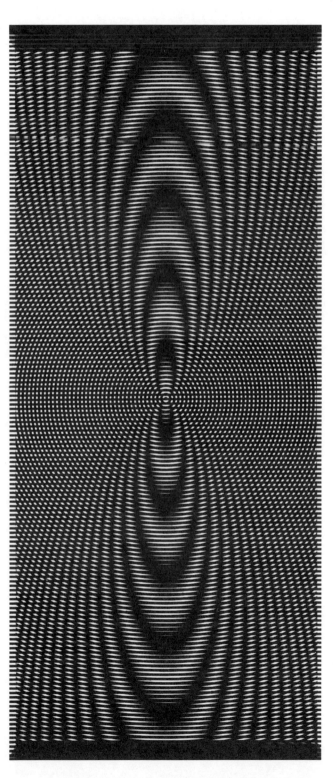

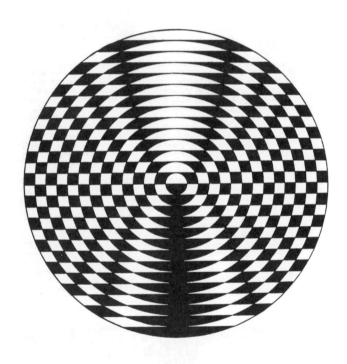

At right: Moiré effect produced by the kinetic optical combination of two superimposed patterns of parallel lines and concentric circles. Gerald Oster. *Conic Section II,* 1964. Courtesy Howard Wise Gallery, New York.

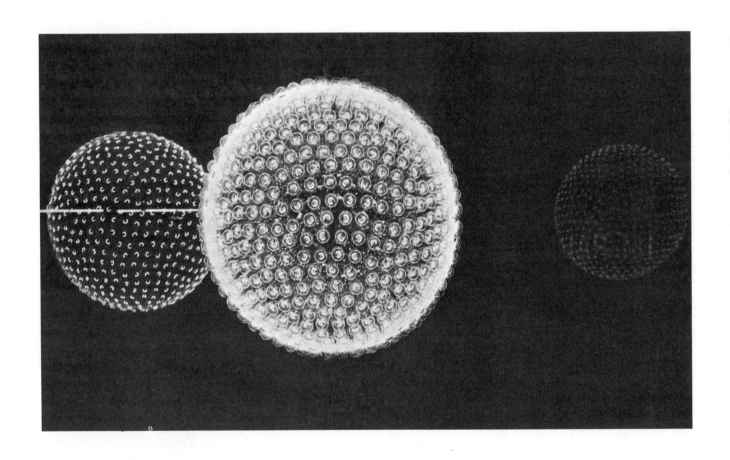

Otto Piene. *Light Planets,* 1964–1965. New City Theater, Bonn.

Below: Piet Mondrian. *Broadway Boogie-Woogie,*
1942–1943. Museum of Modern Art, New York.

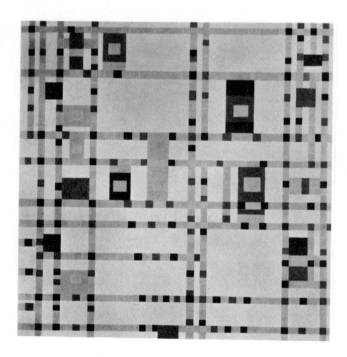

At right: Theo van Doesburg. Design for stained
glass window, 1924. Courtesy Rose Fried Gallery.

Le Corbusier. Façade of the Secretariat, Chandigarh, India, 1951–1956.

LAWRENCE B. ANDERSON

MODULE: MEASURE, STRUCTURE, GROWTH AND FUNCTION

Dictionaries, reflecting the last generation's usages, confine their definition of "module" to the narrow technical meaning of module as it is used by scholars in analyzing the classic orders of architecture. The Parthenon of Athens had columns almost twice as high as those of the Theseion in the same city, yet in both cases the columns were eleven modules high, the module being one half the column diameter. By applying the module and its subdivisions to all the critical dimensions of column and entablature the proportions of the order could be related to a common measure independently of absolute size. It is astonishing that using the same basic elements the Greeks were able to stretch the fundamental idea of a rectangular building with porticos on all sides from delicate little shrines up to great bulky temples covering two acres of ground.

True to the quality of Greek thought in many other domains, Greek trabeated architecture stands out as a remarkably clear statement of the basic formal problems encountered. For example, the end portico of the temple, given dominance by the diagonal accent of the pediment, requires a whole-number relationship with the more passive, but much longer, side portico. Again, the spacing of triglyphs in the frieze gave two of these to every column, while the mutules still higher up were four to a column. The triglyph centered on the column required a special solution to the spacing problem at the corner of the building. All of these are modular considerations as the term is now understood, for we are now concerned with module not only as a hidden unit of measure, but also as a visible unit

Fig. 1. Theseion, Athens. Photo Agora Excavations.

Fig. 2. Parthenon, Athens.
Detailed measurements of
the portico members.
From Stuart and Revett,
The Antiquities of Athens.

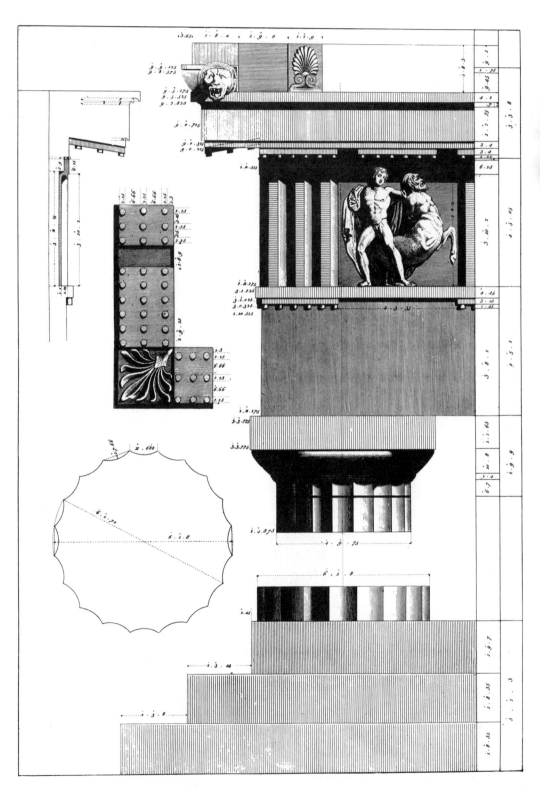

103

Fig. 3. Campanile and Cathedral, Pisa. Photo courtesy Anton Schroll and Co.

Fig. 4. Subdivision of a pyramid. Student work, Massachusetts Institute of Technology.

Fig. 5. Subdivision of the torus. Student work, North Carolina State College.

The unit of recurrence may simply subdivide the surfaces of a geometric solid. The great religious structures grouped together at Pisa are decorated with tiers of arcades. These arcades give unity to four buildings very dissimilar in form. They also supply accurate visual clues to scale and distance, since a feeling for the true size of one module gives a measure to all the buildings. Very strikingly in the campanile, the arcades define the cylindrical form of the tower through the foreshortening of their forms as the curved surfaces turn away from the observer. This effect is independent of light and shade; in no illumination will the shaft appear other than as a cylinder. In contradistinction, the surfaces bounding the nearby cathedral are clearly planar. Thus modular subdivision of a surface is a powerful visual device for emphasizing the geometry and defining the size of architectural forms. Its mere presence intensifies the "thereness" of surface.

The subdivision of the surface of a solid like the truncated pyramid requires distortion of the module to preserve wholeness of units and consistency at the corners without which the feeling of the whole being composed of the parts would be lost. The lozenges seen below continuously change their size and shape as they move over the surface of the pyramid. What would otherwise be a rather static form becomes charged with the tension of change. Surfaces of double curvature will be encountered increasingly as the technology of thin-shell construction becomes more familiar. As both Nervi and Fuller have shown, double-curved forms can be constructed of separate prefabricated units as well as of continuous membranes. Warped surfaces will often be selected on the basis of their subdivision geometry. Straight-line generation, as in the hyperbolic paraboloid, is a factor in aid of subdivision. Surfaces generated by revolution of curved lines are more difficult to subdivide into standardized modules. The torus illustrated below may be broken down into lozenges defined by two sets of lines moving helically around the torus. Here again the module modulates in size, from a maximum at the outer face to a minimum on the inner.

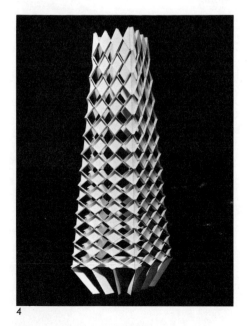

4

5

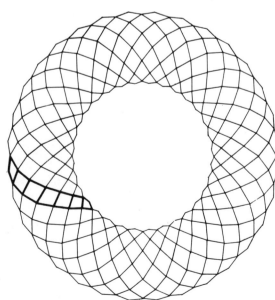

Fig. 6. Alberti, Palazzo Rucellai,
Florence. Photo Alinari Art
Reference Bureau.

The architects of the Italian Renaissance, with their intellectual passion for measure and proportion, were eager to develop the rhythm potentials of modularization. Tradition, climate, and available materials combined in Italy to make plane masonry walls whose solid parts dominate the relatively small openings needed for windows. Such walls the architects proceeded to subdivide in precise patterns of great visual power. Departing from earlier schemes like that of the Palazzo Riccardi by Michelozzo and the Palazzo Pitti by Brunelleschi, Alberti in 1451 revived for the Palazzo Rucellai the ancient Roman device of applying classic orders in multiple tiers to the façade. Supplied thus with horizontal and vertical divisions the wall surface comes to life as a plane completely filled by a system of definite repetitive units of measure, well-proportioned rectangles within which the windows are organized as secondary forms. It is surprising how elegant and strong this device proves to be, even with a very restrained relief; the pilasters give hardly more shadow than the stone joints, yet so true is the proportion that the wall resonates. Half a century later Bramante in the Cancelleria exploited the cadence of a long-short spacing, the windows occurring between pairs of pilasters. The ratio between long and short provided yet another opportunity for the application of proportional measure.

Fig. 7. Bramante, Cancelleria, Rome. Photo Alinari Art Reference Bureau.

As the parade of Italian genius revealed itself, newcomers built on what had gone before. In 1549 the young Palladio, in his design for the façade of the Basilica in Vicenza, a building already a century old, applied orders at two scales, the smaller spaced according to a module one half as great as the larger. The arcades which reflect the vaulting system characteristic of Renaissance building were in Palladio's time combined with the classic orders. Palladio rested his arcade upon the smaller of his orders, but spaced the arches according to his larger module, producing an intricate rhythm involving a sequence of proportional ratios between large and small parts, a façade rich in plastic events, part structural necessity but largely sheer visual intrigue.

An exterior beautification of an existing structure, the Basilica of Vicenza is an example of calculated façade architecture. Contrast it with the west elevation of Notre Dame la Grande in Poitiers, neither Italian nor Renaissance. Three hundred years before Alberti's Palazzo Rucellai, this façade is also modularized; the entire surface is subdivided into modules of similar shape. The common denominator of these modules is the arch, but the range of size of the arches is about 8 : 1. The largest arches are composed of multiple archivolts supported on clusters of columns. Accordingly, as the arcades become smaller they are supported, either on paired columns or on single columns, and finally

Fig. 8. Palladio, Basilica, Vicenza.

only on brackets. There are horizontal tiers of arcades, five in all, yet the central window interrupts the upper three, and the two flanking towers have arcatures supported on grouped columns that break the rhythm of the façade. The whole is crowned by the oval in the gable containing the triumphant Christ and the four Evangelists, bringing to a climax the accumulated curves below. The calculated sequences and proportions characteristic of the Renaissance are entirely absent. One searches in vain for any commensurate ratio between the many different scales of arcades. The two arches on the ground floor on each side of the entrance arch are made narrower partly by making the arches pointed, though none of the other arches has this form. The ratios of size of the three lower arches do not reflect the proportions of nave and aisles of the church. Indeed the whole façade is more sculptural than architectural. These modules have more to do with the hierarchy of sculptural representation than with structural necessity or geometric logic; the arcades are frames for the statues of saints and apostles and for a number of biblical narratives. The designer considered that a unit of recurrence could be treated with utmost freedom, and he allowed the arch to range from a broad and rugged structural form down to the mere cusping of a coping or archivolt, with all degrees between. He achieved richness and variety with a single formal idea diversely stated.

Fig. 9. Notre Dame la Grande, Poitiers, west elevation. Photo Jean Roubier.

Later Medieval architecture did not fail to provide a more disciplined modularization. Consider the interior elevation of a bay in the nave of one of the great cathedrals, Chartres for example. Such a bay is bounded below by the main colonnette clusters and above by the arch at the base of the main vault. Within this as a frame are placed the ground-floor arch, open to the aisle, the small tier of four arches of the triforium, and still higher a pair of clerestory windows surmounted by the culminating wheel window. Even considered apart from the context of the nave as a whole, this complex is highly organized. The progression 1–4–2–1 establishes a clear numerical hierarchy. Each element is complete within itself yet specifically related to its neighbors and to the whole.

Fig. 10. Cathedral, Chartres,
interior elevation of a bay.
Photo Courtauld Institute of Art.

Fig. 11. Cathedral, Bourges, interior view.

It would be myopic to think of modularity in a Gothic cathedral as limited to the analysis of a single bay, for in Gothic architecture structural necessity generates the module. As every student is aware, the cross vault based on pointed arches, intersecting in diagonal ribs, and spanning a rectangle in plan, is the basic Gothic module. Walls hardly seem to be involved at all. Each structural module is open to the next and can expand by duplicating itself in four directions. The adjoining vault compartments are mutually dependent, as they neutralize each other's thrusts, although the flying buttress permits modulating the scale and vertically offsetting the joint to afford clerestory lighting. The system has flexibility, as when the vault cluster becomes pentagonal in order to make a radiating chapel. The extraordinarily flowing quality of Gothic architectural space is due not so much to the repetition of the structural module as to the interlocking type of joinery that binds the modules in a continuous spatial framework. Each element, such as an arch, a rib, or a colonnette, is visibly a member of a family of similar elements distributed throughout, yet also has its own special role in the organization of the bay to which it belongs.

In the end it is space itself which is modularized, and the module is not so much one of subdivision, as in the examples previously examined, but of accretion and seemingly infinite growth. The Cathedral of Bourges is a highly symmetrical, hierarchically organized, and complete form with a progressive scale relationship in the two aisles and nave, powerfully terminated by choir and ambulatory. Yet so vast are the modules and so numerous that in the interior there appears to be no beginning and no end. Iteration of the module has the effect of obliterating spatial limits.

The above are examples of the module as a unit of visual measure, as a way of characterizing surface, and as a unit of structure and growth. Something should now be said about the module of function. Both occupancy and circulation generate modularity in architectural form. Repetitive units dictated by functional necessity occur in all sizes but are more conspicuous at the larger scale of urban design.

In at least the older towns it is easy to see in the residential areas a repetition of the unit of family lodging. When society agrees in the main about the characteristic form of the lodging, a strong visual harmony results.

As a module of circulation we have the street. A network of passageways on the ground sufficiently dense to provide public access to every private plot becomes rationalized in the planned city to a gridiron of equally spaced streets in two directions at right angles to each other, generating rectangular parcels. In order to solve contemporary movement problems, this simple conception must be greatly elaborated. Circulation as a generator of town-planning modules is also evident in vertical movement patterns in high density development. The grouping of elevators into complexes tends to delimit the floor area of tall buildings to the zone that can be effectively served by a single vertical circulation core. Major horizontal circulation is limited to ground level and perhaps one or two auxiliary levels near the ground. Skyscrapers stand as separate modular events, each with its own vertical system. Greater densities may disrupt this system, may prove it outdated, and further technological development may introduce new patterns, not limited to the ground level for horizontal movement, and introducing a richer three-dimensional space continuum.

Modularity in architecture is no respecter of scales. The superb texture of a brick wall is due to units eight inches in length while in Manhattan the north-south avenues are spaced only six to the mile, a difference of over a thousandfold. Yet each unit is in the broad sense a module, a significant repeating element in the man-made environment. What is the special pertinence of modularity in meeting the problems of the 1960's? Two observations are apparent.

Fig. 12. Skyscrapers of lower Manhattan. Wide World Photos.

Fig. 13. Air view of a gridiron
city: downtown Chicago.
Wide World Photos.

First, architectural values can only with great difficulty be adjusted to the ever higher industrialization affecting every aspect of our culture, but one thing is sure: The modularization that was inaugurated with brick manufacture at the dawn of history is being steadily intensified, and the scale of the transportable modular element has increased from what is convenient to the human hand to what can be manipulated by power movers such as the hoist and the trailer truck. As the elements get larger, they are more and more determinants of the design. Therefore the architect cannot limit his form-making to the assembly of elements, but must himself influence the form of the industrially-produced element. The extent of this revolution is readily apparent in the problems of building alteration. Buildings produced by highly industrialized processes cannot easily be repaired, altered, and modernized by itinerant skilled craftsmen, supposing such personnel to be available. When a major part proves defective and in need of replacement, or if additions need to be made, the work requires calling into action the highly organized industrial skills and equipments that were used initially. This is part of the price of industrialization.

Second, technological and social changes are more rapid than ever before, but what is not always linked to this truism is that other time-measured events, such as the human lifespan or the potential life of a building, are actually being prolonged. This change in ratios throws a new light on the designer's task. Think, for example, of school buildings erected before World War II—almost all are static finished compositions aimed at meeting a specific enrollment. Future growth was not part of the conception. Then consider the school buildings since 1945. They have mostly been built in the suburbs, where greatest population increase has been concentrated. The school population may well double every five years. No static closed composition can meet such a situation of rapid change. What is needed is a design for building which can grow easily by successive accretions to several times its original size.

Fig. 14. Construction photo: Gujavat University, Ahmedabad, India. Architect: B. V. Doshi.

Fig. 15. Snowflakes.

This is only one example of many. The history of contemporary architectural practice is filled with illustrations of the failure of the designer's solution in the face of overwhelming expansion of need and unpredictable changes of occupancy. The pace of growth and change is the most important characteristic of the problems we now face, as compared to those of the past.

The problem of growth is to provide open-ended, expansible systems, equipped with methods of attaching new elements which, though predetermined, allow flexibility for future decision-making. The analogies with crystal-forming and biological growth have not been without effect on current trends in design.

Crystalline organization demonstrates how even a single geometric organization-principle can provide infinite solutions (*i.e.,* snowflakes). Biological growth, classified admirably for designers by D'Arcy Thompson, has at least two systematic methods of great interest. Mollusks secrete their calcareous protective shells in a continuously expanding module; each unit increment is larger than its predecessors, in accord with the growth of both requirement and capability of the occupant. Some industrial and institutional corporations grow in this expanding fashion.

The growth of trees is extraordinary. Everything about a tree is modular: an oak leaf is pretty much the same from an oak tree of any size. Each year new shoots depart from points previously established as buds, forming new branch structures. A branch once defined does not change its length from joint to joint but becomes progressively thicker as it needs to support the increasingly numerous progeny branches that have grown from its buds year by year. Within this general system each kind of tree has special rules, and sets its signature on its structural habit so as to be recognizable without other clues.

Arboreal growth is a kind of continuously articulated network akin to the structures applicable in building construction, circulation planning, and urban design. Although in architecture

Fig. 16. Leaf. Photo Tet A. von Borsig.

and planning the elements used are biologically dead, the *design,* as humanly confected, can have the pulse of life if it foresees, permits, and directs growth, without at the same time invalidating the old structure.

Classical and Baroque architecture taught the importance of hierarchy, dominance, and the vista. Every great complex of the past had its epicenter (Stonehenge, Karnak, Baths of Caracalla, Versailles). This is the great form, closed and immutable, heedless of its surroundings. Opposed to it is a kind of network theory structuring space in which man may live in a time of change. Instead of epicenters the network contains nodes of special prominence. A network is a grid, and there are many kinds of grids. A grid with linear elements intersecting at 120° generates hexagons, a favorite agglomeration system in nature, as it permits units to fill all space with least deviation from ideal circular form and with minimal perimeter length. The hexagonal discipline has also proved useful in design. Used as a structure, the similar grid based on 60° intersection has the advantage of being self-triangulating and therefore stable against multidirectional forces.

In general, however, grids based on intersections of 60° and 120° are beset with difficulties. For circulation purposes a triangular three-way grid offers five choices of route at each intersection. A hexagonal grid with 120° intersections is relatively simpler—only two choices are available. However, one cannot move in a straight line through the system—every intersection requires a change of direction.

Compared to these the rectangular grid has distinct advantages. The system separates easily into a warp-woof contrast where one pair of directions dominates the other pair. One may move straight, ignoring the choices presented by intersections. Yet when erected as a vertical space-enclosing frame, the exclusively rectangular grid has serious structural deficiencies. Lacking both diagonality and vaulting ability, even simple gravity produces bending effects that can be countered only by a relatively inefficient use of material, while nonvertical loading produces failure unless rigidity has somehow been added to the joints. But man is incurably addicted to the horizontal plane for his most intense activities. When he stands, he stands erect to stabilize gravity, and this is the natural position for any column. Although the earth's surface is spherical, man senses north-south as different in kind from east-west and only these four directions are cardinal. For all these reasons rectangular space "fits," though at times it seems arbitrary and lacking a desired pliability.

These very general considerations may be pertinent background principles for devising new modular approaches in environmental design. The work of many contemporary architects reflects keen awareness of the role of modularity: as a means for visual discipline, for organizing the industrial process, and for giving to space some intrinsic merit that will persist under changing occupancy. Forty years ago the modern movement dissolved the static space conceptions that inhibited the nineteenth century, but that new architecture with its force, open plan, its inside-outside, its tendency to free itself from structural order, deprived us temporarily of the substantiality inherent in a strong modular organization. The module of academic Neoclassicism had stood for adherence to forms no longer alive, consequently these forms were repudiated. Now the idea of module is again asserted, with emphasis on its capability to encompass growth and change.

EZRA D. EHRENKRANTZ

MODULAR MATERIALS AND DESIGN FLEXIBILITY

The term "module" is indicative of order. It should represent a conceptual framework to operate in, rather than a specific dimension or grid. Its validity is due to the fact that modular components relate to one another like notes on the musical keyboard. The architect, contractor, and mason understand the module as the composer, conductor, and pianist understand the keyboard. It is this sense of order which makes it possible to construct an efficient building. In this context, the module is the stave of architecture. It does not determine the appearance of a building but provides a dimensional framework for its construction. Any design concept used to enclose space requires continuity of both structure and enclosure. The various parts of the building must fit together according to a mathematical relationship determined by the designer of the building. This is not unlike the case of the composer for whom the frequencies of given notes replace dimensions. He may choose his note and key, but the musical scale provides for order and understanding. The musician would not think of cutting ten vibrations per second from a note as we cut ten inches from a building product.

The order implied by the keyboard is absolute, but its capacity for variation is infinite. The module in architecture also denotes discipline and freedom. Building products manufactured in the factory by machine should not have to be altered at the building site by hand. They should fit together to enclose space in a manner desired by the architect. The quality of the design is up to the architect, but the efficiency with which a building is constructed is dependent upon the dimensional relationship of its parts to one another.

In the past this relationship was based on the use of handcrafted components, but today we must achieve order using the tool- and die-maker as our craftsman. The opportunity to obtain a sense of order in our buildings is by no means diminished by the use of machine-made products, for the basis of order both past and present is mathematics. Proportion and dimension have always been related in architectural design, even though a mythology of aesthetics has frequently obscured this fact.

Today we can no longer afford to work with hand-made products wherein the proportion of a component is fixed but the size varies. Modern technology demands that products be produced to fixed sizes. The former freedom to obtain products of any size is not only uneconomical today but will become impossible in future automated factories. As one must combine in a single design the fixed sizes of many manufacturers' products, it is obviously necessary that these components relate to one another.

The easiest way to do this would be to choose a fixed size and have all products relate to it. This fixed size may be thought of by some as a small dimension which may be multiplied any number of times to obtain larger product sizes. Others may consider it to be of greater magnitude and relate it to a structural or planning grid. In both cases, the concept of the module carries with it a simple sense of order.

In design this type of order may be obtained in other ways as well: by rhythms of two or more dimensions, or by proportional relationships of different sizes. It may also be established in a more random manner where no order is apparent to the onlooker but only to the men involved in the construction of the building as the space is enclosed with standard building products. The module then need not be apparent to a casual observer, although, in cases where the sense of order of the building is simple, it may be discerned as a grid, rhythm, or a line along which the corners of many products fall.

The fact that buildings are three dimensional makes it difficult to join the walls of a building together in a simple manner. Fig. 1 illustrates the difficulties caused by the thickness of building products when used to turn corners. If one tries to design an extremely simple modular building where the bay spacing remains constant, the solution of the thickness problem may involve a complexity of detailing which belies its aesthetic simplicity.

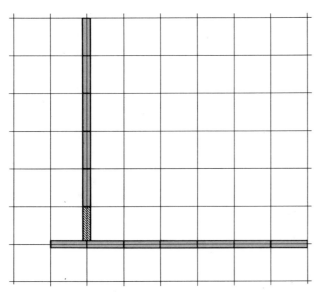

Fig. 1. Single panel size used with center line grid: the joining panel must be a special size.

In earlier periods, proportional systems were evolved that solved the thickness problem. Size was not important, only ratio for the fitting together of large stones and the consequent enclosure of space. Stones of one size could be cut as easily as those of any other, so that the ratios of these stones to one another assumed greater importance than their dimensions. The Platonic Lambda offers a good illustration of this point.

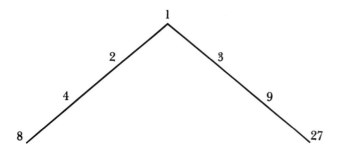

It consists of two series joined, as shown here, one being the doubling series: 1, 2, 4, 8. . . and the other the tripling series: 1, 3, 9, 27. . . . The Platonic Lambda has been surrounded by an aura of mythology which has obscured its logic. The Greeks considered 3 to be the perfect number because it had a beginning, a middle, and an end and $3 \times 3 \times 3$ gave sufficient scope for any numerical expression. Also, these two series provided the ratios used for various musical intervals: 2 : 3 is a fifth, 3 : 4 is a fourth, 8 : 9 is a tone, 1 : 2 is an octave, etc. These two series provided the basis for harmonic proportions which has been described in detail in Rudolf Wittkower's book, *Architectural Principles in the Age of Humanism* (London, 1952). Other proportional relationships were developed by the Greeks based on dynamic symmetry or fractional proportions. The best known of this group of proportional systems is the Golden Section, upon which Le Corbusier developed his Modulor.

The basic value of these proportional systems in terms of building is that a group of product dimensions may be established on the basis of a proportion other than a whole-number ratio such as 3 : 5, and the products of one of these proportional systems will fit together so as to enclose space. Although it would indeed be impossible to enclose space using a group of standard products developed on a ratio of 1 : 1.55 or 1 : 1.64, it may readily be done with products developed on a 1 : 1.618 ratio.

The ratio of 1 : 1.618 may be developed by use of a mathematical series discovered by Filius Bonacci in the sixteenth century, which is termed the "Fibonacci series." In this series the two previous terms are added to give a third term so that $1 + 2 = 3, 2 + 3 = 5, 3 + 5 = 8, 5 + 8 = 13$, and $8 + 13 = 21$. The ratio between two consecutive numbers is 1 : 1.618.

Thus dynamic symmetry does permit products of other than whole-number ratios to be related together so that a building may be constructed with standard elements. The interest of a façade designed on this basis is partially due to the fact that the relationship of the products to one another is more subtle than in the case of the repetition of 4' x 8' sheets of plywood.

The use of these proportional systems and the bonding capacity of masonry construction made it possible to solve the thickness problem in the past. Today we must work with relatively thin mass-produced elements which do not have the bonding capabilities of masonry construction. Unfortunately, industry does not supply groups of standard products which offer architects sufficient flexibility to meet the functional and aesthetic requirements of their buildings, and so they must order nonstandard sizes. This is done to such an extent that many manufacturers cannot set up adequate production lines to produce standard sizes and keep up with the orders for specials. They must therefore set up assembly lines which operate on a comparatively inefficient basis of batch production with a resultant increase in the cost of their products. Their salesmen then offer the architect any sized component at little or no additional increase in cost, as all products are priced as specials. This situation is not beneficial to the architect or to the manufacturer. The difference in cost per square foot between standard and special products is bound to increase with our improving technology.

Actually, manufacturers would produce building products to any size. All they want is direction from architects to determine which sizes to produce and then the cooperation of the profession in using them. Architects, on the other hand, desire product ranges which give them flexibility and choice in design. The nature of lightweight and thin modern construction requires a considerable degree of flexibility to cope with corner and other joint conditions, as we have illustrated in Fig. 1. This situation becomes even more complex when structural elements and doors are added, as shown in the figure here below.

In order to break this impasse of the need for standardization on the part of industry and flexibility on the part of the design profession, it is necessary to develop some sort of keyboard for the sizing of building products so that industry can be assured of sufficient volume to make the production of a variety of product sizes feasible. In trying to develop such a related group of dimensions while working on a modular coordination project at the Building Research Station in England, it was interesting to note that those systems of numbers which appeared to solve the problem best were related directly to the mathematics of previous systems of proportion.

If we try to join the Platonic Lambda with the Fibonacci series we get a pattern as follows:

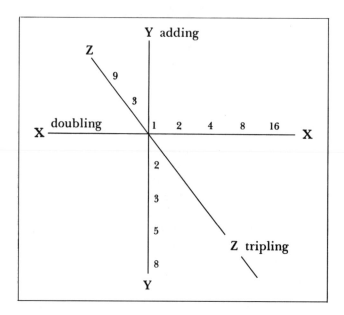

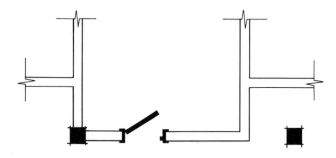

As shown here below, we may then fill in the dimensions based on this pattern, where we double along the X axis, add along the Y axis, and triple along the Z axis.

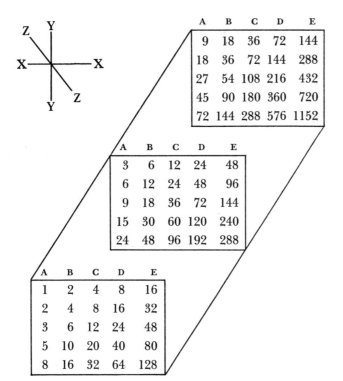

A	B	C	D	E
9	18	36	72	144
18	36	72	144	288
27	54	108	216	432
45	90	180	360	720
72	144	288	576	1152

A	B	C	D	E
3	6	12	24	48
6	12	24	48	96
9	18	36	72	144
15	30	60	120	240
24	48	96	192	288

A	B	C	D	E
1	2	4	8	16
2	4	8	16	32
3	6	12	24	48
5	10	20	40	80
8	16	32	64	128

This grouping of dimensions has been termed the "Modular Number Pattern" and includes the various dimensions shown in Table I.

Table I: Dimensions above 1″ Excluding Fractions

144″	60″	18″
135″	54″	16″
128″	48″	15″
120″	45″	12″
108″	40″	9″
96″	36″	8″
90″	32″	6″
81″	30″	4″
80″	27″	3″
72″	24″	2″
64″	20″	1″

If we analyze this group of dimensions we find that all the prime numbers (odd numbers which cannot be divided evenly) above 5 and their multiples are eliminated. This means that this group of dimensions has the maximum number of combinations for fitting products together in different ways. This allows flexibility in design. From an engineering viewpoint, one could not choose a better selection of numbers as a guide to variety for the building industry. In light of this, it is my belief that the Greeks originally evolved an efficient dimensional basis for construction and then rationalized it in mythology.

We may utilize the dimensions of the Modular Number Pattern to show the musical ratios. Table II shows the scale of C major. At the time that work on the Number Pattern was developing, there was much speculation as to whether the key of E would be as sterile in architecture as it is in music.

The importance of the various proportional systems rests basically in the fact that they provide relationships by which the aesthetic nature of a building may be understood. It is just as valid, however, to design in a random manner creating other less ordered but just as interesting visual relationships. The variety of design approach, be it keyed to a grid, rhythm, proportion, or to a random relationship, may all be modular. Therefore, although proportion and size are the basis of modular construction, the module is not determined by a specific proportion or size. For if products of fixed dimensions and ratios will not fit together at the building site, modular construction is impossible. A sense of order is implied, but the way in which it is achieved is up to the designer. Unfortunately, to date, comparatively little imagination has been used in modern architecture in the development of successful modular buildings. All too frequently, they consist of a simple repetition of a single product so that consequently the use of standard components or prefabrication is generally believed by the public to result in sterile architecture. The same may be said of "Chopsticks" in music which, in its simple state, is actually much more sophisticated than our repetitive buildings.

Table II: Diatonic Scale Using Keyboard of J. S. Bach

Major Scale Key of C				Number Pattern Dimension
C	$1.00\ x^0$	Base	$= 1:1\ = 1.00$	24"
D flat				
D	$1.12\ x^2$	Tone	$= 8:9\ = 1.13$	27"
E flat				
E	$1.26\ x^4$	Third	$= 4:5\ = 1.25$	30"
F	$1.33\ x^5$	Fourth	$= 3:4\ = 1.33$	32"
F sharp				
G	$1.50\ x^7$	Fifth	$= 2:3\ = 1.50$	36"
A flat				
A	$1.68\ x^9$	Sixth	$= 3:5\ = 1.67$	40"
B flat				
B	$1.89\ x^{11}$	Seventh	$= 8:15\ = 1.88$	45"
C	$2.00\ x^{12}$	Octave	$= 1:2\ = 2.00$	48"

If we accept the fact that a single product of a fixed dimension cannot solve the basic building problems, and if we seek to develop a group of products capable of handling the various requirements, it may be possible to find a solution. If, instead of only working with a single product of 4'0", we use two—one of 3'0" and the other of 4'0"—our design flexibility increases from 4'0" to 1'0", as shown in Fig. 2. This results from the fact that the difference between the two products is 1'0". Therefore, if we add a 2'6" dimension, we obtain flexibility to 6", as the difference between 30" and 36" is 6", here illustrated in Fig. 3. With four sizes—24", 32", 36", and 40"—we can obtain 4" flexibility as shown in Fig. 4.

With the development of product ranges that have the potential for design flexibility equal to the thickness of the product itself, it becomes possible to plan a building as though it were laid out on graph paper (Fig. 5). This enables the designer to solve some of the thickness and corner problems mentioned earlier.

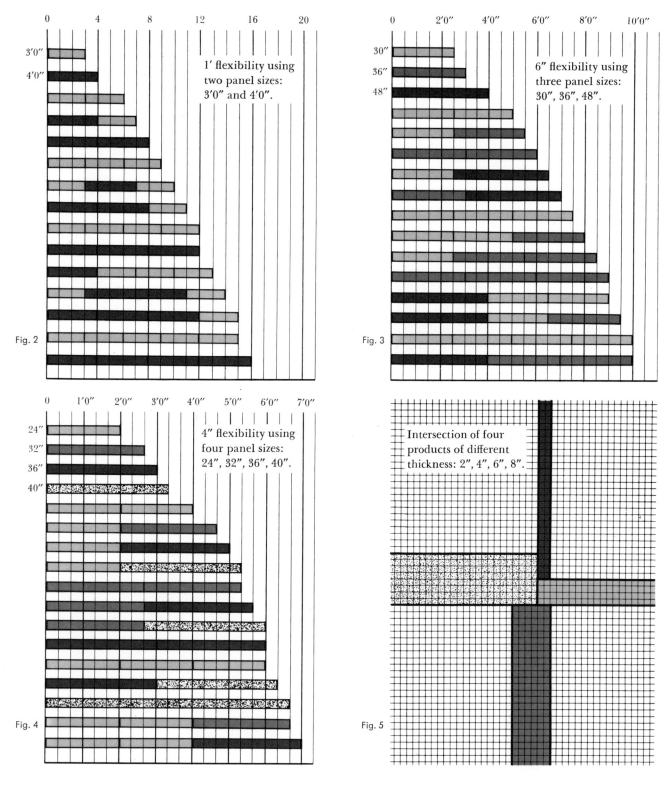

0   4   8   12   16   20

3'0"

4'0"

1' flexibility using
two panel sizes:
3'0" and 4'0".

Fig. 2

0   2'0"   4'0"   6'0"   8'0"   10'0"

30"

36"

48"

6" flexibility using
three panel sizes:
30", 36", 48".

Fig. 3

0   1'0"   2'0"   3'0"   4'0"   5'0"   6'0"   7'0"

24"

32"

36"

40"

4" flexibility using
four panel sizes:
24", 32", 36", 40".

Fig. 4

Intersection of four
products of different
thickness: 2", 4", 6", 8".

Fig. 5

Table III gives an example of the potential design flexibility that may be obtained by working with this type of product range using six product sizes. It shows the combinations of panels to fit each increment of 4" from 5'0" to 10'0".

Table III: 4" Flexibility Using Six Product Sizes

The fact that flexibility to small increments may be obtained by using large product sizes is of considerable significance as the present tendency for mass-produced building components is toward the use of larger and more efficient factory-made products. Neither good nor bad design need result specifically from the use of product ranges developed in this manner. There is clearly considerable scope for the designer. Good design is the result of the effort of a talented person or team of people. A modular system should provide a scale or keyboard which enables the designer to express himself freely while working with a coordinated group of standard products.

124

20	24	36
5'0"	20 + 20 + 20	
	24 + 36	
	20 + 40	
	60	
5'8"	24 + 20 + 24	
	48 + 20	
6'4"	36 + 20 + 20	
	36 + 40	
7'0"	24 + 20 + 20 + 20	
	48 + 36	
	24 + 36 + 24	
	60 + 24	
	20 + 40 + 24	
7'8"	24 + 20 + 24 + 24	
	24 + 20 + 48	
	36 + 36 + 20	
8'4"	20 + 20 + 20 + 20	+ 20
	36 + 24 + 20 + 20	
	20 + 20 + 20 + 40	
	40 + 20 + 40	
	36 + 24 + 40	
	60 + 20 + 20	
	60 + 40	
9'0"	24 + 20 + 20 + 20	+ 24
	24 + 24 + 24 + 36	
	48 + 20 + 20 + 20	
	48 + 24 + 36	
	60 + 48	
	36 + 36 + 36	
	60 + 24 + 24	
9'8"	36 + 20 + 20 + 20	+ 20
	36 + 20 + 24 + 36	
	20 + 40 + 36 + 20	
	36 + 40 + 40	
	60 + 20 + 36	
	48 + 48 + 20	
	24 + 24 + 48 + 20	
	24 + 24 + 24 + 24	+ 20

40	48	60
5'4"	24 + 40	
	24 + 20 + 20	
6'0"	24 + 24 + 24	
	48 + 24	
	36 + 36	
6'8"	20 + 20 + 20 + 20	
	20 + 20 + 40	
	40 + 40	
	36 + 24 + 20	
	60 + 20	
7'4"	24 + 20 + 24 + 20	
	24 + 40 + 24	
	20 + 48 + 20	
	48 + 40	
8'0"	24 + 24 + 24 + 24	
	48 + 24 + 24	
	48 + 48	
	36 + 24 + 36	
	20 + 20 + 36 + 20	
	36 + 20	
	20 + 36 + 40	
	36 + 60	
8'8"	24 + 20 + 20 + 20	+ 20
	24 + 20 + 24 + 36	
	24 + 20 + 40 + 20	
	24 + 40 + 40	
	60 + 24 + 20	
	48 + 36 + 20	
9'4"	24 + 20 + 24 + 20	+ 24
	48 + 20 + 20 + 24	
	40 + 24 + 24 + 24	
	40 + 48 + 24	
	40 + 36 + 36	
	20 + 20 + 36 + 36	
10'0"	20 + 20 + 20 + 20	+ 20 + 20
	20 + 20 + 20 + 20	+ 40
	20 + 20 + 40 + 40	
	24 + 36 + 20 + 20	+ 20
	24 + 24 + 24 + 24	+ 24
	24 + 36 + 24 + 36	
	24 + 36 + 20 + 40	
	40 + 40 + 40	
	60 + 60	
	60 + 20 + 20 + 20	
	60 + 36 + 24	
	60 + 20 + 40	
	48 + 48 + 24	
	48 + 36 + 36	
	48 + 24 + 24 + 24	

The relationships of numbers discussed in this paper have been used in setting out the requirements for the School Construction Systems Development program in California. The prototype for this program, erected on the Stanford University campus, is illustrated here. It has been built with standardized components and embodies several co-ordinated modular systems: 5'0 ceiling modules (appropriate for lighting, ventilation, and structural framing); 40" partition panels (related to doorways, stairs, and corridor widths); and a basic vertical module of 2'0 (a reasonable minimum increment of ceiling height). In the interior view shown here a 2:3 ratio has been used between ceiling and partition products. The former relates to the length of a fluorescent lamp and the latter to a door.

RICHARD P. LOHSE

STANDARD, SERIES, MODULE:
NEW PROBLEMS AND TASKS OF PAINTING

Some of the most meaningful problems in painting are those which deal with the organization of the structure, the standardization of the pictorial elements, and the construction of the module. The following analysis will attempt to point out the essential features in the development of these problems.

THE STRUCTURE OF ANALYTICAL CUBISM

Our analysis begins with structural Cubism. After the era of Pointillism ends, it is in structural Cubism that we first unmistakably discern initial traces of the practice of imposing a structure on the plane of the painting. The characteristics of this particular and important stage of Cubism are that the image is neither created by means of plane elements, nor by means of plastic expression or particular pictorial manifestations. Horizontally, vertically, and diagonally directed short brush strokes, together with elements which impart geometric values, form a dense texture. This method reveals for the first time a vague but nevertheless recognizable parallelism between the pictorial elements and the format of the painting itself. Projected into the painting are figural images taken over from Cézanne: "cone, sphere, cylinder." These spatial elements, however, have been reduced to fragments of irrational, geometric representations of volumes. Two diverging levels of expression begin to appear: on the one hand, the geometric structure which infiltrates the entire plane of the painting and which aspires towards an autonomous form; on the other hand, that level of expression which is bound to the traditional representation of the figural and spatial.

The linear structure of analytical Cubism does not possess a spatial aspect as such, but its figural program, as it expresses itself formally, is marked by a clearly discernible traditional conception of space. This traditional conception of space (the Renaissance conception —the relationship of top and bottom, left and right), which is observable in the entire development of abstract painting, is, in its intellectual foundation indebted to earlier periods of painting. The structural element in analytical Cubism occurs coincidentally, as if it were an unintended side-product. The every-day subjects of Cubism, which have been transformed into skeleton-like geometrical forms—Picasso's *Ma Jolie*, 1911–1912 (Fig. 1), *Le Portugais*, etc.—already represent, because of their titles, a particular aspect of the development toward a synthetic Cubism in which the structural characteristics of analytical Cubism are no longer apparent as a determining factor of style, but possess solely decorative value. Those conceptions of the spatial experience and of the plastic volume which are committed to expression can be detected in the smallest units of the geometrical image, and are present in all projections of Cubism which apparently transform the accustomed vision, and subsequently also in the development of all abstract painting. The pictorial order of Cubism corresponds to the traditional conceptions of support and weight, strength and matter, and is analogous in its terminology to earlier art forms. Outwardly it seems removed from nature, but in its inner constellation, its actual construction, it is indebted to tradition.

In spite of the presence of spatial representation, analytical Cubism develops a vocabulary of its own. Bunches of semicircles, straight lines, and curves slide horizontally, vertically, and diagonally across the plane, dissolve the palpability of the figural conception and form a new structure. A dynamic stratification of geometric-like elements, which is interwoven in the structure of the brush strokes, determines the composition. Based on this process is the beginning of an autonomous structure. This development, which began with Neo-Pointillism and was carried further in structural Cubism, was to be one of the most important contributions to the new way of painting.

Fig. 1. Pablo Picasso. *Ma Jolie,* 1911–1912. New York, Museum of Modern Art, Lillie P. Bliss Bequest.

DEVELOPMENT OF STRUCTURE SINCE 1912

Piet Mondrian. The paintings Mondrian created around 1912, such as *Composition Number 3 (Trees)* (Fig. 2), constitute a decisive step in the direction of a uniform structure of the plane. In these paintings the conflict of curvatures of analytical Cubism with the composition of an always more definite vertical and horizontal structure becomes apparent. What is here basically and characteristically different from its Cubist past is the change which takes place in the traditional spatial relation, and which is in contrast with Cubism where the so-called natural laws were always latently present. In these works of Mondrian, structure, which determines the composition of the painting, is made up of approximately similar values: those circular forms of Cubism which still remain are fragmented and reduced to open curves, thus lessening the differences between the diverging elements. The composition is achieved by shattering the picture plane with the horizontal movement of its structure. This destroys the vertical composition, inherent in the Cubist formulation of space, and introduces movement.

Fig. 2. Piet Mondrian.
Composition Number 3 (Trees), 1912–1913.
The Hague, Gemeentemuseum.

2

130

The elimination of diagonal elements and curved forms is continued in *Color Squares in Oval*, 1914 (Fig. 3). A further breakthrough toward the standardization of the structure, which was to be of great significance for subsequent development, occurs in *Pier and Ocean*, 1914 (Fig. 4). Here the composition consists only of horizontal and vertical elements. A number of them intersect and exhibit a certain similarity in their dimensions. The result is a more or less uniform structure. This is a decisive advance toward the systematization of the pictorial elements and their congruence with the format of the picture itself. The development of the *Pier and Ocean* paintings, as well as the *Church Façade* paintings, in which similar problems are attacked, comes to a close around 1915–1916.

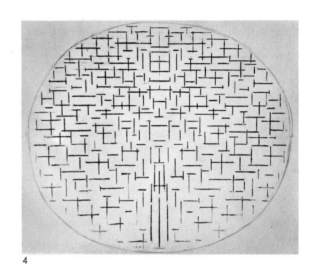

4

3

Fig. 3. Piet Mondrian. *Color Squares in Oval,* 1914–1915. New York, Museum of Modern Art.

Fig. 4. Piet Mondrian. *Pier and Ocean,* 1914. New York, Museum of Modern Art, Mrs. Simon Guggenheim Fund.

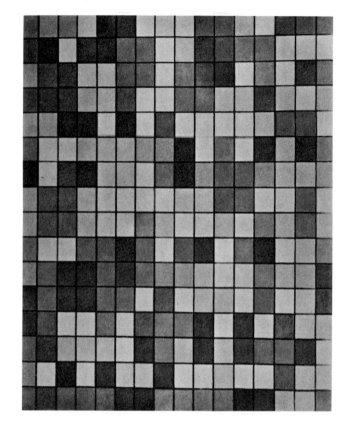

Mondrian's first experiments with more or less un-equivocally rectangular elements on a plane began in 1917. Examples are the *Compositions with Colors on a Plane*. Geometrically undetermined rectangular elements are distributed rhythmically over the width of the painting and a number of them—within the entire group of rectangles—are of just about the same size. The tendency to uniform elements on a plane becomes apparent. Pictorial elements and the format of the painting itself approach the form of a square.

A certain systematization of the pictorial elements, with a directness and consistency of purpose which cannot be found in any of the later works of Mondrian, is found for the first time in the Damebrett paintings of 1919. An analysis of the Damebrett painting, *Composition: Checkerboard, Bright Colors* (Fig. 5), will clarify this point. Identical-size rectangles, positioned vertically and arranged sixteen by sixteen, are the forms which determine the composition of the painting. Evenly distributed across the entire picture plane, they determine the actual structure of the painting. The pictorial element and the format of the painting itself have the same proportion. Movement occurs solely because of the free rhythms of the colored rectangular elements. Measurements show that the transposition of the width onto the height ends exactly at the upper margin of the fourth group, counting downward.

Fig. 5. Piet Mondrian.
Composition: Checkerboard, Bright Colors, 1919.
The Hague, Gemeentemuseum.

The *Compositions* of the years 1919, 1920, 1921 all exhibit similar proportions in the network and also, they repeat certain plane elements. A network of bands made up of equal numbers of rectangular elements, again arranged sixteen across and sixteen down, constitutes the basis of *Composition in Gray*, 1919 (Fig. 6).

Fig. 6. Piet Mondrian. *Composition in Gray,* 1919. New York, Collection Harry Holtzman.

The square is the basis of the network forming *Composition in Black and Gray*, 1919 (Fig. 7). Eight small squares, and ten which are four times larger, all formed by means of lines, as well as seven, one, and three rectangles which have the same proportions (disregarding the square and rectangular forms on all four sides which have been intersected), can be considered as an attempt to systematize the pictorial elements.

The group of paintings entitled *Bright Color Planes with Gray Lines* and done around 1919, are among Mondrian's structurally most interesting works. In *Composition: Bright Color Planes with Gray Lines*, 1919 (Fig. 8), a network of squares again constitutes the basis of the composition, which is developed in practically the same manner as that of Fig. 7. Beginning at this time, the compositions are organized by means of a free construction of plane and linear elements. From now on, only in very few works do the dimensions of the pic-

torial elements stand in a congruent relation to the proportion of the format of the painting itself. There are similarities in the widths of the bands of the compositions, but these similarities are not carried through uniformly, and furthermore they show varied relationships among themselves. The relationship between the dimensions becomes irregular, and the plane elements, which have the effect of squares, actually constitute irrational values. An analysis of certain pictures will show that one of the black bands, which is supposed to be a line of demarcation, is actually part of the measurable area of the square. This period of an apparently rationally determined form, which is actually based on an irrational method, extends to 1937.

At a crucial turning point, structural Cubism was led into an expressive (Picasso), a crystalline (Gris), and a pictorial (Braque) phase, and the goal of the pioneers of Cubism became the synthetic formulation of the ob-

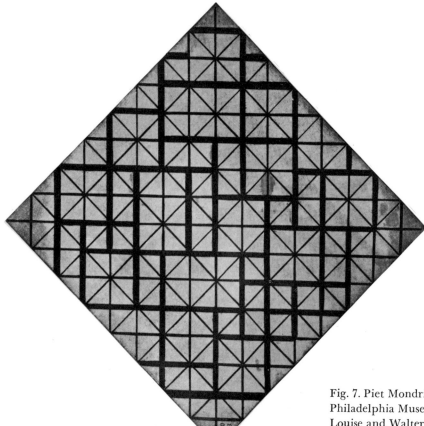

Fig. 7. Piet Mondrian. *Composition in Black and Gray,* 1919.
Philadelphia Museum of Art,
Louise and Walter Arensberg Collection.

ject. Yet the problem of additional elements, which presses itself with inescapable logic on Mondrian, is not developed further by him. The different sizes of the elements are not systematized; their position and placement on the plane is determined emotionally. These elements, as a result of being superimposed on one another in the form of crosses, similar to loose wickerwork, give the effect of a shallow space. The colors of this period, are the same as those of the analytical stage of Cubism: brown, gray-brown, ochre, bright blue, and pink are varied from the lightest to the darkest shades.

The result of this whole development we have traced —a development which is a preparation for the systematization of the anonymous structure—is the transformation of the interconnected, still pictorial structure of structural Cubism into a meaningful linear structure. The expressive forms of Cubism, with their various geometrical fragments, become a linear structure that has a uniform effect, something which is developed into the actual pictorial means. Measurements of particular paintings of this time show that the horizontal lines make up one sixth of all the lines. On the other hand, the vertical lines of the same length are considerably fewer in number. The *Pier and Ocean* paintings, from the period around 1914, give the most consistent expression of and make the clearest contribution to the problem of the formation of additional elements. Typical of this same period, when the uniformalization of the pictorial elements is in process, is the demarcation of the structural forms; they are restricted within an oval format. This phase clearly indicates that progress toward a uniformalization, toward a systematic conception of structure, occurs in stages, from each of which it is difficult to advance any further.

Fig. 8. Piet Mondrian. *Composition.*
Bright Color Planes with Gray Lines, 1919.
Otterlo, Kröller-Müller Museum.

There is a return to the equalized band structure of the year 1919 in *New York City,* 1942 (Fig. 9). The thin bands have the effect of a uniform network. The conflict between the consistency with which the geometric means are employed—in this case the linear bands—and the intention to subsume this consistency under free rhythmic laws again becomes visible. The prevading band elements have partly the same widths, yet the intervals between them do not; they are irregular.

Even the visual consistency of the band elements in Fig. 9 yield different measurements. The apparent unity of the horizontal-vertical network of bands is threatened by the effective real "background." The illusion of the third dimension, the undesired element per se, is created by means of yellow, red, and blue bands which lie on top of one another. The consistency, which might possibly be part of the band idea if it were carried through, is interrupted, and the unity of the plane —one of the basic aims of *de Stijl*—is negated. The result is four different planes.

The band elements, broken up by square elements, but running through the entire picture plane, are again systematized in *Broadway Boogie-Woogie,* 1942–1943 (Fig. 10). The linear principle of 1919 is here taken up once more and laid widthwise across the picture plane as an equalized element. The result is several different intervals which lead to a visual displacement and to a second level, the light background.

With this analysis we are attempting to point out the difficulties which confronted the development of a sys-

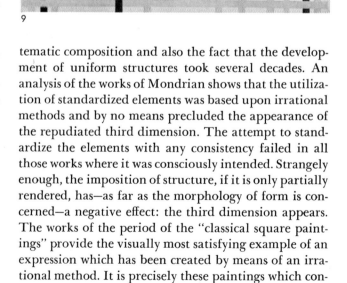

9

tematic composition and also the fact that the development of uniform structures took several decades. An analysis of the works of Mondrian shows that the utilization of standardized elements was based upon irrational methods and by no means precluded the appearance of the repudiated third dimension. The attempt to standardize the elements with any consistency failed in all those works where it was consciously intended. Strangely enough, the imposition of structure, if it is only partially rendered, has—as far as the morphology of form is concerned—a negative effect: the third dimension appears. The works of the period of the "classical square paintings" provide the visually most satisfying example of an expression which has been created by means of an irrational method. It is precisely these paintings which constitute the fundamental importance of Mondrian.

In order to keep the complexity and the difficulties of this entire development in mind, it should be remembered that the elimination of the third dimension was a decisive and conscious aim of all *de Stijl* painters.

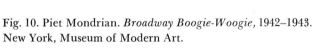

Fig. 9. Piet Mondrian. *New York City,* 1942. New York, Collection Harry Holtzman.

Fig. 10. Piet Mondrian. *Broadway Boogie-Woogie,* 1942–1943. New York, Museum of Modern Art.

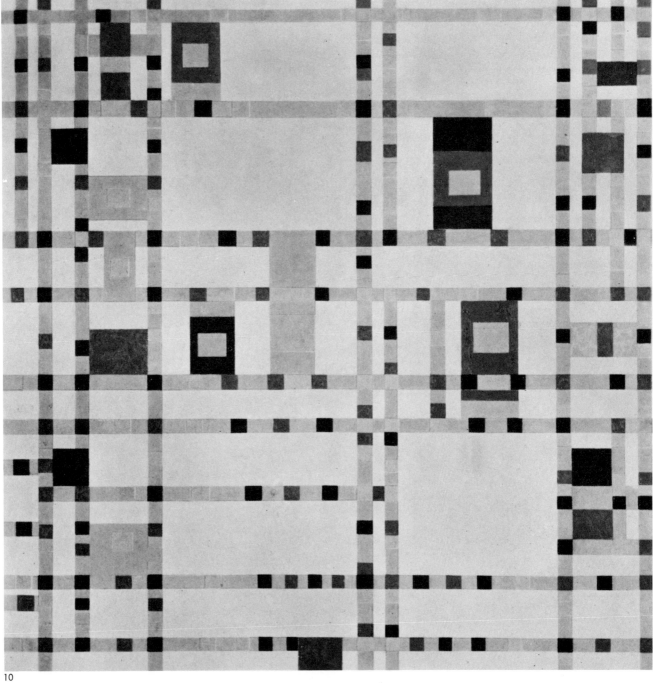

10

Theo van Doesburg. Certain works by Theo van Doesburg come closer to fulfilling the demand for a systematization and are more unequivocal in the application of their methods than those of Mondrian.

An example is *Rhythm of a Dance,* 1918 (Fig. 11). Here a network constitutes the basis of the composition. Pictorial elements of different lengths but of the same widths, and always set at a specific crossing of the network, determine the rhythm. One detects the intent to systematize; yet the arrangement of the elements is not systematic.

Fig. 11. Theo van Doesburg. *Rhythm of a Dance,* 1918.
New York, Museum of Modern Art, Lillie P. Bliss Bequest.

Fig. 12. Theo van Doesburg. *Simultaneous Composition,* 1929.
Collection Miss Katherine Dreier (Société Anonyme).

Fig. 13. Theo van Doesburg. *Composition,* 1925.
Amsterdam, Collection F. Vardemberghe-Gildewardt.

11

Now let us analyze *Simultaneous Composition,* 1929 (Fig. 12). In this work the following units can be identified: two square planes which are the same; one rectangular plane which is repeated in a similar dimension as part of the linear network. Narrow rectangular forms are also repeated, both vertically and horizontally. The construction is based upon a network, all the lines of which have the same width. This network contains square elements arranged ten by ten. The measurements of these elements can be found approximately in all the proportions of the painting.

A work which is exemplary for its consistency is *Composition,* 1925 (Fig. 13). Van Doesburg achieves a con-

gruence of method and structure in this instance which, from a historical point of view, is unique in the development of structure. Squares arranged ten by ten constitute the basis of the construction. There is also a network of four complete, two half complete, and five complete rhomboidal elements. These elements are arranged alternately in a vertical and horizontal direction.

Thus a number of van Doesburg's works show unmistakable signs of a systematization as well as the intent to organize the picture by means of standardized uniform elements.

12

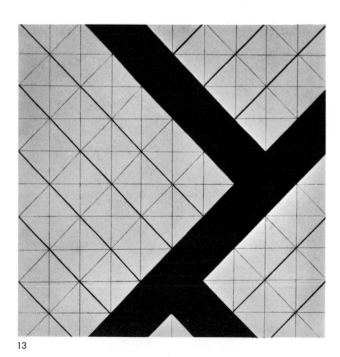

13

Bart van der Leck. Composition, 1917 (Fig. 14) by **Bart van der Leck** is characterized by the extraordinarily distinct standardization of its pictorial elements. Seventy-three elements are apportioned in a specific order across the plane. Nine, four, eleven, nine and three of these elements have similar dimensions, the rest are different. Noteworthy is the combination of these elements partially into loose and partially into concentrated groups. At the top right there is a first group of nine matching horizontal elements which is divided by a group of four matching vertical elements. On the left-hand side at the top there is a group which contains two as well as four matching elements. At the center is a group of eleven matching elements, and lower down a group of nine elements of the same size. All these groups and elements are anchored to the plane visually, not by means of a systematic structure. As in certain works of Mondrian, the outcome is two levels: one with more or less systematically arranged elements, the other—the one on which the work is performed—the ground or surface on which the elements are arranged.

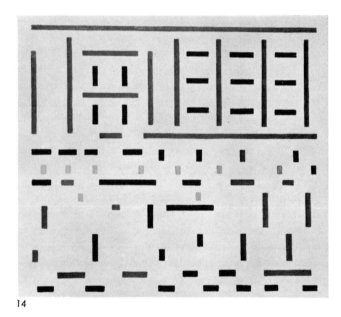

14

Fig. 14. Bart van der Leck. *Composition,* 1917. Otterlo, Kröller-Müller Museum.

Fig. 15. Josef Albers. *City,* 1928. Zurich, Kunsthaus.

Josef Albers. Josef Albers' paintings of the Twenties also constitute an important contribution toward the systematization of the pictorial elements.

In *City,* 1928 (Fig. 15), for example, the static elements of systematization and repose, formed by a reticulated foundation of equalized widths and intervals on the horizontal plane, are activated by a rhythmically accentuated movement in the vertical direction. In the vertical plane there is a clearly expressed tendency to accumulate matching elements.

Albers' manner is peculiar to this kind of construction. One could say that it has an essential intellectual affinity with *de Stijl,* but that it is distinct from it because of its different conception of the pictorial elements and structure. The intention to retain the pictorial rhythm by means of a sequence of matching elements constitutes an early, tentative advance toward the systematic methods of contemporary painting. The vertical rhythm, which determines the actual move-

ment of the picture, is achieved by multiplying the elements. Even though it is often not visible as a pictorial element, the rectangular element resulting from the vertical sequence is the basic form out of which the systematization of the elements and the rhythm grows.

This composition has a twofold basis: first of all, the network with the equally situated elements; secondly, and in opposition to the first, there is the rhythm which has been created by means of freely accumulating vertical intervals. Groups are formed by arranging elements in a sequence. These have the effect of planes in the construction of the painting, especially when larger numbers of the shortest rectangular elements are concentrated into tall, narrow rectangles of ten, twelve, thirteen, or more elements. Basic to all of these operations is the aim to establish a connection between a freely chosen principle of order and an emotional assimilation; the latter, in spite of the normative intension, predominates.

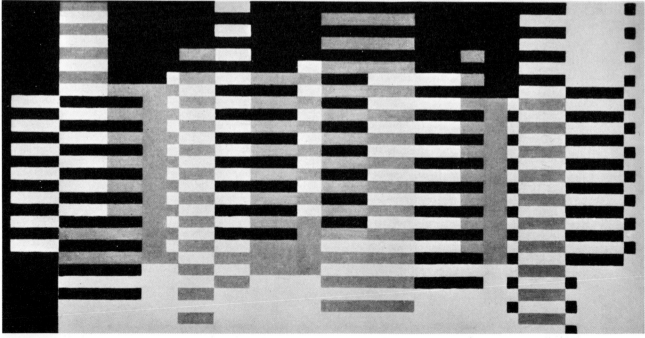

15

Georges Vantongerloo. One of the most significant attempts to achieve a standardization of the elements can be seen in Georges Vantongerloo's *Function of Lines,* 1937 (Fig. 16). Variously situated horizontal and vertical elements have been combined into groups: a first group at the left has eight elements, a second, four, a third, again four, a fourth and largest group has eleven, a fifth group of narrow dimensions, at the top right, has four elements, and a sixth group has three. Within each of those groups which determine the structure of the painting, the length of the elements is the same. Noteworthy also is Vantongerloo's attempt to be consistent in the standardization of the width of the elements, but these do vary. Thus the structure of the elements differs from group to group, thereby disrupting the systematization. The attempt to establish a systematic relationship between the single elements which have been combined into groups fails.

The systematization is more successful in those works in which the same lengths and widths are repeated and thus, as specific values, again stand in a proportional relationship to one another. These visually recognizable relationships constitute the actual potency of such works. The intentions to rationalize the elements and to create standards are both accomplished by irrational means. But what counts here is the fact that the problem of rationalizing the pictorial structure is given serious consideration.

These analyses serve to clarify how these problems evolved and also attempt to determine the meaning of the results. The following statements hold true for the entire period as it has been described here: The intent, both mentally and emotionally, is to create the picture with rational means. Primary tectonic elements are simultaneously used as expressive elements; elements used in the construction as well as the method of construction itself are a mixture of the rational and irrational, *i.e.,* the attempt is made to organize rational pictorial elements with irrational means. Size and number of the pictorial elements are only partially rationalized, a systematization of the latter only appears sporadically. A uniform method for the organization of the picture does not exist. The organization is based upon a subjective disposition and conception; character, structure, number, and size of the means are determined by irrational procedures (a simultaneous identity between the pictorial element and the dimension of the painting occurs only in isolated instances). The organization of the painting is based on a geometriclike procedure which does not appear in the resulting painting. Method and result are not congruent.

Fig. 16. Georges Vantongerloo. *Function of Lines,* 1937.

The second half of this paper will attempt to describe how the contemporary situation manifests itself in the results of the author's own work.

The development and goal of early Constructivism, which was to proceed from the structure of Cubism to a tectonic formulation of the painting, are analogous to the development of new foundations and methods which lead to the standardization of the pictorial elements. The methods themselves are plainly visible. The analyses and experiments led first of all to the results described below.

THE STANDARD ELEMENT

During the first stage, the differentiated pictorial elements, a typical feature of the greatest part of early Constructivism, were standardized. Normative elements were developed, providing the basis for the pictorial structure. The controllable normative element was introduced as a primary device into the process of the actual creation of the picture. The pictorial elements, between which a specific connection exists because of the ratio of their dimensions, were standardized, so that only a few sizes remained, and the attempt was made to use as actual pictorial devices only elements of the same type and size.

During the second stage, the possibilities inherent in these standardized elements are submitted to analysis. A crucial problem of this analysis is to grasp the character of the standardized elements as well as the character of their quantity. And just as problematical is the question of their dimensions, of the direction in which they point, and the relationship of the elements to the expanse of the pictorial surface.

THE ANONYMITY OF PICTORIAL MEANS

The standard element constitutes an anonymous entity which possesses no expressive qualities in the sense in which this was understood in Constructivism. As a result of its anonymity and its new dimensional quality, the points of view are altered. And the new point of view is fundamentally distinct from that of the earlier philosophies of art. The anonymity of the element becomes typical of the methods of organizing the painting. The newly formulated concept points the way for all further developments. Simultaneously we note that the standard element can only function within a combination—as the member of a group. And for this reason it is endowed with a basically different quality, one which is fundamentally distinct from the quality of the elements in the freely arranged constellations of the preceding Constructivist period. The anonymity of the pictorial element and thus of the pictorial structure itself produces a new law.

THE ADDITION OF PICTORIAL MEANS

The law of the standardized elements reads as follows: the maximal use of all possibilities to add these elements one to the other. It becomes necessary to organize the standard elements, to bring them into a meaningful and logical connection with one another, *i.e.,* to create among the elements—and without disrupting their normative character—an order based upon a rhythmic arrangement. The organization of the elements becomes possible once it is realized that the additive procedure constitutes one of the most important steps in the development of the new structure. The addition of elements provides a substance for the creation of the form. At first the additive procedures are based on the principle of accumulation and multiplication, as well as on the rhythmic arrangement of the elements. From these methodical transactions it results that the problem of rhythm is one of the most important factors in the composition. It becomes apparent that the painting will not be completely organized until it is possible to transform the additive principle so that it will introduce order into every level at which it operates.

Inherent in the additive procedure and indeed its primary result is a split between form and method; *i.e.,* the size of the element remains constant while at the same time the addition of elements is compulsory. The freedom which has been won initially contains the danger of the lack of control, of automatism, and of the accidental. Only when the standardized elements are combined into groups does it become possible to create a logical pictorial law in which the additive principle will operate in an orderly fashion.

THE GROUP

Combinations of a specific number of standard elements result in vertical and horizontal structures. These structures determine the relationship of the elements within each group as well as the relationship of each group to the others. The isolated element loses its anonymous quality and becomes functional—it creates order.

An example is *Concretion I*, 1945–1946 (Fig. 17). Eighteen vertical standard elements which are pointed in the same direction have been concentrated into groups. The position and the color of the elements determine the rhythm of the groups. The vertical arrangement is sevenfold. The height of the standard element consists of four of those parts. The proportion of the standard element to the entire height of the painting is therefore 4 : 7. All vertical and horizontal intervals are composed of specific dimensions which have been derived from a multiplication of the widths of the elements.

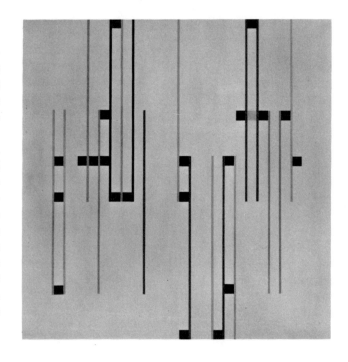

Fig. 17. Richard P. Lohse. *Concretion I*, 1945–1946. 70 × 70 cm. *Colors:* yellow, red, black, white.

What has evolved from the straightforward manner in which Constructivism handled the tectonic elements is this: the uniformalization of the pictorial means; the creation of groups; and potentially, the possibility of creating a new structural law and the application of uniform methods.

The positive result of these analyses and experiments is that the pictorial elements are no longer compelled to be expressive and that they no longer represent a stylistic expression of the *Weltanschauung* of early Constructivism.

These investigations and operations are significant because problems which are intrinsically systematic, and structural, and methodical in kind, constitute the basis of the working process. Also, these problems reveal qualities which were unknown during the preceding, Constructivist period.

In the early stages of Constructivism the desire to combine expression with construction prevented the uniformalization of the pictorial structures, the consistent adherence to a single principle, and the application of a consistent method. Because the problems are so much more concentrated now, their solution has become incomparably more complicated. Much greater demands are made on the imagination. The elimination of the subjective aspects in the creative process, as they predominated in the early Constructivist period, leads first of all to an inhibition of the customary intuitive processes. The intuition must undergo a longer period of crystallization and be correlated with the method. A new attitude toward the act of creation itself becomes necessary. The new methods require that the pictorial organization take place simultaneously on more than one level. The process of creation is subsumed under a set of entirely different presuppositions. The new principle dictates its sequence to the intuitive process. The process of creation takes on the aura of a patient and drawn-out experiment.

The use of uniform standards and the creation of groups necessitates a new concept of the motif. The organization of the elements of the same size, their concentration into groups, and the correlation of groups leads—as the groups begin to play an increasingly more active role—to a new kind of group motif.

But in spite of what had been accomplished, the organization of the structure and of the colors remained imperfect and had to be developed further. The pictorial surface was still the plane on which the groups could be arranged in a relatively free way. The quantity of elements resulted in specific possibilities of choice and placement. Even the use of color was left relatively undetermined, *i.e.,* a comparatively large number of irrational possibilities remained.

The systematization of the elements is unquestionably a significant accomplishment when it is compared to the lapidary-like technique of using units with different dimensions, different quantities of units, and different volumes of color. Nevertheless the element and group was still in conflict with the pictorial plane, the surface. Once this discrepancy as well as the possibilities inherent in the new methods become apparent, the problem of the congruity of the organization of the color with the organization of the form takes on primary importance.

FLEXIBILITY OF SYSTEMS OF CONSTRUCTION

In the new development the picture cannot be completely formulated by using differently oriented, similar elements. What is required instead are values which have been systematically determined. These constitute the starting point of all operations and the basis for the entire formal structure, as if one of these values were a single cell within a system of cells which still had to be built, and in which each cell and the system of cells constitute a congruent unit, a module.

One of the most important and difficult tasks consists in the creation of flexible systems in which extensibility of the basic elements is controllable and where a logical development exists. This requires, once the system is completed, that its components are completely congruent with one another. Otherwise these components will not permit the use of the same proportions at every step of the operation. Sequences, additions, progressions, digressions, permeations, etc., must be able to take place on the same level, that is to say, they must have a common basis. The greater the flexibility of the modular basis, the greater the field of action, and thus freedom in the organization of the picture.

In the years 1943–1944 it was possible to make an advance which was to prove very important. In *Twelve Vertical and Twelve Horizontal Progressions* (Fig. 18), painted in these same years, it was possible to systematize the groups of colors. In this work twelve vertical standard elements are arranged in a horizontal progressive sequence. Each of these twelve standards consists of twelve color elements, the size of which progressively increases from top to bottom. These twelve color elements are arranged in such a way along the twelve verticals that each of the twelve colors—horizontally as well as vertically—appears at only one point which has been arrived at by means of the sequential principle. The principle underlying the sequence is variable and can be extended for an infinite series of colors.

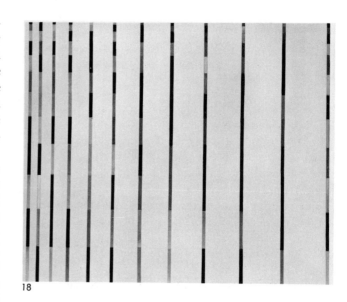

18

Fig. 18. Richard P. Lohse. *Twelve Vertical and Twelve Horizontal Progressions,* 1943–1944. 78 × 90 cm. *Colors:* light yellow, yellow, vermilion, light blue, cobalt blue, light green, yellow-green, dark green, light violet, dark violet, light gray, black, white.

Fig. 19. Richard P. Lohse. *Ten Similar Themes in Five Colors,* 1946–1947. 64 × 200 cm. *Colors:* yellow, red, blue, black, white.

148

THE MODULAR CONSTRUCTION

An example of a concentrated modular construction is *Ten Similar Themes in Five Colors,* 1946–1947 (Fig. 19). Ten matching themes, which are structurally the same and which are arranged in two rows of parallels, one above the other, have their basis—viewed horizontally—in a system of dimensions with the proportions 5 : 4 : 3 : 2 :1. This sequence of proportions is repeated in vertical interval elements, which have the width of proportion 5. This creates a second horizontal rhythm which has the proportions 5 : 4 : 5 : 3 : 5 : 2 : 5 : 1. The diagonal rhythm is analogous to the horizontal rhythm of the second structural field, the horizontal rhythm of this second structural field being created by turning it 90°. Structure one is the basic theme; structure two, which contains the interval elements, is the inversion of structure one and takes over the basic theme without altering it. The vertical interval elements connect the upper with the lower sequence. The structure is actually unlimited and only receives its formal value through the organization of the colors.

The five colors, which actually provide the structure with movement, arrange the ten similar themes in a logical sequence. This is done in such a way that each theme is differentiated from every other. This differentiation takes place because each element within each motif has a different color, *i.e.,* each element within each motif—viewed horizontally—is of a different color than the same element of the previous or subsequent motif.

The decisive task here was to activate the systematic sequence in such a way that a dynamic formulation is achieved and that the organizational principles arrange themselves in this process. This was the decisive artistic aim. The principles had to be related to one another so that their properties and capacities would supplement and permeate each other. On the basis of the first level of activity a second, third, and further levels of activity came into existence, and these are again coordinated with one another. Because none of the colors are repeated in the same element of the same sequence, the following rule is developed: Each of the five colors has the same portion—that is to say, each represents a fifth of the entire mass of color—and each covers a fifth of the entire surface area.

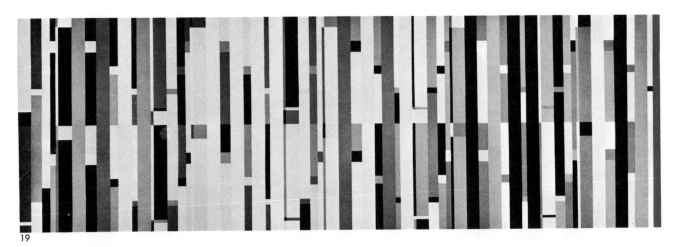

19

THE SERIES

An example of the uniform composition of a structural field is provided by *Serial Elements Concentrated into Rhythmic Groups,* 1949–1956, I (Fig. 20). Three times forty-five elements of the same form constitute the tectonic groundwork. Developing the work further led to an order of specific groups of colors and intervals so that these permeate each other.

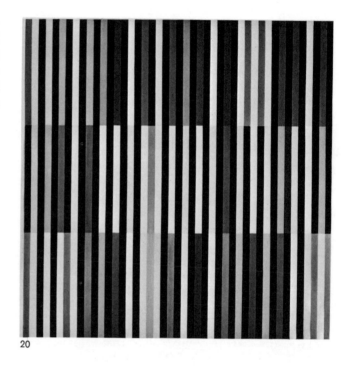

20

Fig. 20. Richard P. Lohse. *Serial Elements Concentrated into Rhythmic Groups,* 1949–1956, I. 90 × 90 cm. *Colors:* yellow, red, blue, orange, green, violet, black, white.

Fig. 21. Richard P. Lohse. *Systematic Series of Colors in Fifteen Self-Repeating Shades,* 1950–1954. 72 × 135 cm. *Colors:* gradations of the primary colors yellow, red, blue.

A second more highly developed example of the same problem is *Systematic Series of Colors in Fifteen Self-Repeating Shades,* 1950–1954 (Fig. 21). Fifteen different colors, arranged in a horizontal series, constitute the motif. This motif determines the entire organization of the form and of the colors of the painting consisting of two hundred and twenty-five colored segments. The sequence of the colors remains the same in all the other fourteen horizontal series. Each colored segment is situated—horizontally as well as vertically—at a specific crossing, which is determined by the structure of the composition. Each color is fixed in a net of relationships by means of the displacement of the color sequences. It was possible to develop the basic structure to the point where an infinite series of colors with the same ordering principle throughout could come into being, *i.e.,* it is possible with a particular operation to multiply this structure and to create an infinite series which will extend into all four directions. All the colors have an equal share of the entire amount of color and an equal share of the entire pictorial surface.

21

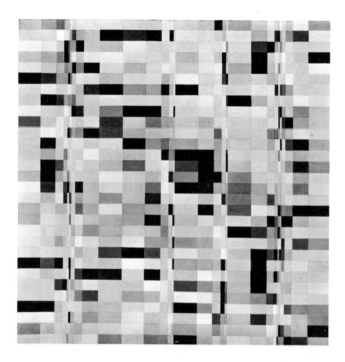

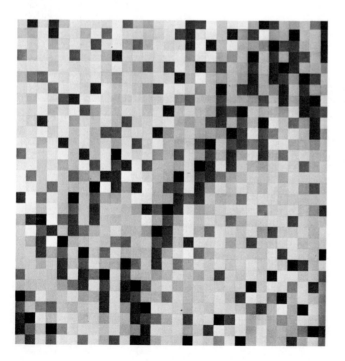

The entire complex of the creation of infinite series undergoes a further intensification in *Thirty Systematic Series of Shades,* 1950–1955 (Fig. 22). Thirty elements in the horizontal proportion of 6 : 4 : 2 : 1 : 0.5 : 0.5 : 1 : 2 : 4 : 6 : 6 : 4 : 2 : 1 : 0.5 : 6 : 4 : 2 : 1 : 0.5 : 6 : 4 : 2 : 1 : 0.5 : 0.5 : 1 : 2 : 4 : 6 constitute the formal groundwork of the thirty horizontal series. Thirty colors, each of which is represented by thirty shades, from the darkest to the lightest—making altogether nine hundred shades —are the basis for the organization of the color. A specific shade of each color is allotted for each horizontal sequence.

A transformation of the arrangement, which determines the pictorial organization of the thematic series, is found in another *Thirty Systematic Series of Shades,* 1950–1955 (Fig. 23). Here, in contrast to *Systematic Series of Colors in Fifteen Self-Repeating Shades,* which we have seen in Fig. 21, the organization of the form and the color is determined by a vertical series. The succession of colors of this vertical series is the principle which determines the expression of form and of colors in the entire painting. A prerequisite for this is that all thirty colors and their nine hundred color points form a harmonic relationship to one another within each constellation. This system contains the possibility of unlimited variability which, as long as the principle is observed, will always produce a new expression of colors and forms.

Fig. 22. Richard P. Lohse. *Thirty Systematic Series of Shades,* 1950–1955. 81 × 81 cm. *Colors:* gradations of the primary colors yellow, red, and blue.

Fig. 23. Richard P. Lohse. *Thirty Systematic Series of Shades,* 1950–1955. 60 × 60 cm. *Colors:* gradations of the primary colors yellow, red, and blue.

An analogous example of these principles is seen in *Thirty Systematic Series of Shades,* 1955–1963 (Fig. 24). In contrast to the structurally composed series, these color series are based on a continuous and steady increasing and decreasing of the spectrum. The forms result from these changes in the spectrum taking place vertically along the bands. Each of the thirty bands has the same number of thirty shades, equalling nine hundred color squares. Each of these color squares is fixed at a specific axis and is not found again in either vertical or horizontal direction.

Fig. 24. Richard P. Lohse. *Thirty Systematic Series of Shades,* 1955–1963. 120 × 120 cm. Spectral colors.

Fig. 25. Richard P. Lohse. *Six Horizontal Bands of Six Formally Similar Color Groups,* 1950–1951, II. 72 × 72 cm. *Colors:* yellow, red, blue, orange, green, violet.

One example of the use of a group theme is *Six Horizontal Bands of Six Formally Similar Color Groups,* 1950–1951, II (Fig. 25). A group of three elements with the proportions 1 : 3 : 2 constitute the basic formal theme. This proportion is repeated six times—both horizontally and vertically—in each sequence of bands, and results in thirty-six parts for each of the proportions 1, 2, and 3. The proportions of the groups—together with the organization of the colors in vertical and horizontal bands—result in six squares for each color. The basic proportion 1 : 3 : 2 is repeated for each color in each of the six horizontal bands. The one hundred and eight elements are organized in such a way that each of the six colored groups which have the proportion 1 : 3 : 2 is represented only once in each sequence.

The problem of transposing and creating new groups is dealt with in *Eight Color Groups with a Light Center,* 1954–1962, V (Fig. 26). Four differently colored square groups, above and below, on the left and on the right, each containing four elements which are symmetrical with one another, are alternately distributed across the plane and constitute a closed group. In addition there appear five other differently colored groups, and these are altered in such a way that the four squares which lie at the center, and which form a closed group, are of a lighter color. Thus a ninth group of four elements and a third constellation of colors come into existence.

Fig. 26. Richard P. Lohse. *Eight Color Groups with a Light Center,* 1954–1962, V. 96 × 96 cm. *Colors:* pink, red, dark olive-green, dark blue, dark red-violet, dark gray-blue, dark green.

The problem of shifting groups is treated in *Six Similar Color Groups,* 1958, I (Fig. 27). The formal structure is created by means of a standard which measures 15 × 2.5 cm., and which has the proportion 3 : 1 to the single groups which measure 45 × 7.5 cm. Each group consists of nine standards arranged in threes, one above the other. Thus each group contains the previously mentioned sequence of nine colors. Six groups, which have the same forms and the same number of colors, constitute the entire tectonic groundwork. Groups one and three develop the nine colors in a vertical sequence from top to bottom; groups four and six in a sequence which leads from the left to the right; group two, at the top, introduces the movement from bottom to top as a contrast to the movement of groups one and three; but group five, although it points in the same direction as four and six, in contrast with these groups, moves from the bottom to the top.

Fig. 27. Richard P. Lohse. *Six Similar Color Groups,* 1958, I. 90 × 22.5 cm. *Colors:* yellow, pink, ultramarine, turquoise-blue, dark violet, orange, dark green, light blue, white.

One of the most difficult modular problems, the continuous growth of a group, was solved in *Systematically Ordered Color Groups,* 1954–1959 (Fig. 28). One hundred and eight standard elements are here arranged in such a way that the groups, beginning with the smallest one of three elements, are augmented by three elements with each progression. The groups which have been created in this manner—groups containing from three to twenty-four elements—contain a specific number of colors which correspond to the number of elements in each group. The basic groups of colors are again subdivided into lighter and darker shades, always in the proportion 1 : 2 or 3 : 6. All shades are arranged according to this proportion and this creates another level of activity. All color groups contain the proportions 3, 6, 9, or are a multiplication of these values. The result is a principle which allows an extreme variability of colors.

Fig. 28. Richard P. Lohse. *Systematically Ordered Color Groups,* 1954–1959. 180 × 54 cm. *Colors:* lemon-yellow, light red, dark red, light turquoise-blue, dark turquoise-blue, light green, dark green, light violet, dark violet, light pink, dark pink, light orange, dark orange.

Fig. 29. Richard P. Lohse. *Sixteen Progressively Asymmetric Color Groups within a Symmetric System,* 1956–1960, III. 96 × 96 cm. *Colors:* gradations of the primary colors yellow, red, and blue.

The last example of complicated group operations is *Sixteen Progressively Asymmetric Color Groups within a Symmetric System,* 1956–1960, III (Fig. 29). A symmetrical system, consisting of two similar vertical and two similar horizontal serial progressions, constitutes the basis of the construction. The colors, eight altogether, are arranged in a rhythmic sequence. Four asymmetrical groups of the same size are located at the center; they permeate each other and are responsible for the pictorial activity. In addition to the four asymmetrical central groups, there are three smaller groups which are developed in a diagonal progression toward the center in the proportions 4 : 2 : 1 : 3. Each of the four asymmetrical central groups contains the same amount of color. Each plane area, in the neutral zone surrounding these groups, has a color which is particular to the area and is not repeated in any other.

Characteristic for the possibilities of a flexible system is *Four Similar Asymmetric Groups within a Regular System,* 1962, IV (Fig. 30). In contrast to the progressive-degressive development seen in Fig. 29, here the sixteen groups at the center, differentiated by form and color, are brought together into four equal color groups. The construction results from means of equal size square elements. The number of elements in both constellations is equal to one hundred and forty-four. The resulting formations are distinguished from each other by form and by color.

Fig. 30. Richard P. Lohse. *Four Similar Asymmetric Groups within a Regular System,* 1962, IV. 120 × 120 cm. *Colors dark groups:* dark blue, red, blue-green, olive-green, violet. *Colors light groups:* white, light blue, light violet.

Fig. 31. Richard P. Lohse. *Four Similar Groups,* 1965, II.
120 × 120 cm. *Colors:* dark blue, dark green, light violet,
and yellow.

An example of a synthetic group formation is *Four Similar Groups,* 1965, II (Fig. 31). Each of the four groups is constructed from four equal right angles and four equal squares. These are ordered in such a way that the same formal conception exists on each side. This is activated by the color combinations of blue and green and yellow and violet; each of the two has always the same color value. The groups are linked with each other in such a manner that a complex whole results.

One has sought with the above visual examples and their explanations to present problems which are significant for their principles and potency. The following are additional theoretical remarks on these problems and their development between 1940–1964.

A prerequisite for a new style is the understanding and perfection of the means.

Only open secrets are efficacious.

The creation of a new style becomes possible when the means are basically anonymous, possessing a structural quality which permits their extension or reduction in every dimension.

The creation of a new style is rendered possible by the infinite variability of the anonymous elements.

The anonymity of the elements is the primary condition for their infinite extensibility.

The proportion of the pictorial element corresponds to the proportion which rules the entire tectonic area, the law of the sequence of colors. The dimension of the picture determines the size, proportion, and number of pictorial elements.

The elements are shorn of their individuality and become objective.

The tectonic areas must be developed in such a way that they can contain what as yet does not exist.

Simplicity no longer arises spontaneously but is created by means of a long and complicated process. Why? Actually because we are no longer interested in simplicity. Instead we are trying to create modular elements which can be used to make structures and which can be either reduced or extended.

The idea alone is not enough; what counts is not the individual quality, but that a process functions smoothly.

A dialectic of the method of construction is needed.

Transferable into another plastic medium would be at most the method, but not the expression.

Variable systems were developed, possessing simultaneously the highest degree of elasticity and a maximal capacity to order. One of the main problems is to introduce logical continuity into the flexibility of the elements, and to keep flexible the principle which provides order.

A work has several logical sequences which pass over into and are connected with one another. The "first" logical sequence passes over into the "following" ones. They have specific values in common, are related to one another according to the sequences, and establish a new group principle.

The principles should be correlated in such a way that their properties and capacities supplement and permeate one another. For example, the first level of activity produces a second, third, and further levels of activity; these levels again are reciprocally coordinated with one another.

It was possible to develop structures which permit the creation of an infinite sequence of colors, while simultaneously ordering this sequence. An infinite series which simultaneously retains its principle of order is made possible by using a specific proportion to multiply the structure. The infinite series can be integrated into any network of proportions.

Small groups make possible large operations.

From small cell systems develop larger systems, in which the small ones are integrated as part of the whole.

More and more the task of form is taken over by color, which shapes the rhythmic foundations of a composition by its differentiation.

The number of colors is no longer enough.

Color shapes form.

Form is anonymous.

The pictorial elements become bound together in the theme. The theme takes over the function of the individual element. The anonymous form becomes endless and absolute.

Similar themes line up to form a whole, which is the same as its parts.

ANTHONY HILL

THE STRUCTURAL SYNDROME IN CONSTRUCTIVE ART

I have chosen to illustrate what I call the "structural syndrome" in constructive art with one type of constructive or constructional art: the relief. This inquiry will be limited to a few of the features associated with this approach in plastic art and the examples used will be exclusively from my own work in this field.

The abstract constructional relief has a life history that started with works of Braque and Picasso at the peak of the Cubist explorations, around 1912. These were Cubist works and not abstract, but they were followed a year or so later by the reliefs of Tatlin which were entirely abstract.

The relief was to play only a small role in the developments of the two most important abstract movements, Constructivism and Neo-Plasticism. Later, however, when something amounting to a synthesis of aspects of both these movements emerged, the relief—the constructional relief—became the relevant technique or form of art work.

The constructional relief is neither relief painting, relief sculpture, nor is it a form of three-dimensional space construction. The relief defines a spatial domain that detaches itself from the situation whereby a work is either a flat plane concerned with a surface, or an object totally embedded in space.

Needless to say, it is not sufficient to simply posit a new spatial-plastic domain and/or technique. This brings with it further consequences to be faced: the role of the art work, born as intention and actual performance or function, what may be called the orientation, the sources of the manner of organization, from whence they come and why they are chosen. These are but some of the threads in the network constituting the artist's system or approach.

I am bound to say that in appropriating the term "syndrome" from the biological and medical sciences, I mean to imply only, that generally speaking the topics under discussion in this volume—the module, proportion, symmetry, rhythm, etc.—seem to justify being considered as concomitant factors. That is to say, an inquiry into these topics from the point of view of creative art, rather than attempting some sort of scientific exposition, should deal with an integral part of the work of art per se.

It is also possible to approach all these topics from other directions and, in fact, impossible to ignore the other viewpoint, for a work of art presupposes that these topics under discussion have already become the subject of considerable systematization in the hands of mathematicians and others.

Much of what is perceived and every aspect of what is fabricated in a constructionist work can be charted in a series of drawings amounting to the ordinary specification drawings for architecture. It is often the case that the artist prepares these drawings so that the work can be repeated.

The artist may also undertake a detailed explanatory exposition of the work and it may seem that he might be expected to provide an exhaustive thesis covering every aspect of the work and its function, including an account of the origin of its conception, etc. This, although in principle not unfeasible, is not yet a noticeable practice. Indeed the bit by bit analysis of a plastic work of art by some dependable person is still a rare thing, be it by the artist himself or some other person.

A data sheet concerned with a constructional work may seem complete when the dimensions and physical structure of the work have been accomplished, but there is still little point in such a thing unless it serves another purpose other than "topographic." As already noted, the work of art is born from specific interests on the part of the artist, and these are not always so evident or deducible by cursory inspection.

To the experienced musician the score of a work of music may be said to contain a complete description or account of the work, and one that is provided by the composer at that. In this sense the score is the "music in instruction" and contains codified all that is required to reveal the organization of an autonomous structure. By comparison, works of plastic art of the kind I shall consider here are both simpler and more complex at the same time, and in this can be found part of the reason for their unsuitability to this form of codification and exposition. Furthermore, we have a paucity of acceptable terminology available for the task, and thus we tend to move from borrowing from the specialized sciences to overstressing the obvious.

The physical object that is a work of art, the idea of the work, and the thematic structure controlling the idea, all these aspects of the work employ and exhibit the structural syndrome. The work is embedded in a physical context and so is the spectator who brings to the work his own perceptive mechanism. In all this too we are in the domain of the structural syndrome.

The art work can be regarded as an autonomous structure, but it is finally seen to be a mechanism that is completed by a physical context and its interaction with the spectator. Thus its domain can be said to be an artificial one, suspended between that of its physical context and that of the beholder. The factors of the syndrome are themselves located in the mind, in active perceptive apprehending and the mechanisms by which this is possible. They are also displayed in the structure of events and systems around us, from the phenomena directly perceivable to the complex phenomena investigated by tenuous chains of indirect inference.

Probably the most obvious example of the structural syndrome is to be found in all the activities concerned with the man-made environment, a large part of which are the outcome of physical needs, the results of which are an "unquestioned" part of our visual environment.

The role of much art in our era has been directly conceived to the end of widening physical consciousness, and doing so in the name of an unfettered humanism, undirected by the myths that run riot in every epoch.

The heightening of awareness is not the reason such works are made, but it is forced upon the visual artist as a prerequisite for the understanding of his works, since what he makes can be said to be competing with everything else in "the light world."

Music offers an alternative to the light world; visual art is in the light world and must impose itself through its identity. Thus it is linked to the man-made visual environment and to the visible forces of nature. And such art cannot avoid involving a moral directive to our visual behavior, directly or indirectly.

Analyzing a work of the constructional type shows how much more related to music and architecture it is and so how much more available to analysis than most other types of art.

Constructional work falls into the category of being an assemblage of components, and often the method of fabrication allows it to be taken apart in actuality.

Even if no "plan" of the work exists, one can be made. When this is done, the results provide the material for the next phase, which may amount to a detailed account of the relationships of the parts to each other, and to the whole.

Results of this phase of the analysis may include no more than clues and speculation as to the artist's intention (the idea of the work), the theme, and the structure of the theme. If the investigator is already familiar with the work and ideas of the artist, he may be able to present a complete account of every aspect of the work. Such investigations have the immediate purpose of showing how a work of art functions. They also make available findings of interest to those who may want to know the extent to which an artist employs such factors as constitute the structural syndrome. There is then a sense in which to ask about the role of anything is meaningless unless it is answered in the context of a total analysis.

The task of this paper will be to focus on the structure of themes in constructional work. In this way what is presented can be appreciated without direct knowledge of the work of art, photographs being a very poor substitute. This investigation will offer evidence of the structural syndrome at one of the least often explored levels in works of plastic art. While everything points to the value of taking a single work and making it the subject of an extensive exposition, I have decided upon a selection, so that by comparing the works some idea of the variety, even within what may seem severe limitations, can be taken into consideration.

EXAMPLE ONE

This first example is the relief shown in Fig. 1. My records show that I made two reliefs, the first was subsequently destroyed, being a project on which the second was based. The scheme, as shown in Fig. 1a, was the same in each relief executed and dates from 1957.

The work is small in size and simple in conception. It consists of four components comprising two types: a white formica-faced slab of chipboard and back P.V.C. extruded sections. The sections are of two types, rectangular and T-shaped.

The theme or idea of the work involves the articulation of a tall slab by vertical elements producing "fields" of horizontal tensions across the surface. The physical features of the work are the light-reflecting surface and the relation of two types of section to the slab.

The standard components are selected for their availability, subsequently they determined not only the scale of the work but the final realizing of the theme. The two types of black sections do not appear in any run of standard manufactured stocks, they owe their existence to the remains of a special order and were obtained from the factory as scraps.

The dimensions of the elements, the T-shaped and rectangular sections, can be considered as more or less arbitrary; the structure of the theme did not embody any module consciously employed. However, when the theme is expounded this seemingly arbitrary quality gives place to a precise scheme, that of the fields of tension.

In this first example my intension is to focus primarily on the physical arrangement that is presented, from the point of view of symmetry, proportion, etc.

Considered as a partition of an area, the three white areas, none of which are equal, and the three black areas, none of which are equal, may suggest various readings. It may be wondered if all the areas have a common module.

The rhythms or partitions of the white surface by the black not only result in areas of differing widths, three white and three black, but each black element fixed to the surface gives three different types of black region.

Thus seen in relationship to the surface and volume of the slab, each black element is operating differently, and the T-shaped section on the left combines the functions of the other two, by being itself a combination of the two positions of the rectangular section and involving the articulation or affirmation of the slab's volume.

Fig. 1. Anthony Hill. Constructional Relief, 1957. Chipboard, Formica, P.V.C. Collection Dr. Michael Morris, London.

Fig. 1a. Scheme of relief shown in Fig. 1.

The proportion of the T-shaped section is that of two rectangular sections of equal thickness fixed in the right-angle relationship, which can be seen as either two identical limbs or three, one of which is longer by the addition of a common width.

The dimensions of the rectangular extrusions are 0.4 × 1.2 cm. The T-shaped section is rather unstable, with the side faces cut at an angle, but its dimensions can be taken as 0.2 × 8 cm.

The over-all dimensions are 23.6 × 39 cm.; the slab of 1.27 cm. chipboard measures 22.86 × 38.74 cm.; the over-all thickness of the board plus formica is approximately 1.4 cm.

The proportions of the slab and the intervals across the surface were not predetermined. In the case of the slab the *exact* ratio of height to breadth to width plays no important part in the surface articulation or the physical idea.

The fact that after the work was completed the measurements showed a module that tied in and reinforced the theme simply points to the fact that a theme, even when conceived "intuitively," will express itself "metrically," in the general sense of the word.

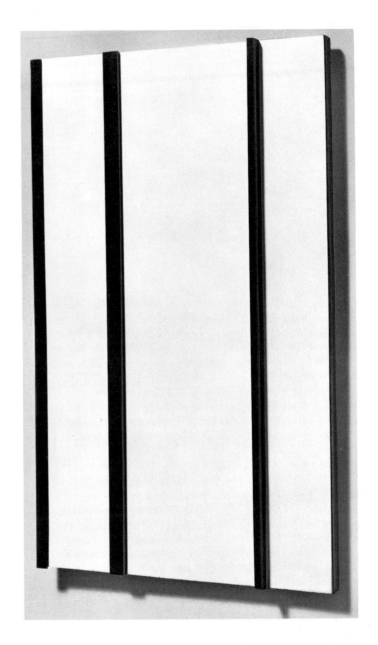

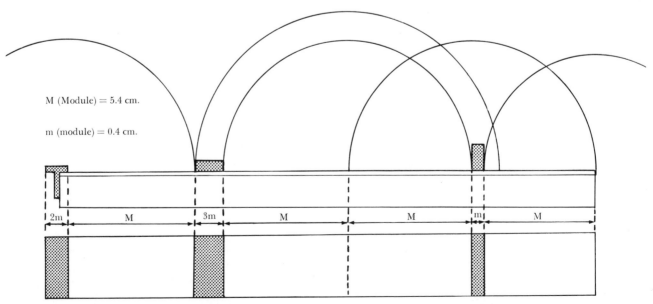

M (Module) = 5.4 cm.

m (module) = 0.4 cm.

2m   M   3m   M   M   m   M

EXAMPLE TWO

The project version of the relief used for this second example dates from 1956. The relief shown here in Fig. 2 was made in 1960, at the time I completed the project version. Fig. 2 has the same proportions as the first version, but is rendered half-scale larger and differs in a few details from the earlier relief.

The idea here is similar to that of Example One in that it involves the affirmation and articulation of volume and surface, the main difference being that in this second example the scheme and dimensions are both simple and involve a module.

The scheme of arrangement, that is, the structure of the theme as a separate entity from the ideas and functions of the work, reveals itself in an account of the proportion of the surface defined by the array of the angle-section elements. The over-all area is a rectangle, $12'' \times 19''$. The white perspex is a square $12'' \times 12''$, and the transparent plane measures $12'' \times 7''$. The implied inner rectangle comprises a square $5'' \times 5''$ plus a rectangle $5'' \times 2''$, the over-all measurements of this implied inner rectangle are $5'' \times 7''$. Thus the progression of magnitudes 2, 5, 7, 12, 19, exhibits a Fibonacci-type series: $U_n = U_{n-1} + U_{n-2}$.

The physical components of the relief are eight in all: they comprise a blockboard slab, two sheets of perspex, one opaque white, one transparent, and five aluminum angle sections. All the aluminum sections and the perspex have the same thickness, $3/16''$, including the one black element, which is black anodized aluminum. The thickness of the blockboard slab is the same as the outside dimension of the aluminum sections.

The components in the theme are less in number than the physical components: the theme concerns only seven elements, the slab, an extended plane, and five sections.

It would be possible to conceive a physical scheme with just these seven elements. This would result in all the four sections facing forward to be on a common plane, and this plane would be the axis of symmetry between the slab and the implied slab.

In the scheme used, the drop in level of the one black element serves to further individualize it and increase its isolation. The scheme results in two unequal areas to the left and right of the long sections, while the left-hand area is the larger and contains two small elements, the movement of all the small elements is to the right.

Fig. 2. Anthony Hill. Constructional Relief, 1956–1960. Perspex and aluminum.

Fig. 2a. Scheme used for relief shown in Fig. 2.

Among the ratios set up between horizontal and vertical, etc., is the following: If the vertical limbs of each section are counted as being a vertical element, *i.e.*, a plane at right angles to the horizontal plane, and computed in area, the ratio of the vertical elements on the left to those on the right is 2 : 1. If, however, the two long sections are counted as part of either side, the number of elements is an equal 3 : 3, but in area the vertical element is slightly greater on the right.

The choice of a square for the left-hand area was deliberate, but the right-hand area (the transparent plane) was not predetermined, the intention was simply an area *greater* than half.

The height of the small angle sections was similarly chosen to be less than half. The placing of the angle sections at equal distances is part of the theme, the width of the sections being equal to the thickness of the slab.

The exact relation of the areas was not discovered until after the work was completed, as with many other features. Here the module of the theme is embedded in the module of the dimensions.

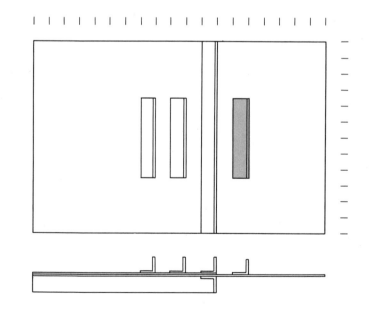

EXAMPLE THREE

The interests of the next two examples include employing a greater number of elements and an increase of structural homogeneity. Both examples have a thematic which, more than in Example Two, can to some extent be detached.

For the purpose of analysis I make a distinction between the "interest of a work" and its "thematic," as opposed to the theme, its intention. The reason for making this distinction is to isolate the thematic structure. Indeed, as yet, there are no accepted terms with which to make a clear distinction between the theme or idea *of* the work and the theme or idea *in* the work. One is left with such awkward notions as "the structure of the structure," "the theme of the structure," "the structure of the theme," etc.

In these next two examples I will focus upon the *thematic ideas* used in a series of works, rather than describing the *structure and function of individual works,* although ultimately the validity of the former depends upon the latter.

It may be thought that the "arrangement" of the black and white elements in the relief shown in Fig. 3 is all (or nothing). So I shall furnish an explanation of the scheme which was used in this relief. That is to say, I shall explain what it really is that underlies the ordering of these elements.

The scheme seen in Fig. 3a explains the structure of a "number spine" where "clusters" (in the main, "twins") of primes and composites are arrayed on the left and right. "Fins" are made by "webbing" across "ribs," and the result in this case is a structure of a unit area forty-nine by forty-nine. The scheme derives from the numerical diagram accompanying it. The density of black is equal on each side, although the number of "fins" is greater by one on the right. Just over one sixth of the total area is black. The number of white regions is greater on the right, but the density of white is subsequently equal.

The sequence of operations on the "number spine" amounts to reducing the interval of 1–100 by removal of the even numbers, thus reducing the number of primes from twenty-six to twenty-five, leaving the number of primes to the remaining composites at exactly twenty-five to twenty-five.

Finally, the remaining fifty integers undergo reduction to leave thirty-two, fifteen primes and seventeen composites, by leaving only those that are consecutive. When these are "webbed," equality is restored for the separate webbings, nine each side, while the webbed regions are seven to nine, the larger being the seventeen composites. Apart from the axial symmetry, the decision to utilize the square and the module

Fig. 3. Anthony Hill. Constructional Relief, 1958–1960.
Perspex and vinyl sheet.
Collection Adrian Heath, London.

Fig. 3a. Scheme used for relief shown in Fig. 3.

of forty-nine intervals, what is presented are positive and negative areas (the white and black, the black being a continuous area and the white located at a small distance in front). But what is presented physically is in no sense a simple demonstration of the primes theme.

The observer is soon likely to see that the black intervals are not all uniform (the two exceptions are those respectively twice and three times that of the others). He will also note that each white area is an interval co-mensurate with the module. Moving from the top down on the left, the white areas are respectively 2, 2, 5, 5, 8, 5, 13, and so on, and on the right they are 12, 3, 7, 2, 3, 5, 4, 2, 2.

The white areas exhibit a 4 : 6 change ratio, sets of common areas, and a ratio of 2 : 4 of unique areas. The horizontal axis finds the bulk distributed so that the top-right and bottom-left quarter each have two blacks and the remainder in the opposite quarters, although the axis runs through a black interval on the left.

Thus, apart from the symmetry, the module, etc., what is exhibited is concerned with distribution, deviation and density ratios, equalities and inequalities other than those of symmetry.

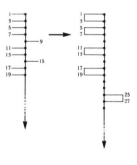

At this point it might serve to recall some general points concerning the distribution of primes:

The number of primes is like the number of integers, infinite. The average distribution of primes is very regular, its density shows a steady but slow decrease. On the other hand, the distribution of primes in detail is extremely irregular.

The so-called twin primes become rarer and rarer.

The statement that there are infinitely many twin primes is believed to be correct. The proof or disproof of this conjecture is, at present, beyond the resources of mathematics.

These are some of the well-known facts to take into consideration before attempting to formulate a description of the type of thing the prime series is. It is clearly unique in one sense and the subject of one of the most fascinating theorems in Number Theory.

It may very well be thought that here the whole question is begged. I am bound to be asked why and how I was prepared to accept my resulting work when it was "derived" from something as recondite as the prime-number theme. It may even have presented something entirely unacceptable. Let me answer this indirectly.

Consider the sieve of Erastosthenes—a square block of the first hundred numbers giving the primes starting with 1, 2, 3 (three consecutive primes), giving a total of twenty-six primes. The pattern is not very arresting. Seen, for example, as a random scattering of negative-positive areas at the approximate ratio of one quarter blacks to whites (or vice versa) it is rather disappointing. Furthermore, there is no clue as to the essential factor of a sequence. However, this can be brought in by such devices as refolding the assembly, in a spiral for instance.

Whatever is thought about such a thing and putting it to work, the important point is what is done with it, with the theme as an integral part of the ensuing idea and its function in the work—which, of course, may very well have other "themes" emanating from other aspects of the work.

As to the "rule of the theme," this may well become "modified" or dictate a structure that may then be "modified."

An example of this at the level of the theme itself is the question of whether 1 was to be considered a prime, and this apart from my decision not to utilize 2 and the "padding out" with even numbers. (It is important to observe here that

1 is not a prime: D. H. Lehmer's list of primes from 1 to 10,006,271 brings forth G. H. Hardy's comment, "our numbers of primes are one less than Lehmer's because he counts 1 as a prime.")

What remains is to characterize the prime series in its role of embedding an unending distribution criteria on an unending series, utilized within a special stretch—the first one hundred integers. This in turn leads to the secondary and final controlling theme, that of twin primes, another distributive criteria embedded in the prime series.

Its function was to overlay "unpredictable" rhythms over a very simple modular beat. By unpredictable I mean visual, even the module is only perceivable through the appearance of the "off-beats."

In some versions of this scheme I have introduced a gap between the left- and the right-hand sides, an accentuating of the vertical "axis" by a gap of one unit, and have also located the whites on a transparent sheet, or two sheets lying at a distance from the black back plane. In no version are the "prime rhythms" realized by locating the blacks over the whites, or reversing the original decision of blacks for the "prime beats."

I mention these things as some examples of the extent to which a theme imposes itself into the physical structure, and the extent to which its realization is open to possibilities of transformation without losing its identity. Certainly other procedures could have been found to achieve the same sort of end, but the satisfaction of the one chosen lies for me in the fact that it had to be worked on and did not involve chance or "aesthetic trial and error" at every level, nor did it carry with it some notion of finite ideal order.

In saying that the primes theme imposed a compelling fascination, I must stress that it arose to be employed for a specific function and that is what matters, not that the work is based on the idea.

EXAMPLE FOUR

In this last example I shall show a theme with some of the developments that I have used, to be seen as variations.

In the sequence of drawings shown on the following pages, the first (Fig. 4a) is a grid of twenty-five squares. In Fig. 4d the twenty-five unit squares have given place to five rows, one of which contains five of the unit squares; in the rows below the units increase in area and in the row above they decrease. This tessellation exhibits the fact that the square of N odd is the sum of N consecutive integers:

$$e.g., 3^2 = 2 + 3 + 4 = 9$$
$$5^2 = 3 + 4 + 5 + 6 + 7 = 25$$

If this is set out on the original grid, as in Fig. 4b, another demonstration of this can be made.

In Fig. 4c, the original grid (Fig. 4a), with its sixteen 4° nodes in the interior and sixteen 3° nodes on the boundary is changed into one with five 3° nodes on the boundary and three 3° nodes in the interior. The grid transformed (Fig. 4d) has forty-eight nodes, all 3° nodes, sixteen on the boundary and thirty-two in the interior. When five regions are picked out, counting from the top left and moving down and back to give regions growing in area, another map is obtained with the same structure, Fig. 4b, which has eight nodes, five regions, twelve boundaries.

The next phase treats the separation of the five regions by treating the seven-line graph in the interior as a network of canals. The "canals" or pathways comprise four vertical stretches of unit 2 length, and four horizontal stretches of unit 7, 6, 5, and 5 respectively, moving downwards.

If a unit of width is given to the system, one stretch will have to be twice the width.

The last phase comprises embedding angle pieces in the pathways and/or on the regions, the angle sections having their limbs the width of the pathway.

The constants in all schemes have been the five regions, a unit width pathway, and angle sections.

The variables have included two other progressions (Figs. 4e, 4f, 4g); progressions and four standard lengths for the angle sections; the use of black and white for the regions and

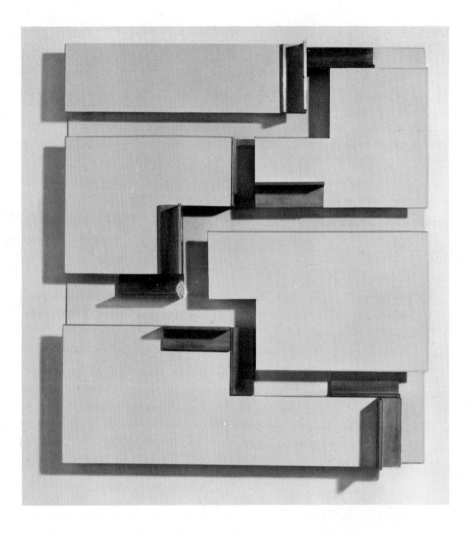

Fig. 4. Anthony Hill.
Constructional Relief, 1960.
Vinyl and aluminum.
Calouste Gulbenkian Foundation.

Figs. 4a–4g. Developments and
variations of the same theme
used in Fig. 4.

pathway; white throughout; space between the plane of the regions and the back plane; different orientations for the schemes, *i.e.*, rotations so the movement of progressions is either downwards, upwards, or lateral. The orientation of the angle sections have incorporated alternative levels and left and right alternation.

Finally, the initial scheme can be treated in another way, the five regions can be located on a grid of one hundred squares. Here each region is comprised of unit squares of respective areas:
14 (7 × 2), 16 (8 × 2), 18 (9 × 2), 22 (11 × 2), 30 (15 × 2).

In the two schemes that can occur in square, the first and its "variant," referred to above, allow the substitution of the third for the fourth region. In fact, it is essential to draw the scheme in this way on the sheet material used in order to cut the region out of one piece using no more material than is required. This can be achieved by a sequence of eight cuts, corresponding to the eight stretches of the pathway network when drawn this way.

The variations illustrated by no means exhaust all the possible tesselations or (strictly speaking, tilings), depending upon which of the rows are to be made up of squares. The possible over-all can be 7 × 5, 6 × 5, 4 × 4, and 3 × 5; arbitrary dimensions could be used and a variety of progressions.

In the example illustrated in Fig. 4, the lattice is the static progression seen in Figs. 4d, 4c and the width of the pathway chosen was the module plus a half, so that this dimension also determines the height of the angle sections (in all variations the angle sections are equal sided). The over-all format which leaves it taller than it is broad is contained in an outer square panel.

A complete discussion of the series of works from which this example comes would have to take in, in particular, the question of scale. I will only mention that the work illustrated— the over-all dimensions of the outer square being 3′ × 3′—is the largest of the series and that an increase in scale brings problems concerned with the critical perceptual threshold of a work of this kind.

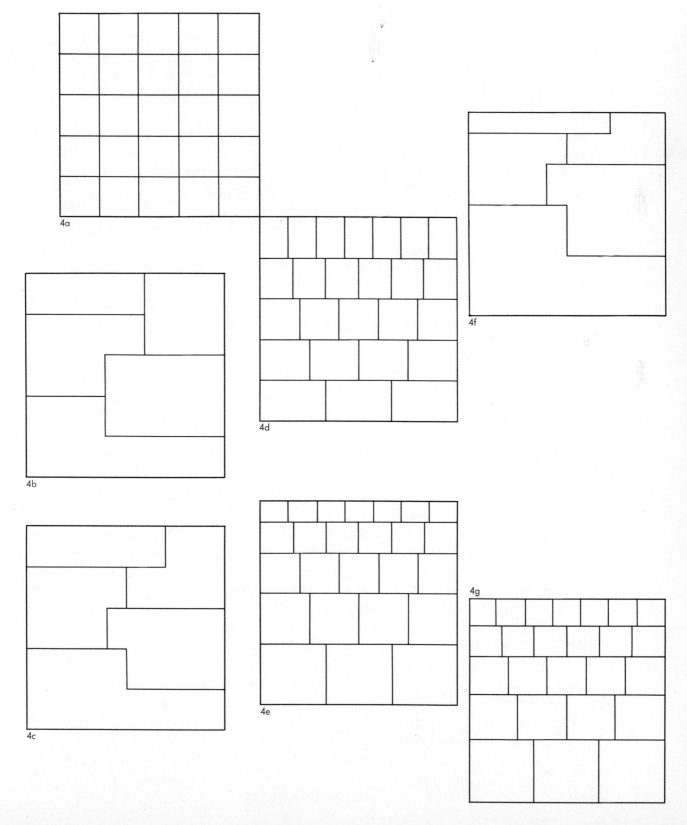

4a

4b

4c

4d

4e

4f

4g

ERNÖ LENDVAI

DUALITY AND SYNTHESIS IN THE MUSIC OF BÉLA BARTÓK

"There are many persons to whom it gives pleasure to behold a cathedral, who are delighted with pictures and poems," wrote Bartók, "but who will never take the trouble to find out who was the architect or the author of the work. Naturally—or at least it should be so—interest is shown for the works and not for the names of authors and details of their lives. One may well wonder whether it would not be better to play compositions without mentioning the names of composers." This statement would seem to lend itself readily for a motto to which I should like to add Schweitzer's remark on Bach to the effect that his works would be the same even though his life had followed a radically different course. Characteristically, Bartók said nothing or very little about his own compositions (though he liked to emphasize the relations of his music to folklore, chiefly with the intention of propagating folk music). "Let my music speak for itself; I lay no claim to any explanation of my works." With these words he meant to avert curiosity, for there was nothing more abhorrent to him than any prying into his private life or the possibility of infringement on the independence of his personal feelings. In all things he laid stress on what bound him to humanity in general, the element common to everybody. His music aspired toward the medium of universal laws. I would like to add a few strokes to this aspect of Bartók's portrait.

In the line of Bartók's works, his opera entitled *Bluebeard's Castle* (1911) is perhaps the first to present his music in full maturity. Bartók's style took shape suddenly, virtually between one day and the next —it burst forth, to put it more accurately. About the time he composed his *First String Quartet* (1908) he produced a final style which, in regard to essential features, continued unchanged to his latest works. His later style does not display a single significant element that was lacking when he composed *Bluebeard's Castle*. With him, unity of personality implied that of style, as well as of his musical mother tongue. It was by no means accidental that the moment when Bartók found himself, and the magic of Strauss and Reger vanished, coincided with the discovery and study of peasant music. On one occasion Denys Dille addressed the following question to Bartók: "Is there any difference of technique or trend between the famous string quartets, piano concertos, and the three stage works and the compositions based on original Hungarian tunes or melodies of your own invention, such as the *Dance Suite* and the two rhapsodies for violin and orchestra?" "This difference is only apparent," Bartók replied. "The melodic world of my string quartets does not differ essentially from that of folk songs, except insofar as the setting of the former is more severe. Folk songs should be known as we know them, and then the existing distance will be undeniably diminished. In the string quartets I go in for excessive concentration." An astonishing result of my studies on Bartók relates to the unity of style in his music, which is at least as organic as that of, say, Bach or Mozart: *Bluebeard's Castle, Music for Strings, Percussion and Celesta,* and the *Concerto for Orchestra* permit analysis by the same means. This is the characteristic that distinguishes Bartók from most of his contemporaries (Stravinsky, primarily); his lifework is void of arbitrary turns, for he always remained constant to his principles.

Any attempt to explore the strata underlying this style and the meaning of what is known of Bartók's world of form and harmony calls for inquiry into the relationship of Bartók's idiom to a) folk music, b) functional harmony, c) impressionism, and d) atonal trends.

I

The words of Bartók's musical language stem from the deepest layer of folk music. He himself strongly believed that every folk music of the world can finally be traced to a few primeval sources; in creating his musical idiom he was demonstrably inspired by the possibility of such a "primeval" music. Now, what is to be denoted hereafter as the "golden-section system" is simply an integration into a system of pentatonic primeval motions and primitive affinities. Bartók's most characteristic chords can be traced to simple pentatonic basic steps. Moreover, from stylistic analysis of Bartók's music I have been able to conclude that the chief feature of his chromatic technique is obedience to the laws of golden section in every element.

Golden section (*sectio aurea*) simply means division of a distance in such a way that the proportion of the full distance to the larger part should correspond geometrically to the proportion of the larger to the smaller part. That is, the larger part should be the "geometric mean" of the full distance and the smaller section. As shown by computation, when full distance constitutes the unit, the value of the larger section amounts to 0.618 and that of the smaller section to 0.382. (Accordingly, the larger portion of any distance divided by golden section may be expressed by the product of the figure reflecting distance and the proportionality factor 0.618.) Golden section is a no less significant constituent element in Bartók's creation of form, melody, and harmony than overtone harmonization and construction in periods embracing eight or four bars in the Viennese classical style.

For example, in an earlier study ("Bartók's Style," published by Zenemükiadó, Budapest, 1955) I demonstrated that every unit of the *Sonata for Two Pianos and Percussion,* from the whole of the work to the tiniest cells, is divided according to the rule of golden section. I performed nearly a thousand geometrically satisfactory measurements. Thus, golden section of the first movement indicates the center of gravity in the movement: the beginning of the recapitulation. (Since the movement consists of 443 bars, and $443 \times 0.618 = 274$, recapitulation sets in precisely in the 274th bar!) Golden section may be observed to touch, in every case, the most important turning point of form in the analyzed unit. For instance, the principal theme of the finale shows the following articulation: $A_1 + A_2 + B$. The main section naturally determines the place of the member "B" ($43.5 \times 0.618 = 27$), while the two members "A" are adjusted to each other with golden section ($27.5 \times 0.618 = 17$).

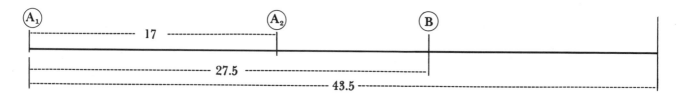

Golden section may be further observed to follow one of two courses, according to whether the longer or the shorter section comes first. Let us call one of the possibilities *positive* (long section followed by the short one), the other *negative* (short section followed by the long one). The best example is offered by the fugue movement (first movement) of *Music for Strings, Percussion and Celesta.* From pianissimo the movement reaches the boiling point by a gradual rise to forte-fortissimo, then gradually recedes to piano-pianissimo. The 89 bars of the movement are divided into parts of 55 and 34 bars by the pyramid-like peak of the movement. From the points of view of color and dynamic architecture, the form is proportioned within these units, by cancellation of the sordino (in the 34th bar) and its repeated use (from the 69th bar), with the part leading up to the culmination showing a relationship of 34 + 21 and that from the culmination onward, 13 + 21. Thus, in the rising member the longer section comes first (34 + 21) and in the falling member the shorter section (13 + 21). The points of junction condense around the culmination. Positive and negative sections embrace each other like the rising and sinking of a single wave.

It is no accident that the exposition ends with the 21st bar and that the 21 bars concluding the movement are divided into parts of 13 + 8. We shall shortly return to the series of numbers that figure here (8, 13, 21, 34, 55, 89).

The measurements can be continued all the way down to the smallest units. As a final example the golden-section scheme of the introductory part of the *Sonata for Two Pianos and Percussion* may be cited (first movement, 2 to 17; for detailed analysis see the author's article in the volume, *Bartók. Sa vie et son œuvre*. Edited by Bence Szabolcsi. Corvina Publishing House, Budapest, 1956).

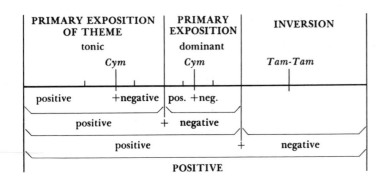

As may be seen, in form units of both higher and lower orders the positive and negative sections are associated as if reflected in a mirror, so that ultimately the details merge in a large positive section. Therefore the process is coupled with a powerful dynamic increase (from *pp* to *fff*). Analytical studies permit the conclusion that the positive section is accompanied by enhancement, dynamic rise, and intensification or condensation of the material, while the negative section is marked by sinking and ebbing.

These studies lead directly to the questions presented by melody and harmony formation. Bartók's chromaticism, as mentioned, follows the laws of the golden section, more particularly of Fibonacci's numerical series. This series is characterized by the fact that each expression is the sum of the two preceding numbers and, further, by containing the simplest golden-section series expressible in whole numbers:

$$2, 3, 5, 8, 13, 21, 34, 55, 89 \ldots$$

(For instance, the golden section of 89 is 55 and that of 55 is 34.) Compare this series of numbers with the proportions of *Music for Strings, Percussion and Celesta,* analyzed before. (Calculated in semitones, 2 means a major second, 3 a minor third, 5 a fourth, 8 a minor sixth, 13 an augmented octave, and so on.) For the present the musical tissue may be imagined to be built up of cells, 2, 3, 5, 8, and 13 in size, with cell division following the pattern provided by the proportions of the above series. Thus, the 8 may be broken up only into 5 + 3. The supplement below shows the themes in the first movement of the *Sonata for Two Pianos and Percussion.* The leitmotif includes 8 semitones, divided by the fundamental note C into 5 + 3. The principal theme comprises 13 semitones, divided by the fundamental note C into 5 + 8. The first phase of the secondary theme embraces 13 semitones, the second phase 21 semitones. Hence the various themes develop in golden-section order.

leitmotif	3 + 5 = 8
principal theme	5 + 8 = 13
secondary theme	13, 21

From the point of view of harmonic architecture, this exposition also bears witness to a systematic arrangement. The principal theme gains its characteristic tone from a pentatonic harmony (scheme "a" prevails also in melody: bars 37, 39); the formula might be 2 + 3 + 2. Toward the middle of the principal theme a unit built on 3 + 5 + 3 is added (scheme "b" from bar 41), while the fourth,

E flat—A flat, is divided by an F sharp into $3 + 2$. Parallel fourths (5) and minor sixths (8) join the secondary theme (scheme "c," which grows more clearly discernible in the recapitulation, from bar 292); finally, the closing theme is accompanied all along by parallel minor sixths: 8 (scheme "d," from bar 134 to 160). Thus each new harmony rises one golden-section step higher.

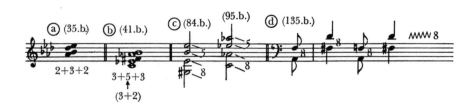

principal theme	$2 + 3 + 2$
principal theme, middle part	$3 + 5 + 3$
secondary theme	$5 + 8$
closing theme	8

Golden-section cell division can be clearly followed in the last movement of the *Divertimento*. The principal theme appears in the following variations (the quotations have been grouped according to size and typical division has been denoted in connection with every variation):

Since the fifth line is the continuation of the fourth, in bar 4 the melody rises not by a minor third (3), as in the preceding line, but by a fourth (5)—in conformity with the augmentation. The same correlation of motifs is encountered in the mime-play *The Miraculous Mandarin:*

The harmony type shown below occurs in Bartók's music perhaps even more frequently than did sevenths in nineteenth-century music:

Now these are marked chiefly by being built up exclusively of golden-section intervals (2, 3, 5, 8).

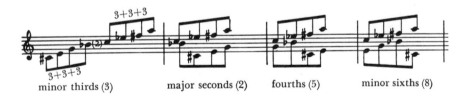

minor thirds (3)   major seconds (2)   fourths (5)   minor sixths (8)

It is typical that whenever Bartók used a triad in a chromatic movement he placed the minor third over the fundamental note and the major third below it, tuning the chord to acquire the proportions 8 : 5 : 3.

major   minor   chord typical
3+5=8   5+3=8   of Bartok!
                              "major-minor"

That golden section is not an exogenous restriction but one of the intrinsic laws of music is evidenced most convincingly by *pentatony,* perhaps the most ancient human sound system, which may be regarded as the purest musical conception of the principle of golden section. Pentatony, particularly the more ancient form of minor pentatony, rests on a pattern reflected by the melody steps of major second (2), minor third (3), and fourth (5).

From this aspect, golden-section architecture is extremely interesting in the *Dance Suite,* which appropriately has been given the name of *Eastern European Symphony.* Construction of the golden-section system can here be followed virtually step by step, for this work actually demonstrates this technique in its genesis; starting from the elements, the world of multifarious tones rooted in pentatony is developed before our very eyes:

At first it may seem astonishing that with Bartók pentatony is so closely tied to chromaticism. This relationship is, however, natural; where the element of stress has access to chromaticism, animated tension is expressed by golden section, and an atmosphere of a more "humane" world is created. A great value of Bartók's music, as perhaps most nicely phrased by László Németh, lies in its exploration of "sub-European geology," in his having discovered and drawn into his art the laws governing depths of the human soul which have not been touched by civilization. The place of popular romanticism was taken by a deepening of the prehistoric memory of man, with a sort of excavation of the soul and an attempt to find beneath the deposit of modern times the sound and desirable basis of a new civilization, the "common human element" alive in everyone.

It has been said that the more recent a style the farther it goes back into the past: "Early romanticism to the Middle Ages, Wagner to Germanic polytheism, Stravinsky to totemism," writes an eminent commentator on modern Western music. In a figurative sense this applies also to Bartók. In the course of my investigations, I have come to the conclusion that Bartók's art represents a logical continuation and, in a certain sense, a conclusion of the development of European music; the circles of harmonic development are fused into a single, coherent, closed unit in Bartók's sound system: the "axis system" (to be discussed later). This circle is, however, closed in the opposite direction as well; Bartók's art goes back to the remotest past of music, and it can be said to penetrate to the core of music, to the most elemental interrelations. The most intricate has been traced to the most primitive; the "excessively concentrated" string quartets were enriched by simple folk songs. This was the breakthrough for which the majority of his contemporaries longed in vain.

II

Another clear feature of Bartók's music is its wide European horizon. "Every art has the right to stem from a previous art; it not only has the right to but it must so stem," declared Bartók. His sound system grew out of functional music; from the beginnings of functional music through the harmonies of Viennese classicism and the tone world of romanticism a line proceeds without a break to the development of the axis system. By this system Bartók set down the final results of European harmonic thinking. As revealed by analysis of his compositions, this axis system can be traced to the peculiarities of classical harmonies: a) functional affinities of the fourth and fifth, b) the intimate relationship of parallel major and minor keys, c) relationship of overtones, and d) the role of leading tones. Here I should like to sum up briefly a few characteristic traits of this system:

First, in classical harmonies (in the case of C major tonality) the circle of fifths F—C—G—D—A—E corresponds to the functional series S—T—D—S—T—D. When this periodicity is extended over the entire circle of fifths, the scheme of the axis system may be clearly recognized.

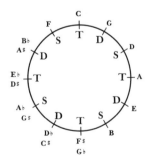

Chords resting on fundamental C, E flat = D sharp, F sharp = G flat, or A possess a tonic function; those based on E, G, B flat = A sharp, or on C sharp = D flat have a dominant function: and chords built on D, F, A flat = G sharp, or B have a subdominant function.

Second, Bartók is generally known to have shown a preference for the use of so-called major-minor chords (with neutral third), for instance, the following form in C tonality:

C minor

C major

Function remains unchanged when the C major mode comprised by the above chord is replaced by the parallel A minor or when the C minor tonality comprised by the chord is replaced by the parallel E flat major; this process occurs at every step in Bartók's music:

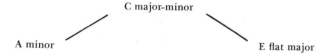

C major-minor

A minor   E flat major

These substitution chords may also be employed in major-minor form, which brings the system to a close, because the parallel of A major, F sharp minor and that of E flat minor, G flat major arrive at an enharmonic meeting (F sharp = G flat):

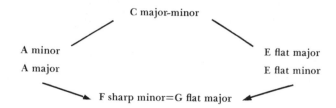

C major-minor

A minor   E flat major
A major   E flat minor
           F sharp minor=G flat major

Thus the axis extends the use of parallels over the whole system. (Naturally only major and minor keys of equal signature may be regarded as parallel, *e.g.,* C major and A minor, or C minor and E flat major.) Application of these parallel connections to dominant and subdominant function leads to the scheme of the axis system.

Third, the acoustic precondition of arriving from the dominant to the tonic is to reach the fundamental tone from an overtone (this results in the affinity of various cadences). Accordingly, the dominant of C is not only G but also the near overtones E and B flat (therefore the circle of tonic-dominant relationships is expanded to include E—C and B flat—C). Since the D—T relationship corresponds relatively to the T—S and S—D relationships, overtone-to-fundamental-tone attraction prevails between the T—S and the S—D. When these conditions are applied to the circle of fifths, the results agree completely with the axis system.

Fourth, in the simplest cadence—in the affinity of the fifth-degree-seventh and the first degree —the chief role is played by the so-called sensitive sounds: the leading tone strives to reach the first and the seventh the third degree of the tonic—that is, the leading tone B is resolved by C and the seventh, F, by E or E flat. These two characteristically sensitive tones, however, stand in a tritonic relationship to each other, the tritone being distinguished by the characteristic that it persists when its tones have been exchanged. Thus, if the B—F relationship is converted into an F—B relationship—as is frequently done by Bartók—it results that the F (E sharp) assumes the role of the leading tone (striving toward F sharp instead of E), while the seventh, B, strives toward A sharp (or A) instead of C; thus, instead of the expected tonic C major, the "counterpole" but equally tonic F sharp major (or minor) steps in.

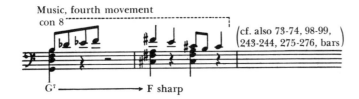

So far I have published some ten sorts of deductions from this system.

A survey of the past and of the development of harmonic thinking is bound to convince us that elaboration of the axis system was a historical necessity. As compared to the past, the advance consisted mainly of Bartók's having extended these affinities uniformly to the entire twelve-tone system. Moreover, his axis system represents not only a development of European functional music but also its consummation and even its conclusion, because by extending functional correlations to the homogeneous twelve-tone series he put the coping stone on further development.

III

Among the influences that affected Bartók in his youth that of the French impressionistic school, particularly of Debussy, was decisive. What is today referred to as the "acoustic" system in Bartók's compositions drew chiefly on the coloristic chords of French impressionism. Bartók himself liked to allude to the wealth of inspiration he owed to modern French music. Without this factor the characteristic duality of his harmonic thinking could never have taken shape. From such evidence as has been given here it becomes clear that Bartók contrived to melt into a comprehensive style material that appeared to be incompatible, and it was this incongruous material that produced the most striking feature of his music: the dualism shown in his technique of polarization, or, in other words, the peculiar visual system which consistently permits things to be seen from two aspects and which, with Bartók, grew into a veritable philosophical standard, as if contrast were the only means to justify the existence of things. Bluebeard's night would be inconceivable without the luminous chord of the fifth door, the F sharp without the C, the Inferno without the Paradiso.

One may well wonder about the source of this tendency to polarize. Sometimes it would seem to flow from the attitude in Bartók of the scientist who knows that no existence can be imagined without positive and negative poles. Sometimes the impression is thereby created of harsh judgment, as with Dante; on other occasions it appears as a crystallized philosophical system. For the most part, however, it serves to mirror life: the unfathomable depths when, from the world of light it plunges us into darkness or (as in the *Music for Strings, Percussion and Celesta* and the *Sonata for Two Pianos and Percussion*) when, from the night it leads us into daylight, pointing the way to solution, to joy.

In my analytical studies I have used the terms "bartokean chromaticism" and "bartokean diatony" to denote Bartók's dual world of harmonies. On the basis of their most characteristic traits, I have named the former the golden-section system and the latter the acoustic (overtone) system. Let us take a look at the properties that ensure the unity and polar division of the two systems. On this occasion we shall have to be content with a few main correlations.

First of all, it is common knowledge that Bartók's most markedly diatonic melodies constitute an acoustic or overtone scale. In the finale of the *Sonata for Two Pianos and Percussion*, for example, the acoustic scale of C—D—E—F sharp—G—A—B flat—C hovers over the C—E—G (C major) chord. This scale is dominated by the major third, perfect fifth, natural seventh, and, further, the augmented fourth and the major sixth, in contrast to the minor third—perfect fourth—minor sixth (3 : 5 : 8, C—E flat—F—A flat) milieu of the golden-section system. Compare, in *Sonata for Two Pianos and Percussion*, the principal theme of the chromatic first movement with that of the diatonic third movement:

These two worlds of harmony complement each other to such measure that the chromatic scale can be separated into golden-section and acoustic scales. Separately each is merely a part of the whole and neither can exist without the other.

			3		5			8		
Golden-section scale:	C		E flat		F			A flat		

Acoustic scale:	C	D		E		F sharp	G		A	B flat
		2		4		6	7		9	10

In the second place, the two systems are in a relationship of inversion, reflecting each other. By the inversion of the golden-section intervals acoustic intervals are obtained—from a major second (2) a natural seventh, from a minor third (3) a major sixth (with Bartók, the "pastoral sixth"), from a fourth (5) a fifth, from a minor sixth (8) a major third—and at that the most characteristic acoustic intervals. Systematically, therefore, they become related by organically complementing and reflecting each other. Their unity rests on mutual interdependence. The opening and closing of the *Cantata Profana* offers a beautiful illustration: two scales mirror each other tone for tone—a golden-section scale (intervals 2, 3, 5, 8, with a diminished fifth) and a pure acoustic scale:

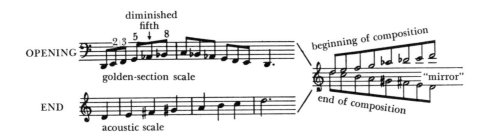

Third, although the features cited seem to concern external factors, this is no longer the case when it is shown that the acoustic system can admit only consonant intervals (because of overtone harmony), whereas the intervals of the golden-section system are tense and "dissonant" (this, by the way, exhibits the contrast between the Western "acoustic" and Eastern "pentatonic" attitudes).

An equally deep secret of Bartók's music (perhaps the most profound) is that the "closed" world of the golden-section system is counterbalanced by the "open" sphere of the acoustic system. The former is inevitably associated with the presence of the complete system (its configurations being representable only in the closed circle of fifths); the latter was molded by Bartók from a single tone derived from the overtone series of a single fundamental note. The former does not respond to the requirements of "up" and "down," and its material is permanently in process of concentric augmentation and diminution. (The above-cited themes of the *Sonata for Two Pianos and Percussion* are, for instance, subjected to incessant increase, the principal theme being augmented from bar to bar and the tone series of the second theme expanding similarly from step to step until it attains a broad sixth; "cornet-shaped processions," "scissor-like" movement of voices, and sequences proceeding by augmented steps are frequent, and even these processes follow a planned course, every detail of the movement showing augmentation up to the geometric center of the movement, after which every step is systematically diminished.)

Bartók's mode of acoustic writing is, on the other hand, marked by permanence; his harmonies radiate their energy for prolonged periods of time with motionless, unwavering constancy. For the closed world the emblem of the "circle" and for the open system that of the "straight line" automatically present themselves (chromatic configurations being bound to the circle—the circle of fifths—as opposed to the overtone system, where the component tones strive upward in a straight line). There is an obvious reference here to Dante, the emblem of his Inferno being the circle, the ring, and that of his Paradiso the straight line, the arrow, the ray. The rings of the Inferno undergo concentric diminution to "Cocitus" whereas those of his Paradiso are widened into the infinite "Empyreum." With Bartók, the themes follow the same pattern: chromaticism is associated with the circle and diatony most naturally with straight lines of melody.

"circle" (beginning)   "straight" (end)

Thus the two systems form unity and contrast; they require and preclude, affirm and deny each other. They constitute each other's negative impression in the twelve-tone system, each being capable of disclosing only one aspect of life. In Bartók's music, ideological unity and a complete picture of the world can be achieved by chromaticism only together with diatony and by diatony only together with chromaticism. It may be interpreted as a poetic symbol that in the diatonic system harmonic overtones develop above and in the chromatic system below the fundamental tone.

C⁷   C⁷
(acoustic)   (golden section)

In some of his works Bartók went so far in the polarization and simplification of the material that material and content, emblem and program, means and expression, were amalgamated to the point of inseparability.

IV

So far, this investigation has sought to establish the ties between Bartók's music and that of the remote and recent past—folk song, functional music, and French impressionism. The question naturally arises now of whether any correlations can be discovered between Bartók's art and the aspirations of the atonal school ("Zwölfton-Musik," as he liked to call it).

These days we may witness a curious phenomenon: formerly, even one or two decades ago, Bartók was attacked by his enemies for "aggressiveness" and "Asiatic gruesomeness"; today his music must be defended from attacks launched from the opposite side. The adherents of the twelve-tone system accuse Bartók of conservatism, compromise, and "convenience" (in a dictionary of music recently published in Western Europe *Bluebeard's Castle,* for instance, was relegated into a class of compositions "intolerably superannuated"). Is it possible that Bartók, whom his contemporaries stigmatized as a barbarous shatterer of form, when regarded from a certain distance should suddenly turn out to have been no revolutionary but the heir and bearer of classical ideals? "In art there is only slow or rapid progress, implying in essence evolution and not revolution," Bartók said in an American interview in 1941.

It is certain that the peculiarities of Bartók's idiom tended gradually to disappear, as they grew more familiar and natural, while firmness of classical form, balance, and proportion, simplicity and clarity of expression came more and more to command admiration. In *Music for Strings, Percussion and Celesta* we are held no longer by peculiar effects of color but by the brilliant and unique grandeur that communicates a deeply human message, taking the listener from the resounding chaos of the first movement, through the biting humor of the second and the nature-bound spell of the third, to the joyous round dance of the fourth and the tones of fraternal love that crown the composition. To ears trained to atonality this music may really sound as if "softened by humanity." It is, however, worthwhile to examine more closely the accusations hurled at Bartók. Extremists like to reproach Bartók for two things in particular: first, for his construction, with the claim that in the organization of material he fell far behind Schönberg and Webern, and second for his failure to attain the perfect "indifference" of the twelve tones and to give up the principle of tonality and achieve independence from harmonies. (One critic said, "he did not recognize the possibility of culmination beyond harmony.")

In this controversy the material analysis of Bartók's works has produced a most unexpected turn; from the point of view of construction his works have been found to rank by no means behind those of Schönberg or Webern. On the contrary, with highly superior and much stricter organization his compositions actually surpass the works of these composers. If, on analysis of Schönberg's music, Adorno could declare, "There are no more free notes!" this statement can apply to the *Sonata for Two Pianos and Percussion,* among other works. Here organization is really extended to everything, to form and proportions no less than to rhythm and harmony and even to dynamics, color, and register. But this constraint did not flow from a speculative tendency, as in the case of the atonal test tube; Bartók's solutions are always and everywhere musical and perceptible and are due to his having been able to reduce music to something extraordinarily elemental, ancient, and fundamental. This is apt to appear with such straightforward bareness as to assume outwardly the form of mathematical formulas or symbols, yet they do not create the impression of abstraction. Rather, this simplification to symbols intensifies their elemental power.

Before proceeding further along this line, let us make a short detour. No one would think of asserting that the *la-so-mi* figures of the oldest nursery songs resulted from deliberate construction, though the notes of the melody are tuned after the "geometric mean," *i.e.,* after golden section. Hardly anyone remembers, when listening to music, that the consonance of the simple major triad results from the harmony of the nearest natural overtones; the perfect fifth and the major third bring to our ears the simplest process of vibrations. Now let us turn again to the *Sonata for Two Pianos and Percussion*. The melody and sound system of the first movement may be traced to the most primitive pentatonic turns; in the principal theme of the finale, the melody simply spreads out the natural overtone scale above a C major chord. Yet this major triad, appearing here, comes as a true revelation. How can a simple major triad be invested with such explosive content?

To approach the issue from the other side: can the contemporary composer avail himself at all of the services of the "major triad," the once vital significance of which has worn off until it has become an empty husk? Actually, the elemental effect of Bartók's music lies for the most part in apparently casual presentation, with plain connections, of the strongest means of expression. The major triad may be in itself a worn-out cliché, but when it is brought into polar-dual relationship with another system —as it was by Bartók—it may promptly regain its original and deep significance. Let us set up the formula of the work and add immediately the explanation: the golden section (geometric mean) between two poles always cuts into the most tense point, whereas symmetry creates balance (the overtone series is void of tension, because its notes are integer multiples of the fundamental tone's vibrations):

Dynamic proportion = golden section = pentatony = opening movement
Static proportion = symmetry = overtone scale = closing movement

In this connection *la-so-mi* and the major triad are not only representative of purest music but also elements of form and organization in construction, which are given the role of restoring to these apparently defervescent forms the fire that they may have possessed only when they came into being. What I should like to denote as the elemental rebirth of music is this reconstruction of musical means. Every element of music has been regenerated in a similar manner by the touch of Bartók; the most ancient element he re-created on the loftiest plane, so that beginning and end form an inseparable unity. There is no reason to question the authenticity of the thought attributed to Bartók in A. Fassett's book to the effect that he believed the very new could be born only of the very ancient and that he had bypassed all the intervening and unnecessary complications separating the present from its origin.

It is inconceivable that Bartók, who applied thorough scientific methods in analyzing, classifying, and systematizing folk songs, should have been naïvely uncritical when it came to his own compositions. I have no wish to prove that he aspired to an arithmetic or geometric system; he did, however, by going back to the roots of music, discover fundamental laws and "root" correlations which may be expressed by formula-like, mathematical symbols. In the last analysis, the whole technique of his music was based on these fundamental laws, and, with a consistency comparable only to that of the greatest masters of form, he expanded the system of laws derived from popular as well as art music over the whole of music, proceeding from the simple to the complex.

It was shown above that in the *Sonata for Two Pianos and Percussion* (as in numerous other compositions) every unit is divided after the rule of the golden section, from the whole of the work to the smallest cells. In these phenomena a much greater role must be ascribed to instinct and musical sensitivity—just as it was unnecessary for Mozart to count bars in order to compose periods of 4 + 4, 8 + 8, or 16 + 16. That Bartók was not inspired by formalistic tendencies emerges from the fact that he treated the secrets of his forms as real "secrets" and never evinced any desire to explain his music. His high-tension message, however, stood in need of guarantees. With him, architectonic bonds implied recognition of the possibilities inherent in the material and of natural attractions; form did not represent a mere "façade" for composition. In the history of music, every truly great composition is imbued with the longing for full possession of the material, for completeness. With Bartók it also involves the triumph of man over unbridled instincts. Does the word "art" not intimate discipline over formless, chaotic material, thus giving expression to man's longing for order, to the healing power of art?

In Bartók's case, however, we have to repulse attacks on two fronts. Let me present a typical instance to those who reproach Bartók for having omitted the "total and radical reorganization of the material." In form the *Sonata for Two Pianos and Percussion* follows the pattern of "slow—fast + slow—fast"; the golden section may therefore be expected to come in at the beginning of the second slow movement. The result fulfills our expectations with astonishing accuracy: the time value of the complete work is 6,432 eighth notes and that of golden section, 3,975 eighths.

Those who speak of Bartók as a romantic retrograde bent on seeking asylum in folklore must have failed to grasp the exceptional coherence of his thought-processes and his all-embracing spiritual vigor. In architecture, his compositions are in no way looser than those of his contemporaries. Bartók's new adversaries are misled chiefly by the fact that these features escape notice, because with him geometry never appears as a sign of outward restriction but flows from the nature of his music, following the natural motion of the musical material. "We follow nature in composition," wrote Bartók, who proclaimed peasant music to be a "natural phenomenon."

Let us return to the second accusation, namely, that he failed to obey the demands made by the twelve-tone system on twentieth-century composers. This issue is answered most convincingly by Bartók's sound system. This system possesses the peculiar, dialectic trait of being approachable from the points of view of both functional and twelve-tone music, since in the axis system the principles of tonality and distance are equally realized—the latter to a degree that could not be surpassed by the use of purely logical methods. In Bartók's chromatic world, functional chief tones step into relationships of the augmented triad (cutting the system into equal thirds); hence with C as the tonic, the chief note of the dominant is represented by E and that of the subdominant by A flat; each of these permits substitution by the tritonic "counterpoles" (dividing the system into symmetric halves), while the poles of single functions rest on the basis of a diminished fourth (corresponding to equal quartering of the system). Thus the axis system can be built up also of mere distance formulas. Indeed the axis system, given the twelve-tone system and the three functions, is the only system that can be realized with distance division. Seen from the historical angle this is an organic continuation of the age-old struggle between the principles of tonality and distance, with the gradual ascendancy of the latter, which finally made it possible for the twelve notes of the chromatic scale to be subjected to equal, free treatment (with introduction of the tempered sound system in the center of development; in some of Liszt's and Mussorgsky's attempts the distance principle was made to prevail faultlessly). Bartók's greatness lies precisely in his having realized his ideas while maintaining tonality and even function, because he was familiar with the surfaces of contact by whose aid these two archenemies could be reconciled. (He traces the minor-third circles of various "axes" to the minor-third relationship of parallel major and minor modes; for models of the augmented-triad correlations linking the three functions, Bartók may have drawn on such examples as are offered, for instance, by romantic harmonies.)

V

Particular significance may be attributed to the fact that pentatony is the most characteristic form of Bartók's chromaticism (golden-section system) and overtone chords, of his diatony. This duality would seem to give expression to the two perhaps most ancient endeavors of music. Clearly, the physiological apparatus of our ears (with the logarithmic structure of the cochlea) is such as to make *so-la-so-mi* (2, 3, 5) congenial at the earliest stage, of which the primitive levels of folk music and the simplest nursery songs provide unequivocal evidence. In such primitive melody cultures, the sense for major tonality and functional attraction are completely unknown. Harmonic thinking arises from a quite different source, from the overtone system, which could have come into its own exclusively with instrumental music (it cannot be considered as accidental that functional thinking is no more than a few centuries old). Pentatony may be deduced from the sound system of Pythagoras, harmonic music from the overtone system.

One wonders if pentatonic (golden-section) and harmonic (acoustic) thinking—these two points of departure for every kind of music—had a double root. If so, Bartók actually seems to have seized music at the very root. On one side is "inner" hearing—based on the form of the ear—and on the other the "external" hearing, so to speak, or physical harmony. The former is more ardent, expressive, and emotionally charged, and the latter more radiant and luminous, richer in sensuous elements.

The above considerations agree with the scientific observation that golden section is associated only with *organic* substances (Fibonacci himself discovered it in connection with an investigation of natural phenomena). Without the contribution of man's emotional world, pentatony, with its tension, would never have come into existence. The acoustic system, on the other hand, may develop independently of the phenomena of human life (a pipe-like column of air or motion of a string-like material will suffice to bring it about).

Pentatonic and acoustic endeavors follow demonstrably contradictory courses. Physiological efforts organize and create tension, while physical efforts disorganize by striving to abolish tension. Here the thesis may be formulated that the golden-section system creates a *closed* world, heavy with inner tension, while the acoustic system is *open* and strives to dispel tension by overtone consonance.

It may be added that this closed-in form is an organic feature of golden section—quite apart from Bartók's sound system. Closure and golden section are related phenomena. The capacity of golden section to organize is due to this property. The following is an illustration of the correlation between closure and golden section. Golden section can easily be brought about with the aid of a simple "knot" on a strip of paper (*cf.* Otto Schubert: *Gesetz der Baukunst,* Seemann, Leipzig, 1954); every proportion of this knot—without exception—will display geometric golden section.

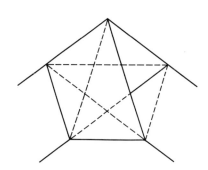

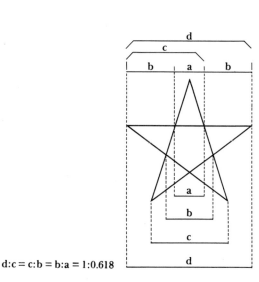

$$d:c = c:b = b:a = 1:0.618$$

It is this property of the pentagram closed form thus obtained that Goethe alludes to in Faust, Part I:

MEPHISTOPHELES: Let me admit; a tiny obstacle
Forbids my walking out of here:
It is the druid's foot upon your threshold.

FAUST: The pentagram distresses you?
But tell me, then, you son of hell.
If this impedes you, how did you come in?
How can your kind of spirit be deceived?

MEPHISTOPHELES: Observe! The lines are poorly drawn;
That one, the angle pointing outward,
Is, you see, a little open.

I would like to attempt here an interpretation of Bartók's dual world, his "yang-yin" technique, in terms of an equation, contrasting some special elements encountered at every step in Bartók's compositions. This interpretation is particularly applicable to the construction and content of the *Sonata for Two Pianos and Percussion*.

First, "Inferno" movement	Third, "Paradiso" movement
chromaticism	diatony
golden-section system	acoustic system
closed world	open world
circular pattern of melody	straight pattern of melody
presence of central tone	presence of fundamental tone
rhythm with strong ending	rhythm with weak ending
uneven meter	even meter
asymmetries	periodicity
F sharp minor beginning	C major end
demoniac world	serene world, festive and playful
instinctive existence	intellectual existence
organic	logic
love—hatred	perfect understanding—irony
tension	freedom from tension
emotional nature	sensuous nature
inspiration	thought
experience	knowledge, solution
feminine symbols	masculine symbols
dependency on fate	law, order, form
permanent change	validity at all times
augmentation—diminution	stabilized forms
occurrence	existence
process in time	extension over space
origin—development—conclusion	division
finite: circular motion	infinite
geometric nature	mathematical nature
(key figure to golden section: irrational figure)	(key figures to overtone system: integrals)

It is interesting to note that Bartók presumably intended—as supported by the date of its composition, 1937—the *Sonata for Two Pianos and Percussion* as the crowning of the *Microcosmos* (1926–1937): the "Macrocosmos."

While the important questions of symbolism of keys and the role of rhythm cannot here be dealt with at great length, a few outstanding features may be pointed out. Bartók's rhythm is also governed by strict laws. The circular course of the first movement of the *Sonata for Two Pianos and Percussion Instruments* is in no slight degree brought about by the "absolute" uneven measure (three times three eighths), while the third movement owes its static character to its "absolute" even measure (twice two eighths); in the second movement, even and uneven bars are intentionally made to alternate between the two. Bartók was greatly interested in the idea of even and uneven meters: *Second Piano Concerto, Concerto for Violin and Orchestra,* second movement of *Music for Strings, Percussion and Celesta, Microcosmos* No. 137—with these, themes presented in even measure recur in uneven rhythm, and vice versa. In addition, the rhythms with a "strong" ending in the first movement have counterparts with "weak" endings in the third movement:

Consequently, the themes of the first movement acquire a closed and those of the third movement an open form. The most interesting circumstance is that the dimensions of the complete work were not accidental—to quote only the final results, the time value of the composition (the above-mentioned 6,432 eighths = 804 whole tones) may also be traced to the symbol of the circle: $2^8\pi = 4^4\pi = 16^2\pi = 804$.

Let us finally take up the role of Bartók's art in the music of our century. Bartók's golden-section system was rooted in Eastern popular music and pentatonic conception; his acoustic system he owed to Western harmonic thinking. His greatest achievement was the integration of these two ways of thinking. Hence those who respect Bartók as the epitomist of the music of the peoples of Eastern Europe are no less mistaken than those who would like to monopolize him on behalf of extremist efforts and condone his relations to folk music as a "regrettable pastime." He himself liked to refer to popular music and the French impressionistic school as the sources of the most decisive influences that shaped his art. Through his compositions we can extend the dimensions of this idea: what Bartók achieved in his art amounts to a synthesis of East and West, where folklore meets the counterpoint of Bach, the forms achieved by Mozart and Beethoven, and Western harmonic thinking. Bartók is a classic master because he aspired to completeness. If his art and his position in the history of music could be summed up in a single sentence it would run as follows: Bartók achieved something that few others have been able to realize: a symbolic handshake of East and West, a union of the Orient and the Occident.

The principal characters in the following text are Le Corbusier, architect of beautiful buildings, inventor of the Modulor, and David Tudor, musician, without whom my later music and the musics of Morton Feldman and Christian Wolff, to mention only three, would never have come into being, not because of his virtuosity but because of what, when his skills are put away, he is. This text is not for him but is an homage to him.

There's virtually nothing to say about rhythm for there's no time. We've yet to learn the rudiments, the useful means. But there's every reason to believe that this will happen and not over dead bodies. When I see everything that's to the right resembles everything that's to the left, I feel just as I do in front of something where there's no center of interest at all. Activity, busyness:—not of the one who made it (his intentions had moved down to next to nothing)—perhaps a speck of dust.

We are constructed symmetrically (with the usual allowances for imperfection and ignorance with regard to what goes on inside) and so we see and hear symmetrically, that is, notice that each event is at the center of the field in which we-it is. This is not so much a democratic point of view as it is equally aristocratic. We only object when someone calls our attention to something which we were about to see originally. He mentioned going backward or to the side and combined this with the notion of progress.

The house in Los Angeles the others visited. They told about it: how the people tried to get it destroyed ("an eyesore") but that it proved to be too great a source of income. She spoke of change in her perception of light. As I pick up my thought now I already know that it is going to slip through my fingers. Its very nature is to evade being caught. That is what thought does (not just this one: that things are in the fluent relationship of life and death, Death coming only to him who wins: nothing stops).

Before leaving the earth altogether, let us ask: How does Music stand with respect to its instruments, their pitches, the scales, modes, and rows, repeating themselves from octave to octave, the chords, harmonies, and tonalities, the beats, meters, and rhythms, the degrees of amplitude (pianissimo, piano, mezzo-piano, mezzo-forte, forte, fortissimo)? Though the majority go each day to the schools where these matters are taught, they read when time permits of Cape Canaveral, Ghana, and Seoul. And they've heard tell of the music synthesizer, magnetic tape. They take for granted the dials on radios and television sets. A tardy art, the art of Music. And why so slow? Is it because, once having learned a notation of pitches and durations, musicians will not give up their Greek? Children have been modern artists for years now. What is it about Music that sends not only the young but adults too as far into the past as they can conveniently go? The module? But our choices never reached around the globe, and in our laziness, when we changed over to the twelve-tone system, we just took the pitches of the previous music as though we were moving into a furnished apartment and had no time to even take the pictures off the walls. What excuse? That nowadays things are happening so quickly that we become thoughtless? Or were we clairvoyant and knew ahead of time that the need for furniture of any kind would disappear? (Whatever you place there in front of you sits established in the air.) The thing that was irrelevant to the structures we formerly made, and this was what kept us breathing, was what took place within them. Their emptiness we took for what it was—a place where anything could happen. That was one of the reasons we were able when circumstances became inviting (changes in consciousness, etc.) to go outside, where breathing is child's play: no walls, not even the glass ones which, though we could see through them, killed the birds while they were flying.

Even in the case of object, the boundaries are not clear. (I see through what you made if, that is, the reflections don't send me back where I am.) But why argue? The Indians long ago knew that Music was going on permanently and that hearing it was like looking out a window at a landscape which didn't stop when one turned away.

Etc. Some time ago counting, patterns, tempi were dropped. Rhythm's in any length of time (no-structure). Aorder. It's definitely spring—not just in the air. Take as an example of rhythm anything which seems irrelevant.

What's marvelous is that the moon still rises even though we've changed our minds about whether or not we'll ever get there. Symmetry. Pure symmetry. Doesn't exist. (He worked for several years and as he worked his technique improved but he preferred to keep the ineptitudes, to reveal, that is, not something perfect but something that showed that he had been alive while making it.) And yet I know when I see something that at least makes the signs of symmetry that I am where measurements no longer have real significance. (Like his flags and targets, alphabets and the cans of ale.) Don't tell me it's a question of mass production. Is it not rather that they want to establish if not the rules of the game at least what it is that one uses to play with when he starts playing? (There is no need for us to agree that play is what it is, since in that case Invention without which we might as well not have been born is a spoilsport.) There was a time (and I would not have minded living then even though I would not for any money change places with anyone past, present, or future) when, in Music, there was a glimmer of perfection—a relationship between the unit and the whole, down to the last detail: so elegant. How did that come about (it was an object)? It was an icon. It was an illustration of belief. Now do you see why what we do now is not at all what it was then? Everything now is in a state of confusing us, for, for one thing, we're not certain of the names of things that we see directly in front of us. (But even if we don't know their names, can we not take our rules—and compasses—and measure them? No, we cannot: remember what he said about the tiger.) And No, again: they've required the campers to leave the park because the fires in distant places were sixteen in number.

Ancient history: *tatami* (material); *tala* (structure open at both ends); isorhythmic motet (closed structure); a rhythmic structure (micro-macro-cosmic) in which the first part had that number of units of which there were subsequent parts, the total number of units being a square, the relation of small parts within each unit being identical with the relation of large parts within the whole (closed structure); the Modulor (material).

She told me she'd dropped in around eleven-thirty in the evening and he said, "Why don't you stay for dinner?" His cooking, she said, was like a performance. There was no running about the room: everything was mysteriously in the very place his hand reached when the need for it arose.

The world in a grain of sand (or is it the universe?) and vice versa. Yes, but when we say as one artist to another, "The unit and its relationship to the whole," we speak of an object, and it is well to remember that the only time the idea of movement on the part of this object entered his head, except as a far-fetched analogy to music of previous times, was when he was forced to accept errors into his calculations. (Rhythm, too, is not arithmetic.) *He* had not made mistakes: it was just that circumstances were overwhelmingly different than the idea with which he was attempting to cloak them. And his idea, actually, he said, was a tool, an instrument—not an object. But it had in it all the elements (present only as measurements) that the object, once made, was to have. Thus it was not a tool, for paper, once cut, is free of the knife which was used to cut it. Not a tool but an instrument, like the piano, which, used, leaves its notes scattered all over the music that was played. (Was that not why it was necessary to change it? Otherwise we would have been faced with a project like that of the Pittsburgh maker of stringed instruments who wanted to so fashion his 'cellos, violas and violins that one wouldn't be able to hear any difference in timbre, passing from one to another. The problem is more serious: we must dispense with instruments altogether and get used to working with tools. Then, God willing, we'll get some work done. It can be put this way too: find ways of using instruments as though they were tools, *i.e.,* so that they leave no traces. That's precisely what our tape-recorders, amplifiers, microphones, loud-speakers, photoelectric cells, etc., are: things to be used which don't necessarily determine the nature of what is done. There are, of course, pitfalls, but so is one's finger when he points at the moon. What we're dealing with is not things but minds. What else?)

We are now back on the ground on our feet. The cars can no longer pass over the bridge. Last week it was a case of uncertain footing, quicksand and, before we got out, plunging through the stream. I remember the story he told of their having to stop altogether—and they were not timid souls. Symmetry's not produced in music by doing something and then doing it backward or by doing something and then something else and then back to what was first done. Exercise: lying flat on your back, your arms at your sides, your legs uncrossed, ask yourself: Among all the sounds I hear, which ones are off balance?

There'll be centrally located pulverized Muzak-plus ("You cling to composition.") performed by listeners who do nothing more than go through the room.

There are those who think or feel that it should never have happened but (disregarding them) the others no longer say, "Perhaps it would have been better had you cut it." They say instead, "I was just getting with it." Some say, "Couldn't you have made it more effective?"

And when that comes about that has not yet been heard will we be able to say more or less than we can now about the unit and its relationship to the whole? In the interior of that space, open yet filled like a dish to the brim with sounds both gentle and terrifying, occurring at unpredictable points not only in time but throughout the space too, will it not be as it is today, spring definitely here (or is it summer?), finally outdoors, deliciously plagued by insects, something to hear on all sides (even back of me), that anything we may think we will have had to say will as now have somehow slipped our minds?

His response to the question was: There seems to be a tendency toward the Good. And what does that have to do with proportion? This, that once the measurements are made (not in rubber but in some inflexible material), the proper relationships determined (Can you believe it? They managed to get an entire family out of the house simply because she raised her children in a way the other mothers didn't), a police force is in order. I quote (omissions and italics mine): "Concord between men and machines, sensitivity and mathematics, a harvest of prodigious harmonies reaped from numbers: the grid of proportions. This art . . . will be acquired by the effort of men of good will, but it will be contested and attacked . . . *It must be proclaimed by law.*" Art this is called. Its shape is that of tyranny. The social inflexibility follows from the initial conception of proportion. The line there drawn between two points becomes first a web and finally three-dimensional. Unless we find some way to get out we're lost. The more glass, I say, the better. Not only the windows, this year, even though they're small, will open: one whole wall slides away when I have the strength or assistance to push it. And what do I enter? (It draws me like a magnet.) Not proportion. The clutter of the unkempt forest. (His music gave me the same experience: it was only one sound amplified and recorded on tape from the action of two people who for twenty-odd minutes rubbed metal ash trays against panes of glass. That is one way. There are as many others as there are people and there are more people now than at any other time in history. Now the increase in population is geometrical; soon again it may be a question of simple addition. There is *ergo* no lack of ideas which we have not yet had. Why then do other people get his ideas before he does? A short circuit? Let them mend their ways, starting wherever they are constantly from scratch.)

Let us list our reasons for having dropped all thoughts about proportion: 1) We are dealing not with the number 2 but with the number 1; 2) During any one year—the record proves it—we worked in at least two different ways: it took in some cases three or even four years, unburdened as we were, to drop those habits; 3) Being slow-witted, musicians were able to observe the effects of thoughts about proportion in the other arts, giving them the responsibility to do otherwise and fortunately they were free of the problems of architecture and civil engineering (the leaking roof and the collapsing structure), the problems of language (meaning of words and conventions of syntax), the problems of painting and sculpture (objectification); 4) Process, pure subjectivity; 5) Consideration of the activity of listening (We do our own listening: it is not done to us)—that to be direct it must not be followed by any other activity formed (intellectual) or uninformed (emotional, kinesthetic, critical, discursive), thus making possible a transformation of experience (which was which? the sounds or I?); so: composition—that to be direct it must not be preceded, etc. until "which was which?" which is crossed out since nothing has yet been performed, *i.e.,* come into existence; 6) We have found ways of composing indeterminately, writing on sheets of transparent plastic which can be superimposed in any way; and

7) (it took three years to realize the necessity) We have found that one notation is all that should go on a single such sheet (no proportion = optimum flexibility = any proportion). This brings to mind the Russian chickens. Fragmentation. We began by increasing the differences between the sounds making a *klangfarbenmelodie*. More and more we left openings in our space of time. What changed matters radically was the willingness to stop work altogether before the structure was complete. After that there was no longer any fixed structure: just parts in any number, superimposition and duration. Time-sense changed. Now he says: The permeation of space with sound.

The copperhead strikes only one hunter. The others go on about his business. Again last night, the bird, was it blinded? Was that my purpose in killing it?

He made an analysis of the sound of a gong and then, in order to make a piece of music on magnetic tape, derived measurements from that analysis so that all the frequencies, durations, etc. would follow from these. And even though "anything can be done" this project had to suffer as the other one did the introduction of approximations. What we are concerned with now is quantity (we get quality automatically), but we don't want to be drowned by it: we insist on being able to feel as though nothing were there even though we can no longer count our possessions. If, and I don't believe it, anything like design took place before they put those rocks in those gardens of sand, then it is high time one of us hunters takes time off to make a garden empty-minded. What would it be? Something else to study?

At this moment if proportion and such matters were uppermost in our minds, harmony and beauty and all the rest of it, we would desire no further change (except we need some rain—six fires yesterday so that two thousand were sent back to the cities they came from): there was an indefinite whiteness sitting in the air around the trees and I was moving along at forty miles an hour. If, as is the case when I look at that building near Chicago, I have the impression it's not there even though I see it taking up space, then module or no module, it's O.K. But don't get me started counting sheep! What we musicians are expecting to discover is not how to stop counting (we've done that already) but how to dispense with our watches. (It's true: I'm always asking him, "What time is it?") It must be that eventually we will have a music the relationship of which to what takes place before and after ("no" music) is exact, so that one will have the experience that no experience was had, a dematerialization (not of facts) of intentions. We already have this, so there's no cause for alarm, but we want it in the future available everywhere, just as it is already. They're beginning to work.

She had a goat. She no longer does. Now they have dogs and the plan to get rid of them. The cat which she's had for a long time has no mother instinct. They're going to buy a horse. Why don't they do as with the view from the balancing rock near the top of the hill, never bothering to see it? Proportion.

Aperiodic rhythm admits of periodic rhythm. (It doesn't work the other way around; that's why it has to be aperiodic, though that isn't how the decision that it should be aperiodic was reached. It was thought that another expression was possible with its own rules and so, though changed, strict control was maintained. —I'm speaking of the people on the other side of the Ocean.) The bird goes on singing repetitively even though the flies are buzzing at the window erratically and intermittently. In all of this, and I do not mention the 9,997 other events, where do we begin if work consists in measuring? And if we begin, say at any point, do we measure each single event, how much time it takes, or do we measure the spaces between events (were there any?) or both? The Northwest Indians began as though they'd lost their powers of singing and dancing (as though they were at Death's door) and then into them came other powers, those of another, a bird or an animal, full of the vigor of new birth. In this case no strict control was maintained. The fire was not avoided. When the dancer could no longer move, others came and carried him back to the place where he had been sitting. Those in Asia also began, but meditatively, as though they didn't know their own minds. The power of another and what other? If, as we needn't, we give an image of it (as they did with the drone for pitches and the proportions of a particular *tala*), what will we in our impartiality give? The others, perhaps, will cite Confucius and the Southwest Indians, but even there the Spider Goddess will not permit the passage of anyone lacking impurities. Apparently we are going North in our sense, that is, of what it is that we must bring in our arts into existence. He called it *allagermanica* and warned against the use of compasses. (I don't have one; the one I borrowed I only used once: to draw the image of a watch—which I trust won't be necessary again. I don't have one because I know perfectly well that once a circle is drawn my necessity is to get outside of it. We begin therefore without it and it is getting urgent by the minute not to erase the clock but to drop the way we used it.)

To change the subject. What do I mean when I say: He has no time-sense? Shifting from one situation to another at appropriate moments? For this reason we made our work experimental (unpredictable). a) We used chance operations. Seeing that they were useful only where there is a definite limitation in the number of possibilities, b) we used composition which was indeterminate of its performance (characterized in part by parts independently made by each performer—no score). Seeing that that was useful only where there was a change of consciousness on the part of each performer, c) we used performance which is indeterminate of itself.

Chopping our way through the forest trying for our own sakes to give the impression that our visit never took place. Our minds are already changed (and they know it: that's why they call us cold and dehumanized); what remains to be done is to find out what tools are at our disposal and how to use them so that our objective is never seen in the distance but rests continually inside each one of us, so that whenever one goes, as he will, in all directions at once, it with him will go polymorphically. They speak of evolution. Where is there sense of proportion? Talk talk talk: is that what we must put up with? What is necessary is to listen to what you say so that the purposelessness of the listening can somehow get into what you're saying. He used the word latent and said that was when he was able to understand. How in heaven's name did anyone get the idea that proportion took place in an object outside of him? A little flexibility of mind and one is able to see it wherever he looks. She objected to the position of the tree on the island and we all laughed. Not the perception of the proportions of things outside of us but the experience of identification with whatever's outside of us (this is obviously a physical impossibility; that's why it's a mental responsibility). When we tell of something in our experience, they answer with evidence to the effect that just the same thing happened to them. Conversation should be more affluent, each remark unfolding unsuspected ideas and turns of thought. Where our sense of proportion was violated, it no longer is, just as the most common variety of anything is nowadays a rare experience. We still have a few prejudices hanging around and even if we don't remove them ourselves dear friends come in and do it for us.

What am I dealing with when I deal with proportion? Going to the store to buy something? Standardization and mass production and containers (this was his most striking evidence) for packing comestibles for distribution anywhere on the globe? But look closely. This idea (and each one of the others too in typical Mediterranean fashion) is earth-bound: the project is not about space but about packing things so efficiently that space is used up. Examples are given from ship-building and one could certainly find others in the machines that today orbit the earth. But I suspect my father is right: that space travel will be facilitated by not going against gravity but by going with the field—not the gravitational one but the universal electrostatic one. No great expense or force will be required. One will in a wasteful American way simply move off into space inefficiently, *i.e.*, with enough room in the vehicle so that he won't feel cramped during the journey. Furthermore, that wastefulness of space will be a *sine qua non:* size itself will determine whether or not the unforced journey is feasible. You might therefore say that we meet at another point the naturalness of proportion, a law of nature. No doubt there is a threshold in all matters, but once through the door—no need to stand there as though transfixed—the rules disappear. This is not far away from the world of hi-fidelity which in its deadening search for perfection is unintentionally revealing to him the lively musical steps to be taken and in detail. Needless to say, these steps are not only in the opposite direction (when you say do, I'll do don't), they are in all directions. Whenever anyone speaks informatively with precision about how something should be done, listen, if you can, with great interest, knowing his talk is descriptive of a single line in a sphere of illuminating potential activity, that each one of his measurements exists in a field that is wide open for exploration.

Having this view we find fertility in whatever is inappropriate, providing it's practical. (I mean: we don't intend to just do nothing.) Exaggerate the need for no ulterior motives: consider success of any kind a disastrous failure. (Beware of losing what isn't in your head.) They apparently lost their sense of proportion: they blew the whole thing up and yet only presented a fragment. The result is that nothing has the right size. An obvious mistake. Yet that they're brilliant people is proven by the original and useful arrangement of numbers for the days, the weeks, and the months.

FRANÇOIS MOLNAR

THE UNIT AND THE WHOLE:
FUNDAMENTAL PROBLEM OF THE PLASTIC ARTS

The Necessity for a Fact-finding Aesthetic. Salvador Dalì once sent a telegram to Picasso. "Pablo," ran the message, "you have killed Beauty—thank you." Today we might send a similar telegram to all contemporary artists, saying, "Gentlemen, you are killing art."

Why should one sound such an alarm? There have never been so many painters, never so many exhibitions, so many art enthusiasts, so many pictures sold. We might even add, never has it been so easy to paint, to produce works of art. In our times business is so good for art and the artist that anything can be shown and sold. A quick glance at the current exhibitions easily convinces us of this. In Paris there are more galleries than cinemas, galleries where one can see displayed as functional art the perfect mechanism of a complicated machine, as well as a rudimentary machine—or antimachine—of which the sole function is to run badly. A poster is matter for an exhibition, but it would be equally appropriate to exhibit the scratched wall it is pasted on, with the traces of former posters still visible. A car is displayed for its lines, or a broken-down jalopy for heaven knows what. A canvas on which someone has poured a bucket of paint may be hung at the same time as a canvas without a drop of paint on it. Everything, therefore, can be considered a work of art. If this is so, then there is no longer such a thing as a work of art. If everybody is Peter, then Peter doesn't exist. At one time the Dadaists exhibited sanitary objects, *pour épater le bourgeois.* As a gesture, in certain eras, this kind of thing can serve a purpose. The Dadaist capers still have a historic, if not an aesthetic, value. It is an amusing fact that Picabia's urinal is in a private collection where it is admired as a work of art. Imagine the ironic grin of an old Dadaist at the art lover's admiration for some object he had invented just to make fun of the spectator.

The artist therefore is not the only guilty one, if indeed one can speak of guilt. The sanitary utensil has become a work of art by the free consent of the art lover. It is this same art lover who was once the target of the Dadaists and who today accepts extravagant creations. The same man who once snorted at Wagner and treated Cézanne as if he were a besotted garbage collector, now buys a bare canvas or a broken-down car. Has the art lover grown any the more intelligent in a generation or so? Hardly. One says he is afraid of being fooled, one talks about speculators and the shrewdness of picture dealers, and so on. In actuality, neither snobbery nor greed nor salesmanship can in themselves explain the dubious triumph of contemporary painting. The reason must be sought elsewhere. Ever since Romanticism, a historic tendency has tried first to subdue, then to replace, reason by the obscure forces of the subconscious. It is the "terror" of the subconscious that has driven both artist and art lover to this pass, where henceforth, in the name of unconditional liberty, everything is allowed.

This situation is not one we can go into here, but it would not be hard to prove that the artist who preaches total liberty is sometimes more of a slave than the faithful adherent of photographic realism. As for us, we reject that kind of realism, not in the name of some abstract freedom, but in the name of history. Plastic art has come by a historical route to abstraction, and history is irreversible. Still, it is hard to believe that everything the galleries feed us is a work of art. How can we distinguish the art of "anything at all" when we know nothing of art? One can present anything to me as a masterpiece and I cannot refute this judgment. All I can assert with a clear conscience is that I don't like it. (At the same time, I have to admit that somebody else, more "sensitive" than I am, may like it.) To refute its claim to being a work of art, we have to have the facts. Verbal arguments are of no use, they are mere "words, words, words," as Hamlet said. Without an exact understanding of the facts, we are blind.

The art lover's position in front of the painting to be judged, or better, the painter's position in front of the picture he is to paint is like that of any man confronting action, so the philosophers say. In theory such a man has in front of him before he acts an infinity of possibilities, an infinity of paths. He must choose one, but his choice is never, or for the most part never, justified subsequently. Obviously we know this theoretical infinity to be illusory. We are not all-powerful. The question before us painters is: can we through a better understanding of the facts determine which roads are actually possible and avoid the dead-end streets of scratched walls, crushed automobiles, and so forth? To restrict our possibilities is perhaps to limit our liberty; but is it not more worthwhile, instead of slipping into the delusion of total liberty, to be more modest and concern ourselves with problems having some chance of being elucidated? In this way we shall be led—not to spout poetic messages about profundity, the absolute, responsibility, security, incantation, magic, signs, or spontaneity (these terms all come from an eighty-line text written by a well-known Paris art critic)—but to examine objectively certain concrete problems a picture poses.

The Unity of a Picture. According to the most competent opinion, a work of art must have a unity. That famous unity, which has given rise to so many philosophical speculations for centuries and has caused so much ink to flow without our really knowing what it is.

When I stand before a picture, I perceive it at a glance, globally, as a picture. But, if I want to see it better, if it has aroused my interest, I have to look at it closer. At this precise moment the unity of the picture becomes a problem. When I read a page, my eyes are guided by the typography from left to right, according to a habit learned in childhood. When I look at a picture, there are neither typographical lines nor traditions. Yet the eye must have an incentive, a guide, to examine this scattering of colors that is a picture in the last analysis. Moreover, the eye must explore the picture, though not in any arbitrary manner. The composition of a picture, and consequently one's aesthetic emotion, depend to a large degree on the way our eye explores the areas of this surface so as to re-create its totality. Thus we see that the philosophical problem of the total-partial relationship is also an aesthetic problem of the first importance.

Philosophy. The totality and the part, their mutual relation, is one of the oldest of intellectual problems. It goes without saying that this question, put in a general way, soon invades metaphysics and, according to the law of metaphysical thought, never reaches solution. The problem takes on even greater importance when exact science begins to extend its sway not only over mechanical physics but also over chemistry and especially biology. One cannot frame the problems of these sciences in the language of ancient philosophy, yet modern philosophy seems incapable of creating a new language for itself. In examining the relation between totality and its parts, even dialectical philosophy gets lost in the labyrinths of theory and knowledge.

Only after psychology and philosophy are definitively separated can the question of totality and its parts take concrete form and give hope of a satisfactory reply. But before we call on psychological research, let us turn aside to a specifically aesthetic domain.

Esotericism. At the edges of philosophical and theological thought we have always found reflections that particularly interest us. Certain real or imaginary numerical relations between man and the world, or, as they were later termed, between microcosmos and macrocosmos, have richly inspired both profane and religious philosophy for more than two thousand years. In the realm of numbers secrets were suspected to exist that one tried to explain in a more or less esoteric manner.

The root of all these theories is to be found in a verse of the "Hieros Logos," or "Sacred Discourse": "Everything is arranged according to Numbers." This line, though attributed to Pythagoras, was in fact written much later. However that may be, the idea it expresses was intimately linked not only with aesthetics but also with science until relatively recent times. Even today, in modern mathematics, we hear a curious echo of it. We know that certain theories in modern mathematics, such as set theory, were considered typical examples of pure science—like a marvelous yet gratuitous proof of the capacity of man's rigorous thought—up to the day when physicists discovered that to explain certain phenomena of microphysics, the "new numbers" of modern mathematics were perfectly capable of being utilized. Naturally, however, the philosophical question remains: is the atom indeed organized mathematically, or is it rather our consciousness that has discovered a new tool, a new crutch? "When the Universe began to be organized . . . God gave each element its features through the interaction of Ideas and Numbers," wrote Plato in the *Timaeus*. We have no communication with God, therefore we can take no position as to this delicate question, for lack of the requisite information.

But let us leave this task of unraveling the enigma of the philosophers. Our business is with aesthetics. From that point of view we can assert, without any risk of deceiving ourselves, that to the man gazing at a picture it is of no consequence whether the forms—or parts—of the picture are arranged according to numbers or not, or at least not when his gaze seeks aesthetic pleasure. (The situation is a quite different one if he is looking at the picture in order to study it.) Mathematics speaks to our understanding; the picture, to our sensitivity. We by no means want to separate the two domains. On the contrary, we know that feeling is greatly influenced by knowing, and conversely, our knowing by our feeling. Doubtless, however, every visual creation speaks directly to our affectivity. Furthermore, this principle is the chief criterion of all pure plastic art.

Since certain artists and certain modern theoreticians attribute such importance to these "mystic" figures as an organizing force in the totality of artistic creation, we must pause at this point.

The Golden Number. From Pythagoras to Le Corbusier, including Vitruvius, Vuillard de Honnecourt, and Dürer, all the mathematical or geometrical theories of beauty have been based on the Golden Number.

The Golden Number is a geometrical progression whose formula is:

$$\frac{a+b}{a} = \frac{a}{b}$$

and after a slight mathematical manipulation, we get the formula:

$$\phi = \frac{1 \pm \sqrt{5}}{2}$$

This mathematical formula has a number of remarkable aspects. But it is far from being the only interesting formula: mathematics is very rich in curious formulas that play an important role in science.

From our point of view, however, it is immaterial whether the basis of the composition of a work of art is the Golden Number or some other numerical relationship, some other "harmonic series." The mathematical beauty of a work of art is not perceptible immediately but only after long reflection, and furthermore, without mathematical knowledge it is not perceptible at all. Not even a mathematician's head contains any built-in ruler or scale or calculating machine to perform the requisite operations fast enough. One's aesthetic pleasure fades during that brief lapse of time the psychologists call "the density of the present." What goes on in our head in that fraction of a second, we scarcely know. It is hard enough to imagine that we can manage a not very complicated calculation, when we know that the time needed for a simple operation is more than the density of the present, and this even for a man highly trained in mental calculations.

No matter how many rational or irrational properties there are in a pentagon, it is not beautiful because of that. If it is beautiful, the reason for its beauty must be sought elsewhere. Of course, mathematics too has its beauty, but we have to traverse a long road of reflection before we perceive it. We have to "understand" mathematics, in the strictest sense of the word. At the end of the road that we travel to understand it, we can find true joy, true feelings, that belong in aesthetic categories such as "superb," "monumental," "marvelous," etc. On the other hand, the beauty of a work of art must reveal itself, it ought immediately to impart itself, as we have said above. This, of course, does not mean that the beauty of a work of art cannot remain hidden as long as desired under certain conditions—longer, perhaps, than the sense of mathematics to a mathematician. Indeed, mathematics explains itself, conveys itself. The work of art, on the other hand, cannot be explained. Its beauty may or may not reveal itself, but it does not explain itself. It is possible to help someone become permeable to this beauty, but we certainly cannot explain it to him, for there is nothing to explain.

Science. We see, therefore, that if we do not want to shut ourselves up within a blind mysticism, subject ourselves to a dangerous illusion, we cannot a priori accept any mathematical modulor that excludes man. Such a rejection of the priority of mathematical formulas over aesthetics by no means signifies an a posteriori renunciation of mathematical formulation. If the foundation is man, and his sensitivity alone, it is easy to slip into a subjective idealism. To be sure, art is the only terrain where one can eventually accept a subjective realism. But—to paraphrase C. Cherry, "Speaking language, and speaking about language"—to look at painting is one thing, and talk about painting another. When we confront a work of art in order to analyze it, we must have a scientific attitude, we have to distrust idealism. We thus avoid all danger of philosophism. Let us say that all the philosophical consequences (metaphysical, ontological, etc.) do not now concern us. We know that there are numerous problems in philosophy, but if we want to arrive at any concrete result we have to set aside these problems for the time being. According to the rules of scientific procedure, we must define exactly what we are talking about and avoid talking about what we cannot define. Let us abandon vain speculations, a priori theories, and turn to experimental psychology, where we find the problem of totality and its parts at the level of the study of perception.

Classical Psychology. It would seem that the psychologists, in undertaking the problems of perception, in accordance with tradition, have first tried to avail themselves of an especially fruitful heuristic method used in other sciences. They have tried to explain complicated psychological facts by simpler facts. But to explain perception by elementary sensations—that is, an atomistic psychology, as Locke imagined—soon clashes with the observed facts. Indeed, pure sensation has never been demonstrated. Sensation cannot be separated from perception. Pure sensation does not exist. We always perceive something. The red spot I see on a rug is inseparable from its wooly material, which I see at the same instant as the red spot. According to Cézanne, we see not only the color of the apple but also its savor, its fragrance. What we perceive in thunder is not merely thunder but "thunder-light—silence before—silence after," as William James said.

Gestalt. The same idea has been expressed and examined independently of James by the theory of form (Gestalt). This theory considers form as a whole, indivisible. We cannot study a tree, it is said, by beginning with its roots, then its trunk, its leaves, etc., but rather it is the tree as a unity that must be the center of our attention. The forest is quite another thing, something more than the sum of the trees, as popular wisdom has long known. We therefore have to substitute for the idea of sensation the idea of form as the prime value. Furthermore, this substitution is in perfect harmony with the latest researches in physiology. The physiologists have increasingly come to substitute for the differences in cell formation the differences in circuits. Today no one looks any longer for that portion of the cortex where perception takes definite form, but rather for the circuit of the cortex that makes a particular perception possible.

The Gestalt theory has had considerable influence on psychology. Its success is due in large measure to the fact that this theory agreed with the philosophy that was dominant between the two wars. Thus, according to the French philosopher, Merleau-Ponty, form takes on an important philosophical role. Watson, the leading exponent of the behaviorist school of psychology, reproached the Gestaltists for taking over the idea of immanence from Kant.

The Gestalt school has, moreover, formulated laws that seem exact and that can serve for a scientific study of painting. Still, we cannot content ourselves with only general laws. It would appear that for a more precise understanding we have to return somehow to a psychology of detail. Here lies the contradiction of modern psychology: the theory of associational psychology (classical atomistic psychology) is unsustainable because it contradicts observed facts, whereas the theory of form—a more faithful mirror of reality—falls in the last analysis into philosophism. The psychological research of these last decades is based on the awareness of these contradictions.

The Problem of Form. Let us again consider what form is. Spontaneously, we believe that we know what form is. On closer view, we see it is nothing of the sort. The idea of form as an abstraction from the complexity of the real is a vague one that can take on various meanings, depending on the author, on the subject, etc. Let us envisage the simplest example, the perception of a geometric form. I immediately and unhesitatingly recognize a triangle. At the same moment I am shown it, I see one triangle, then another, and again a third. Yet these triangles differ: on the one hand, in size and in their angles; on the other hand, in the corresponding images they make on the retina. In view of the astronomical number of different forms we perceive as triangles, certain astonished philosophers speak of a miracle. Miracle there certainly is not, but we believe that even the psychologists cannot yet provide us with any satisfactory solution of the problem: by what process, what abstraction, do we perceive a triangle? It is hardly likely that we recognize a form after certain mental analyses. We do not say: there is a form whose angles seem to total 180°, it has three sides, etc., therefore this form must be a triangle. On the contrary, we say intuitively, without hesitating, even without reflecting, this is a triangle. Form, therefore, appears to constitute a bridge between art and science.

But what is form? The theorists define it thus: a group of elements perceived in their totality, as it were, and not as the product of any chance assemblage. (I emphasize "perceived," for of course form in reality may well be the result of a chance assemblage.) To create a form thus defined would mean to assume a certain previsibility of this form. In the strictest sense of the word, previsibility, or *Vorsicht,* means to imagine a phenomenon in the future, in terms of the past. Let us imagine a circle we watch someone drawing. At any moment the designer can interrupt the design, while for my part I can at any moment hazard a guess as to what he intends it to be. If, at the instant he stops drawing, the circle was almost closed, I can be the surer that he wants to draw a circle than I can when he is just beginning to draw. Thus there obviously exists a degree of previsibility, a connection that is at least a statistical one between past and future, a correlation between what happened just now and what is going to happen in the immediate future.

It is this connection between the past and the future of a form explained statistically that Wiener has called "autocorrelation." Autocorrelation evidently varies between 0 and 1. It is 0 when the phenomenon is totally lacking in order and its behavior in future is therefore not previsible. As order appears, it tends toward the value of 1, or the autocorrelation of a completely ordered phenomenon—in other words, one that is indefinitely previsible. At first sight, we see that autocorrelation expresses very well the law of good form in the Gestalt theory. The nearer autocorrelation comes to 1, the better the form. However, autocorrelation differs in one essential from good form, since the latter does not separate into parts.

The Eye. Autocorrelation poses a difficult problem. In fact, if we suppose that the actual behavior of a system depends on the past, we must logically admit the existence of a kind of memory that recalls the past. We sometimes say, therefore, that autocorrelation is the memory a form has of itself. That form should have a memory can be said only metaphorically. Form, like Carnap's coin, has neither consciousness nor memory. Memory must be supplied by ourselves, by the receptor. It is in the eye, in the elements of the retina, in the optic channels, and ultimately in the cortex that we must trace memory. Therefore, we must conceive of form on the level of the receptor—*i.e.,* on the level of the eye.

We have noted above the opposition between the two theories of perception: the one is atomistic, and considers perception as an exploration of the object (as in television) combined with a certain memory; the other is global, according to which we see a form in its totality. Doubtless we do perceive quite small objects (the "quanta" of perception), such as letters or diagrams, in their totality. Yet when the stimulus, the object under perception, exceeds a certain size, the system of exploration inevitably loosens. Our eyes are continually moving, they sweep over the surface of what they are perceiving at a relatively rapid rate. If fixed on a point in the visual field, our eyes immediately shift as soon as there appears a point of attraction in the periphery of the visual field.

We need not, therefore, take a position between the two opposing theories. (It would seem that even psychology tries to overcome this antagonism.) Rather, we try to decide at what size we can no longer see a stimulus globally, in what direction our eyes shift, and above all (this is of prime importance to aesthetics) how our eyes select from among all possible movements.

Let us examine this idea at closer hand. Everyone knows that to reproduce a picture we break it down by means of a selected screen into a multitude of more or less tiny dots. Thus in a black-and-white reproduction 19 cm. by 33 cm. made with a 130 line screen, da Vinci's *Last Supper* is made up of 13,000 tiny black dots. The reproduction then is an extended and selective luminous source, that is, it has a dimension, it does not give forth light but is made to reflect light, and finally at no point of its surface does it reflect the same amount of light as at any other. We can place some sort of receptor before this surface (a photometer or thermometer, for example) and measure the amount of light or heat reflected. Undoubtedly, this source of radiant energy constitutes the physical basis of all visual perception. The problem of radiant energy, the fundamental problem of microphysics, is an open one. It may well be that the physicists will yet discover solid theories which will be capable of explaining visual phenomena.

If the receptor is the human eye, what it sees is the *Last Supper,* though objectively speaking there is nothing there except a number of dots. For, when seen at a certain distance, the dots in the reproduction evidently fall below the threshold of the eye's power of spatial discrimination; yet objectively, on the retina, there are always the dots. Even if the objective image on the retina were continuous, it would become discontinuous, for it would break down on the retina into dots according to the number of nerve ends affected. Then one might see any sort of thing. There is no reason why I should not see, instead of an apostle's hand, a white spot, or simply a white hole amid some strange dark shapes. I could relate any one of the dots on the surface in any way I chose. But I have reasoned in vain: the vision persists, I do see the *Last Supper*. Evidently the figures are represented there; these are the images of something. But why do we see things? This may seem a childish question, but it is nevertheless a fundamental one. Why do we see things, and not non-things, asked Koffka. Why do we see a table standing out from the background of this room, yet do not see the rest of the room as object? One will say: this is a table, we experience this table. I know I must pause before it, I cannot pass over it as if it were the empty space behind it. Perhaps as a child I did try to pass over it and had the grievous experience of my own powerlessness. It is true that to a certain degree experience helps us see things as forms. But it has also been shown that there are forms which we see as forms, even if we have never seen them before.

In the same sense, in abstract pictures there are forms not seen and known before, and where representation cannot intervene as an organizing influence. We must therefore recognize the existence of other organizing influences besides resemblance, influences without which an abstract painting, for example, becomes a shifting fog, an amorphous surface eventually suggesting vague contours—in short, anything. As Sartre has said, the eye must find a very powerful incentive for undertaking, without looking for any resemblance, the unification of this scattering that is a picture.

For the moment let us substitute for the eye some sort of receptor that "examines" the surface of a reproduction. This surface (or its image on the retina), as we have just seen, is composed of dots.

```
0  0  0  X  0  0  0
0  0  0  X  0  0  0
0  0  0  X  0  0  0
X  X  X  X  X  X  X
0  0  0  X  0  0  0
0  0  0  X  0  0  0
0  0  0  X  0  0  0
```

When we look at this composition, we can imagine a receptor that "sees" only the square made up of certain signs. A more sensitive receptor might see a cross emerging from the square. Yet another, differently regulated, might see only the cross indicated by the X marks. In theory, we can imagine all sorts of receptors that would group the dots according to their resemblance, their difference, their proximity, or their distance, etc. Electronic apparatuses have been built that select the image on six levels of differing luminosity. Every photographer knows that the quality of his photograph depends on the sensitivity of the film and the paper he uses. We see that form ("the assemblage of dots") depends on the receptor's sensitivity of adjustment. Thus the perception of form depends primarily on the eye. It appears that the "very powerful incentive" for unifying the picture, such as Sartre seeks for the eye, is the eye itself.

The difficulty arises in that our eye is not a kind of optical receptor, nor even a complicated electronic machine, but an "apparatus" strongly influenced by our knowing, our willing, our affectivity—in short, by the whole of our individuality. We know, for example, that a very weak red light, scarcely recognizable as red, becomes distinctly red from the moment it is projected onto the image of a tomato. Here is evident proof that our perception is influenced by our knowing, or, just as children perceive a coin as larger than it really is, this is proof that our perception is influenced by our affectivity. We can now represent the situation by the following diagram:

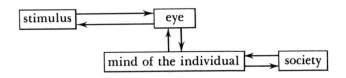

At this point the situation becomes so complex that we have hardly any chance of being able to study it as a whole. The system becomes so vast that it is impossible to extract complete information from it.

Under these conditions we must give up hope of understanding the whole system and apply ourselves to a full understanding of a particular portion of it, partial yet complete, which will suffice as a practical goal. It is legitimate to isolate two elements from our diagram and study them separately, on condition that we never forget that the elements thus studied are part of a much larger whole. We take one element, or group of elements, as a variable, and we try as much as possible to keep all the other elements as invariables. It is this method that makes all scientific experiment possible.

Constraints. Gestalt theory has provided us with a series of laws drawn only from the stimulus-eye relationship. There are stable forms in which the relation of depth to form depends only on the eye and the stimulus. There are ambiguous forms that we see, for example, alternatively as either a black shape standing out against a white background or as a white shape against a black background. And this independently of our will, our affectivity, or our knowing, independently of all social influence, etc. Experiment has shown in an even more striking manner that our perception can be independent of our knowing. Let a suspended object be balanced before a fixed object. In certain conditions we perceive the suspended object, whose actual motion occurs on a plane, as if it were a rotary motion around the fixed object. The movement we perceive is in three dimensions, even though the subject (the spectator) knows perfectly well that the object is really moving in two dimensions.

We must admit, therefore, that it is the structure of the eye that prevents us from seeing certain objective phenomena. Evidently, our eyes on this level are subject to constraints—whether artists intoxicated with freedom like it or not. Now, constraints can be useful. Science has greatly benefited from them. The DC–8, for example, is able to fly precisely because the plane is under constraints: it cannot be anywhere it likes at any moment it likes, nor can it increase its speed at will. If the plane could move without constraint, its behavior seen from without would be chaotic.

The future behavior of a plane is calculated from its previous behavior. Now, we have seen that the role which the relation of past to future plays in the perception of form is defined as autocorrelation. Bergson has spoken of harmony as a line on which at each point we somehow anticipate the future. Can we not, therefore, in studying the constraints our eyes are subjected to, make this anticipation more concrete and thus disclose the first facts so urgently needed for the aesthetics of the visual arts?

Our retina is not uniformly sensitive at all points. Its sensitivity to colors changes according to region, its power of discrimination is greatest in the foveal region. It is to the fovea that we bring the image of the object we want to examine. To see well, moreover, we must have the clearest possible image on the retina, that is, our eyes must adapt well. Naturally, our eyes cannot accomplish this double movement in all directions or at all distances with equal facility. Therefore, the position of our eyes at any moment is determined partly by the previous position.

To understand the topology of the retina, we can set up a "map" of the visual field according to equiprobable zones. This means determining the chance of each point's becoming a point of future fixation from any other point of fixation, and in the absence of all strong stimulus and all evident points of attraction. We can then compare this "map" to a Markov chain, which we know to be statistically determined according to the preceding position of the system. This means that at the end of the count, though we cannot determine in advance each stage of the movement of our eyes, we ascertain, after a certain period of observation, that they always follow an almost identical trajectory.

What happens when our eyes are confronted by an object, a landscape, a picture, where there are several points of attraction of unequal importance? Under every circumstance our eyes will move toward the strongest point of attraction, even if this point on our "map of equiprobable zones" lies at a site of only slight probability. Moreover, it can happen that the importance of the point, its power of attraction, is counterbalanced by its position. Thus we are clearly confronted with two different, though "coupled," systems that function as one: a situation that is analogous to what we often find in the several scientific disciplines. Theoretically, it would not be hard to define the functioning of such a system.

An Example. Since all the foregoing is somewhat abstract, let us try to illustrate it with a concrete example. Let us consider Rembrandt's celebrated picture, *Dr. Tulp's Anatomy Lesson* (Fig. 1). This is an arbitrary choice, and we could equally choose any other picture based principally on "values." The actual measurements of the picture are 216 cm. by 162 cm. A canvas of such a size must be looked at from a certain distance, say, from three or four yards. The painting is seen at a visual angle of from $25°$ to $30°$. The retinal image of the picture is far from covering the whole surface of the retina, but it greatly exceeds the foveal region, where, as we said, the separative power of the eye is greatest. It is to the center of the fovea that we "automatically" carry the image of those details which we want to see accurately. The dimension of the fovea is of the order of $1°$; but to have optimal visual acuity, the center of fixation must nearly correspond to the center of the fovea. When we look at Rembrandt's painting, the width of $1°$ corresponds almost exactly to the surface of one of the faces of the figures of the painting.

Now let us suppose that our gaze shifts, quite by chance, to a marginal section of the painting—the upper left, for instance—where there is "nothing" but dark coloring, more or less uniform. At this moment, on the periphery of our retina there emerge several bright spots (the students' heads) that serve as a point of attraction to our eyes. In other words, our eyes are drawn—fascinated, so to speak—by the bright spots. We inevitably turn our gaze to one of these points of attraction. We cannot foresee in any sure sense where our gaze will land, what place it will select from the numerous possibilities the picture presents. Suppose it moves to the face of the first student standing in the upper part. Our eyes explore the head, with the tiny movements necessary for a clear sight. At the same time, part of the periphery of our retina is filled with new points of attraction, all situated near the center of the picture. Thus our eyes are led little by little to the professor's hand, and thence to the thorax of the cadaver. But our eyes cannot remain fixed. When we look at the cadaver, our retina is filled with new points of attraction, then it begins a continuous movement that lasts as long as our contemplation of the picture. These movements will never be identical like the movements in a drill, but are varied in detail. No matter at what portion of the picture we begin looking, sooner or later our eyes will arrive step by step near the compositional center of the picture. Then the movement begins again, exactly like a weight hung on springs in a state of equilibrium. We can disturb this state of equilibrium by giving the object some degree of motion. The object will return to its state of equilibrium after making a series of movements that depend, in part on the suspension system which is always constant, and in part on the location and strength of the agitating force. Practically speaking, this is the sort of equilibrium we find in a well-composed picture.

Unfortunately, contrary to mechanics, the movement of our eyes is far too undetermined to put it into an equation. If a girl in a blue coat comes into the museum where I am looking at the *Anatomy Lesson*, my gaze will certainly be taken by the moving blue color (be assured I mean the blue, not the girl), that is, if I am not a real art lover, for such a man would not allow himself to be distracted by even the prettiest . . . blue in the world. We can nevertheless determine the succession of

Fig. 1. Rembrandt, *Dr. Tulp's Anatomy Lesson*. The Hague, Mauritshuis.

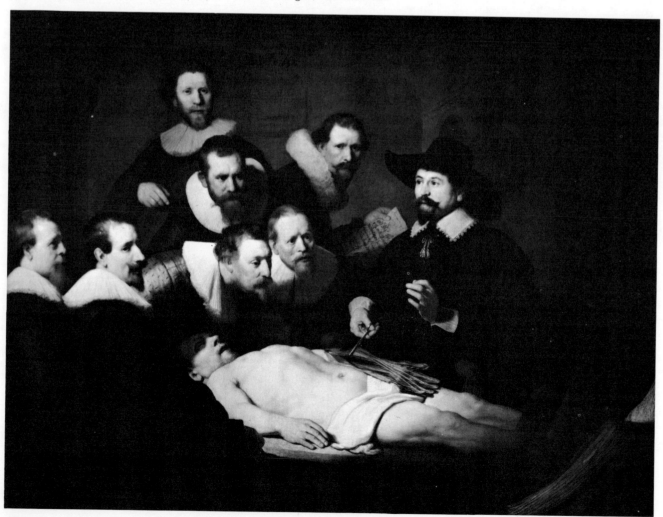

the movements of our eyes, but only by means of statistics. We can determine—calculate—the final equilibrium in the Markov chain to which we have already compared the random movement of our eyes. To establish the ocular movement in a Markov chain, the only condition necessary is that the points of attraction be in a hierarchy. If all the points had the same chance of becoming the next point of fixation—that is, if our gaze could pass indifferently from one student's head to that of any other, we could not speak of a final equilibrium; but the composition of Rembrandt's painting would no longer exist. In other words, the previsibility, and therefore the autocorrelation, of the picture would be very weak. If our eyes were solicited at every moment by a multitude of points of·attraction, all of equal importance, we should no longer know where to look, and the picture would then really become a mere scattering of colors that not only would give us no pleasure, but would also be quite intolerable.

Fig. 2. "Point of attraction" organization in *Dr. Tulp's Anatomy Lesson*.

If the behavior of our eyes can indeed not be likened to a television apparatus that explores a surface according to a rigorous and pre-established order, this does not mean that their behavior is chaotic. Even when they lack any point of attraction, as before a bare canvas or a blue sky, our eyes follow a kind of trajectory. (In the case of the bare canvas, our eyes seem to travel first to the center, then to the right and up, and so on.) Thus the bare canvas or the blue sky can give our eyes a certain satisfaction, since in this "empty" visual field there is no point that could require an unnatural movement of the eyes. One might even ask whether the beauty of the sky, so often sung by the poets (which, after all, is not so beautiful as it is blue), does not lie partly in the fact that our eyes can roam across it without constraint, not only on a surface but even in a sense in "depth."

However that may be, the least we can ask of the composition of a picture is that it not be in contradiction with the natural movement of the eyes. This does not mean that it is sufficient to judiciously place points of attraction in order to create a masterpiece. But if the points of attraction are employed in opposition to the needs of the eye, the contemplation of the picture will be difficult, even painful.

Rembrandt used every means to put his points of attraction into a hierarchy, first of all by representation. In order to learn, all the figures (except two) look in the same direction; they look at the dissected arm of the cadaver, which is indicated likewise by Dr. Tulp's scissors. If we too use some means of restricting our vision, that is, if we try by artificial means to make the image less clear, we see that the composition of the picture is not destroyed even when we can no longer see the individual expressions of the figures. Instead of faces, we then see bright oval shapes (Fig. 2), ellipses, grouped so that if we look along their axis they seem to converge toward one common point. These ellipses seem to "go" in the same direction. We know that their common goal is an important organizing force in Gestalt theory.

We could pursue this reasoning, but our purpose is not a formal analysis of Rembrandt's painting. We have tried to draw attention by a concrete analysis to the fact that the composition of a picture depends first on the exploratory movement of our eyes, no matter how we come to "hierarchize" the surface of the picture, whether by form, by value, or by color. The essential thing is the movement imposed on our eyes.

This problem takes on greater importance in the art called "abstract." A picture delineating a war horse or a nude woman will always have a certain unity because it represents something with which we are familiar. In the abstract picture, there is only "a plane surface covered with colors arranged in a certain order," in Maurice Denis's celebrated phrase. In this case it is the "certain order" that plays the chief role. And this order—as we hope to have shown here—depends primarily on our eyes.

Conclusion. The behavior of our eyes (which to a large degree determines the relation of totality to parts) is actually very complicated. Even in presenting only a small cross section of the problems of vision, we have had to simplify and schematize. We have tacitly ignored chromatic vision, we have chosen Rembrandt as our example, a painter of "value." In his case it has been easier to neglect the problem of color.

Above all, however, we have kept silent as to all that goes on in psychic nature—a higher level than that of the retina. Furthermore, it is beyond question that in studying perception, higher levels do intervene. We have noted in passing that our perception depends on our knowing, our affectivity, and also, in the last analysis, on the society in which we are rooted.

We have avoided these problems because they are too complex. It is to be hoped that in time a future "science of art" may explore areas as yet ill understood. Experimental psychology, now barely a hundred years old, social psychology, which is even younger, and other pioneering sciences have already produced valuable clues. It is evident that if we want to understand the *facts,* so as to refute the scratched walls or compressed cars as works of art, it is on the science of art that we shall have to rely.

One of the basic visual experiences is that of right and wrong. In particular, the subdivisions of lines or other linear distances and the shape of rectangular surfaces or bodies impress us not only as what they are but also tell us whether or not they are what they ought to be. The shape of a house, a shelf, or a picture frame may repose contentedly or show a need to improve by stretching or shrinking. The sense of proportion is inherent in the experience of perception, and—like all other perceptual properties—it is dynamic: rightness presents itself not as dead immobility but as the active equipoise of concerted forces while wrongness is seen as a struggle to get away from an unsatisfactory state. Well-balanced shape is a main source of the harmony found in many products of nature and man and of the pleasure given by that harmony.

How are we to account for our capacity of judging spatial relationships? We may contend that, like all other kinds of ethical judgment, this capacity is imposed upon the individual by authorities and thus declare the sense of proportion a gift of the superego: good shape is simply what we have been taught is good. But this theory nips curiosity in the bud. It passes the problem to the science of social interaction and declines to ask why some patterns, rather than others, are selected for transmission. It is ill suited to explain the universal validity of such judgments, which enables us to understand and appreciate the art work of other individuals and civilizations, regardless of whether or not they agree with our own preferences.

It seems more fruitful to assume that properties inherent in the perceptual patterns themselves impinge upon the organism in a way that largely accounts for its reactions. Such a theory must take two different forms. First, we acknowledge that the organism has certain general biological needs. It requires clarity and simplicity for the purpose of orientation; balance and unity for tranquility and good functioning; variety and tension for stimulation. These needs are better satisfied by some patterns than by others. The square and the circle are simple and balanced. A slight deviation from a simple shape is ambiguous, hard to identify. A rectangle of the ratio 2 : 1 may disturb us by pretending unity and rectangularity while threatening to break up into two squares. The proportion of the golden section—in which the smaller part is related to the larger as the larger is related to the sum of both, and which yields a ratio of roughly 8 : 5—may successfully combine unbreakable unity with lively tension.

It may be objected that such desirable or undesirable properties in geometric shapes provoke a strong reaction even when they are of no conceivable biological value. To be sure, the balance of a house or the dynamic tension in a well-proportioned human body indicate stability and vitality, which are profitable to life, but why bother with a rectangle on paper? In reply, recent psychological experiments have suggested that certain general needs of the mind will manifest themselves, by analogy, even in reactions to perceptual situations that have no practical import. For instance, Frenkel-Brunswik[1] found that people whose social insecurity made them demand clear group distinctions were disturbed by a harmless series of pictures in which a cat gradually changed into a dog. This may mean that central tendencies of the mind impose themselves upon peripheral ones—a theory likely to be correct in cases in which the observed tendency makes sense at the higher level but cannot be understood from what we know about the mechanisms operating in perception itself.

The situation is different when the tendencies in question can be shown to result not only from the behavior of motivational forces but also and independently from that of perceptual forces. In that case, rather than assuming a mere imposition upon perception on the part of the central powers of personality, it seems suitable to think of one and the same principle functioning at various psychical and physical levels throughout the organism. Balance, which is at the root of the sense of proportion, would seem to be such a principle since it serves not only to explain motivation but can also be expected to govern the physiological forces that organize the processes of vision in the brain.

In the following, I shall assume that an optical pattern when projected upon the pertinent cortical field of the brain will there produce a corresponding configuration of forces. The static pattern will thus be translated into a dynamic process governed by the principle of balance, and the resulting tensions in the physiological field will have their counterpart in visual experience. This theory explains how we can judge spatial relations without measuring the lines or planes involved. Intuitive judgment, based simply on the inspection of a pattern as a whole, is assumed to rely on the strength and directions of the tensions experienced in the perceived object. Such intuitive judgment can be most sensitive even to compositions of geometrically or numerically complicated structure because instead of piecemeal figuring out the single elements and their connections the mind can rely on the tensions resulting from the integrated action of all the forces concerned. More generally this means that whereas the calculating mind can only approximate the Gestalt by establishing a network of relations, the perceiving mind can fully realize it by relying on the field of interacting forces itself.

However, the intuitive procedure has serious drawbacks. It is delicate, easily disturbed by external influences, and its findings do not offer proof to the intellect. An observer's assertion that the shape of an object is "good" can be confirmed only by exposing other observers to the same object with a similar result. Fortunately, the simpler the pattern the surer becomes the judgment and the greater is the agreement among observers. The surest result is obtained when we compare the lengths of lines or distances placed side by side. The simplicity of such a pattern of parallels is so strong that disturbance is almost powerless and disagreement negligibly small. Therefore, it is most tempting to reduce complex visual judgments to combinations of this simple one. Here, then, we have the beginning of measurement by yardstick.

There is no difference between the basic act of measuring and any other intuitive judgment. It is purely visual, only simpler and safer. But its application makes for grave differences indeed. Measurement dismembers any pattern and therefore must be handled with caution when it is used to analyze the spatial structure of a whole. Also measurement introduces numbers into spatial relations, and numbers can be manipulated abstractly without any reference to the object to which they were applied. Hence two risks, amply documented by examples from the study of visual proportions. The roving compass, blind to the Gestalt qualities of the object, uncovers identical distances here and there, regardless of whether or not such correspondences are based upon true structural kinship. A scaffold of units is expected to produce an organized whole. Secondly, numbers, obtained by measurements, are juggled about independently, with arithmetic relations replacing the forgotten visual ones. Pyrrhic victories of calculation over vision.

Yet, abuses do not disqualify procedures, and the persistent attempt to find the measure of beauty has not remained without encouragement. Some simple measures are obviously related to visual goodness, notably the ratio 1 : 1, basis of all symmetry. Most spectacular was, of course, the Pythagorean discovery that the perceived harmony of musical intervals is paralleled by simple numerical ratios of spatial distance on the string and the flute. This discovery—made more substantial by our present-day knowledge of the simple relations between the wave frequencies of musical sounds —established for all time to come the conviction that harmony depended on spatial measure. When Le Corbusier takes pains to legitimize his studies in proportion by pointing out that he comes from a family of musicians, he speaks in the same Pythagorean mood that made it imperative for the Renaissance architects to study the theory of musical harmony. "More than these thirty years past, the sap of mathematics has flown through the veins of my work, both as an architect and painter; for music is always present within me."[2]

According to the Pythagorean doctrine, simple numbers and their mutual relations, as well as the simple geometrical figures that obey such measures, represent the innermost secret of nature. All existing things, complex as they may be, are made up of the geometric building stones. The human body, masterwork of nature, soon came to be considered the revelation of perfect measure. "For without symmetry and proportion," says Vitruvius, "no temple can have a measured composition; that is, it must have the exact measure of the members of a well-shaped human body."[3] Once an ideal human figure, which obeyed the demanded simple numerical measurements, had been constructed, it served in turn to prove the sanctity of the canon: the law of the cosmos could be read off from that of the microcosm. This piece of circular reasoning has maintained its power to our day.

The rationalization of proportion, designed to overcome the uncertainty of intuitive perceptual judgment, suited the demand for scientific exactness, which arose in the Renaissance. It satisfied the yearning for objective description and yielded the rule governing the bewildering complexity of things. It helped to make art respectable by demonstrating that the shape of its products was not arbitrary. And wherever the scientific ideal and procedure weakened the intuitive powers of the artist or the connoisseur, the crutch of measurement offered to replace the untrustworthy eye.

At the same time, the reduction of shape to measurement recommended itself for the practical purpose of identifying and reproducing a given product. Mass production demands standardization, and standard shapes are impractical as long as they are not defined by measurement. The ancient Egyptians used a network of vertical and horizontal lines to manufacture statues of specified shape, and in the treatise of Vitruvius the Pythagorean metaphysics of number is transformed into a set of recipes, designed to meet the demands of the imitative Roman style of architecture.

It seems natural that a modern architect, endeavoring to revive the art of proportion, should insist on the aspect of standardization. Le Corbusier is aware of the responsibility involved in selecting standards that suit the functions of the object. His aim is: "To standardize, which is to run the risk of arbitrary choice, and the reverse of that risk: a wonderful freeing of the methods of economic production."[4] Le Corbusier believes that a suitable set of standardized units is offered by his "Modulor," which he obtains in the following manner. In the Vitruvian tradition, he starts from the human body.

He divides the total height, from the feet to the hand of the vertically raised arm, into two equal parts, at the level of the navel, and he assumes that this total height is divided according to the golden section at the wrist level of the downward hanging arm (86 : 140). Similarly, the distance from the feet to the top of the head is also divided by the golden section, in this case at the level of the navel (70 : 113). These two ratios are used as the bases for two independent sequences of numbers, both meeting the condition of what is known to the mathematician as the Fibonacci series. Each element is equal to the sum of the two preceding ones, and throughout the sequence neighboring values roughly approach the proportion of the golden section. (Thus the ratio 86 : 140 gives rise to the sequence 20 .33, 53, 86, 140, 226, 366. . . , continued *ad infinitum* in both directions.)

Adapted from Le Corbusier, *The Modulor,* Cambridge, Mass., Harvard University Press, 1954.

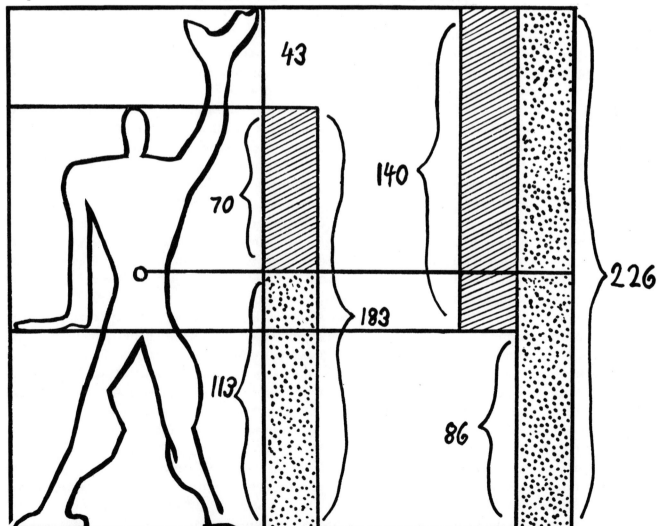

How well does this set of sizes suit the purposes of standardization? Standardization demands that the number of units employed be as small as possible and that the units combine readily with each other. The first condition seems to be met by the Modulor since within any range of size the number of the proposed values is small. Thus for the opening of a normal door the Modulor, if I am not mistaken, practically restricts the choice to a breadth of 70 cm. and a height of 226 cm. This would limit production severely to only one size. The combination of units is much less well taken care of because only a very few are multiples of each other. Within each of the two series, units can be combined only by means of their neighbors. For example, the three contiguous values 33, 53, 86, fit nicely together (33 + 53 = 86), but no multiples of either 33 or 53 match 86. This weakness, which follows from the nature of the Fibonacci series, has also aesthetic consequences, to be discussed shortly.

Standardization aims at facilitating the functional relations between things. Since most manufactured objects are "either containers of man or extensions of man," they must be related functionally to their user. Of course, in an informal way, houses, furniture, tools have always been adapted to the human body, but Le Corbusier hopes to standardize these relations by deriving his scales from the main proportions and dimensions of the body. Unfortunately, however, the human figure cannot be standardized, and since the stature of any population is distributed statistically in a bell-shaped curve, it seems ludicrous to specify the relation between man and his objects to the fraction of an inch. In fact, Le Corbusier worked with a scale custom-tailored for an average 175 cm. Frenchman, until he remembered "that in English detective novels the good-looking men, such as the policemen, are always six feet tall." Since the Modulor is meant to apply to world-wide production, the inventor settled for 6 feet (182.88 cm.), explaining that it would be better for a measure to be too large rather than too small, "so that the article made on the basis of that measure should be suitable for use by all"—an argument unlikely to be appreciated by the smaller specimens of mankind.

Le Corbusier's insistence on his particular scale becomes understandable if one ignores its pretended functionalism and interprets it instead as a romantic variation of the Pythagorean philosophy. The traditional doctrine of proportion related architectural shape to man because his body was an example of perfection, not because he was to live with the building. The architect was expected to create in the image of man, and therefore the relative proportions of the model, not its absolute dimensions, were considered. Whereas, in this view, man, the child of nature or God, revealed the secret of cosmic harmony to the builder, the more recent theory of empathy viewed the humanization of architecture as the means by which man "compels inhuman nature to his need."[5] A stranger in a chaotic setting of plants, streams, and mountains, he creates in his buildings something of his own kind, orderly shapes he can understand; he "transcribes in stone the body's favorable states."[6] Both theories implied a division between man and his work: the first saw man as the model to be contemplated and copied from a distance, the second saw the building as the remote object of sympathetic appreciation.

To Le Corbusier, man and the world he builds are an indivisible unity. Just as man is an outgrowth of nature, so the building, the furniture, the machine, the painting or statue, are outgrowths of man. The builder and his work are interdependent like the snail and its shell. Man enlarges his scope by his works, and the works receive their meaning from his use of them. It follows from this romantic view that man and his creation must be conceived as one integrated organism. Hence Le Corbusier's preference for the golden section, which to his forebears was the essence of cosmic mathematics, while to him it is the formula of life, discovered by scientists in the body structure of plant and animal. Hence also his two proportional series, which embed the human body in a continuous scale from the infinitely small to the infinitely large, presenting man as *natura naturans* and *natura naturata*.

This is an eminently modern philosophy, well suited to provide our biological outlook with an aesthetic superstructure. But it is a philosophy—applicable to the arts only if it assumes visible form. The reasoning mind may find coherence and consistency satisfactorily symbolized in the arithmetic properties of the Modulor series. Are they equally evident to the eye? Obviously the virtues of the system must be tested in practice and can hardly be evaluated in the abstract. Only a few general considerations can be advanced here tentatively.

If one particular ratio of spatial distances is to be chosen, the golden section certainly makes a good candidate. Art historians and psychologists can testify that the eye distinguishes this particular relation—in the twofold sense of recognizing and preferring it. Similarly, the ratio 2 : 1, introduced into the Modulor by the fact that the values of the one series are twice as large as those of the other, is easily recognized by the eye and can be put to good visual use. Continuity, by which a series of steps leads the observer from the smaller to the larger units and thus helps to knit the whole structure together, is a basic prerequisite of all artistic composition. To reaffirm and codify it, with explicit inclusion of the human dimensions, seems particularly welcome in view of a modern preference for "monumental" buildings that make the visitor feel lost like a beetle in a cigar box. However, Le Corbusier's arithmetic progression of values does not guarantee continuity; it merely suggests it. Since it remains for the artist to pick from the scales the values he wishes to combine, he still must rely on his intuitive judgment for obtaining those unbroken chains of relationships that produce the unified hierarchy of any good composition. Within each of the two series, only the contiguous values have a simple relationship to each other. The more distant ones have not. And as far as the relations between the two series are concerned, each value of the one has the ratio 2 : 1 to its opposite number in the other, but otherwise the relations between members of the two series are far from simple. For example, Le Corbusier picked for a cornerstone, designed to symbolize the principle of good proportion, the ratio 183 : 86, one value from each series. No simple relation between the two is apparent, and if the resulting shape "possessed dignity and elegance," this does not seem to be explainable by the fact that both values lie somewhere on the two series.

It looks as though in Le Corbusier's system the harmony of the compositional whole is pieced together by a creeping sequence of concords between neighbor and neighbor, thus neglecting the cross connections of distant elements. A comparison, which may or may not be appropriate, will at least illustrate the point. The musical diatonic scale provides for the unity and density of the compositional fabric not by simply equalizing the intervals between neighboring steps. One does not have to walk the scale in order to connect one tone with another. Any two tones are directly connected by more or less simple auditive and arithmetic relationships, and the varying degrees of concordance make for a rich palette of expressive values. Also, transposition of pitch—which may be compared to the transposition of visual size—produces patterns that are related to each other not only by homology, that is, by similarity of proportion, but also by a comprehensible harmony between each tone of one pattern and each of any other. Every tone of the C scale is directly relatable to every tone of the D scale. Not so the values of Le Corbusier's two series.

The publication of *The Modulor* raises again the more general questions: Is there any justification for applying measurement to visual proportion? If so, when and in what way should it be applied? Not for very long has this subject been controversial. In all advanced civilizations artists and other craftsmen seem to have felt little hesitation about using all the faculties of their minds—perception, intuition, thinking, calculation—wherever they served the purpose. The fear that formulae might interfere with the freedom of the eye did not come up as long as the eye was strong. Only when there was suspicion that calculation, instead of the eye, was being used for tasks that required constant and final visual control, did intellect and intuition come to be viewed as antagonists. Needless to say, no fully developed artist has ever been prevented by such controversy from using conceptual thinking to sharpen his intuitive generalizations, to cast them into less perishable shape, and to make them communicable. And if there is no objection to making a mental note of the fact that, say, "blue recedes and red advances," there should be none to the rule that the golden section creates a good proportion, since the former statement is no less intellectual than the latter. The problem is not whether or not abstract operations are applicable to the arts but whether those involving number and calculation are.

The objection can take two forms. Either the adversary may say: "It is possible and perhaps likely that simple arithmetic or geometric relations are at the bottom of all visual harmony. However, the search for such formulae should remain a hobby for the theorist. They are harmful to creative work because the artist can attain harmony by intuition only." I shall consider this form of the objection a prejudice, based on false dichotomizing and refuted by the artistic practice of the centuries, particularly in architecture, which by its very nature involves constant measuring and figuring. A second kind of objection does not question the procedure as such but protests against some ways of its application. It raises the basic question of what in the nature of the things that are measured justifies measurement and which kinds of measurement can be shown to be more appropriate than others.

It is useful to reformulate the question as follows: To what extent are the objects of rationalization rational? The term "rational" as used here does not mean what it means to the mathematician. By "rationality" I mean the extent to which the visual structure of a pattern and the parts that make it up are simple, clear-cut, identifiable. If, for instance, the lengths of all the parts in a given pattern are multiples of a given unit, the pattern is fully rational in terms of such measurement. This is one kind of rationality, based on measurement. There is another kind, based on geometric simplicity. A pattern shall be called the more rational, the simpler are the geometric relationships by which it can be defined. In this sense the relationship of a circle to its diameter or of a square to its diagonal is highly rational, even though in both cases the algebraic ratios lead to infinite fractions. The question is, then, to what extent and in what way visual objects can be reduced to rationality.

In the history of art both criteria of rationalization have been used. One is based on measurement by yardstick. In its most elementary version it relies on the single module, that is, it defines all parts and relationships as multiples of one unit. This procedure, as we shall see, affords only a minimum of structural understanding. The opposite method of measurement starts from above, rather than from below, by defining the parts as fractions of the whole and thereby making the whole, as it were, the module. For instance, in Vitruvius' analysis of the human body the head is 1/8 of the total height, face and hand are 1/10 each, the foot is 1/6, the cubit 1/4, and so forth.[7] Here, then, are several different units of subdivision, pointing perhaps to a number of different structural levels and thus representing a subtler analysis than the crudely equalizing technique of the single unit. At the same time, this latter procedure creates, at its own primitive level, a unity that the more complex one lacks; for the measurement "from above" relates the various subdivisions of the body only indirectly to each other, namely by their reference to a common whole, whereas the relations between them are neglected. It is as though several incongruous networks had been superimposed upon the same pattern.

In the same analysis in which Vitruvius uses modular measurement he also applies a fundamentally different method by pointing out that the body with outspread limbs can be inscribed in a circle. Here the procedure is geometric. Rationality is obtained not by applying a linear yardstick but by fitting the object to some other simple shape. Geometric planning with the compass and the ruler was practiced by the medieval masons. While not excluding the yardstick, they freely profited from such incommensurable relations as that between the circle and its diameter or that of the golden section.

Le Corbusier's Modulor represents an uncomfortable compromise between the two methods. Being based on the golden section, it is by nature geometric. But all ratios are translated into numbers, which requires a rounding off of the infinite fractions. By this artifice a geometric principle of structure is forced into arithmetic shape. An even more serious ambiguity is introduced by the fact that in order to obtain a continuous sequence Le Corbusier uses the Fibonacci progression, in which the relations between neighboring units meander toward the golden section but are not identical with it. Thus in the twilight of arithmetic approximation two different structural principles—one based on addition, the other on ratio—are made to fit each other.

As a system of measurement, Le Corbusier's scale is a sophisticated variation of the module principle. Instead of keeping the size of the unit constant, it increases it gradually according to an arithmetic progression. This procedure—as was pointed out before—limits rationality to contiguous units and makes distant ones incommensurable. It shares with most of the other systems the weakness of not doing justice to the integrated structure of a whole pattern, in which parts are directly interrelated even when they belong to very different size levels. Instead, one might say, it merely traces linear paths of rationality through such patterns.

Whatever the virtues and flaws of particular methods, the conviction that search for rational shape is justified has been greatly encouraged by the scientific discoveries about the nature of matter. The Pythagorean trust in number was derived from the human mind's yearning for order and was based on little evidence. The confidence of modern science is better founded because its rational models are confirmed experimentally. To the modern scientist simple number and geometric shape as such are not the ultimate principle: they are only the formal manifestation of physical forces holding each other in balance. The atomic model is, of course, the prize discovery of the rationalist. If at the foundation of all matter there is so regular, simple, and symmetrical a pattern as any order-loving mind could dream up, then it may seem sensible to expect that the shape of the things around us is based on rationality.

Such reasoning, however, has to be met with caution. It is modular thinking, based on the over-simplified assumption that the macroscopic world is a mere multiplication of a smallest unit. Crystals come closest to confirming this view because their regular shapes do indeed reflect an extension of the atomic order. Commonly, though, we find even at the molecular level a structure more nearly chaotic than orderly, and if a drop or a large body of water exhibit regular shape, this regularity comes about despite molecular disorder and through the action of macroscopic forces, which, by the way, are not the same in these two examples. "The spherical surface of the rain-drop and the spherical surface of the ocean (though both happen to be alike in mathematical form) are two totally different phenomena, the one due to surface-energy, and the other to that form of mass energy which we ascribe to gravity" (D'Arcy Thompson).[8] When it comes to organisms, "the forces which hold the elementary parts in a certain orderly relation to each other are not derived from the affinities of just a few kinds of units but arise from the interactions of very numerous active entities" (C. H. Waddington).[9] In other words, what I have called "modular thinking" is defeated by the fact that as we ascend the scale from the atom-ically small to the astronomically large we encounter levels of near-chaos, which disrupt the continuity of order. And we also find "integrative levels" at which the whole is not the sum of its parts: "Knowl-edge of the laws of the lower level is necessary for a full understanding of the higher level; yet the unique properties of phenomena at the higher level cannot be predicted a priori from the laws of the lower level" (Novikoff).[10] A landscape is essentially chaotic, but it lies in the scale of sizes between the orderly shape of, say, a flower and that of the terrestrial globe.

Thus, while the order of things cannot be derived from the atomic module, we find the prin-ciple of balance producing orderly shape at various integrative levels. This confirms the soundness of our search for rationality. It also indicates, however, that more often than not the order of structure is not of the purely additive, "modular" kind but involves an integrated organization of the whole pattern. The structural models we invent and apply must take this fact into account. The closer they come to Gestalt principles, the more adequate they are likely to be.

What has been said holds not only for the physical shape of the things around us but also for perceptual patterns, which are produced by the sense of sight and are reflected in the work of artists. Here again we have a gap between integrative levels: the patterns that are seen are not mere extensions of the perceived physical objects. But the gap can be bridged by a reference to the projection area in the cerebral cortex which, as I said in the beginning, can be assumed to translate retinal patterns into con-figurations of field forces. If the physiological field is controlled by the tendency toward balance, the structure of patterns will assume the simplest possible shape, that is, strive towards the greatest possible rationality. And since here again we are dealing with an integrative level, the patterns perceived, created, and understood by the eye—in either nature or art—are again more likely to be analyzed ade-quately by a system that envisages features of the total structure rather than operating with an accu-mulation of units. This means, for instance, that the patching together of pictorial compositions by means of rectangles considered perfect for one reason or another is unlikely to produce a visual whole; nor can it be expected to do justice to a good work of art—even if the mosaic of modules fits the structural seams and corners of the work fairly well. For it is one thing to construct a rational model that serves to make a reproduction of a pattern, and another to hit upon the particular model that reveals the pattern's essential structure. Vitruvius' measurements make it possible to copy a given Greek temple quite faithfully but tell us very little about the underlying principles that render the over-all appearance of such buildings so harmonious.

Although we must demand that the geometric or arithmetic model, constructed for the purpose of rationalization, be adequate, we should not expect it to fit with mechanical precision, unless, of course, the model itself served for the construction of the pattern, as has been the case so often in architecture. But the sculptured or painted human figures that were constructed in strict obedience to compass and yardstick—just as the mechanical applications of central perspective in pictures—exhale a deadly chill. Architecture can afford a simple order because instead of portraying reality it has the more limited task of representing lawfulness in a natural setting. But no portrayal of reality—be it representational or "abstract"—can present the law itself instead of its embodiment in things, for it is in the nature of existence that the manifestations of each lawful process should be interfered with by those of other such processes. Without such interaction an object becomes complete and therefore isolated, and nothing can be complete except the universe, or the total work of art (which is an image of the whole), or the rational model (which isolates some features of the whole so that we may understand).

The rational model, then, is related to its referent the way any law is related to the things in which it is active. Just as the norm of the oak leaf is not perfectly realized in any one specimen so no rule of proportion can be expected to appear perfectly in any thing. This makes the task of finding such a rule harder rather than easier, for instead of being satisfied when a model roughly applies, we must find out, through the judicious examination of many specimens, toward which principle the species converges. To a given human body any number of structural principles can be applied approximately, and "the" human body patiently stretches and squeezes itself to accommodate this or that theory. The paintings of the masters have been interpreted with many and often contradictory schemas. This does not mean that there is no law but that to find it takes more than mechanical measuring and fitting. It requires the scientific methods that permit distinction between the essential and the accidental.

The simpler the configuration of forces to which an object is subjected, the simpler its shape will be. The smallest organisms are less controlled by gravity and therefore more regularly shaped than the large ones; it is easier to be symmetrical in the water than on land—but the more rational the shape, the less "real" does the creature look. At primitive or early stages of organic development, there is little differentiation of function and, therefore, simple shape. As the configuration of the forces that control the organism becomes more complex, so becomes shape. When the human mind is young, the simplicity of its functioning is reflected in the simple shape of its controlled manifestations, for instance, in the drawings of children. These drawings are made up of near-geometric patterns, and it is for this reason—not because they are not faithful likenesses—that they look unrealistic. As the mind grows, so increases the complexity of its creations. The typical product of the mature artist is so differentiated that only intuitive perception is capable of organizing and unifying the multiplicity of forces that make up the whole. If we try explicitly to identify—geometrically or arithmetically—all its parts and relations we are, at best, left with a collection of pieces.

What we can do, however, is to fit to the work rational patterns at various levels of approximation. If we describe a picture as a triangular composition, we let escape almost everything except one feature of the work's skeleton, which may be the key to the whole. And from this most generic level we can descend to more subtle ones and obtain differentiations of the primary pattern. But at a certain point of the approach to rationality we are stopped. It is the point up to which the scientist can find lawfulness in the intricacy of the individual specimen. The compositional schemata with which the artist starts his work on the empty paper or which the art theorist draws on the photographs of paintings or buildings are such approximations. That they are possible is due to the fact that all organized wholes are hierarchic. Such wholes do not grow like unplanned cities, in which each new unit is determined mainly by its direct neighbors and therefore the whole becomes chaotic. They grow by differentiation of a germ structure, and each detail is determined by the law of the whole. This means they have layers of order, which descend from the highest and simplest to more and more complex ones. The order found at each level is true. The edge of a knife is straight even though under the microscope it reveals its irregularities. And when the statistician "smooths" a curve he is not cheating but trying to clean the intrusions of lower orders off the higher one. How deeply our rational understanding can penetrate into the hierarchy of layers depends upon the acuity of our tools, the foremost of which is the mind.

It is necessary here to distinguish between lawfulness and rationality. Every product of nature or man can be assumed to be entirely lawful in the sense that it is composed by the interaction of simple forces. Therefore even the most complex shape is, in the last analysis, a composite of simple shapes. Things are lawful even though the degree of their organization may be low. The chaos of the dancing gas molecules is but the lowest degree of order. Some modern painters limit the organization of their pictures to spot-to-spot relations plus an over-all uniformity: the statement is primitive, the hierarchy is narrow, coherence is weak, but these works are as completely lawful as any other existing thing. This basic lawfulness of all things justifies the search for rationality. But whereas lawfulness is an objective property, rationality describes the extent to which an observer can fit an object to a definable pattern; it is, therefore, always a matter of degree.

We said earlier that the shape of any object must show the effect of interaction in order not to appear isolated and dead. Therefore, perfect geometric shape and very simple proportion are likely to be rare. A potentially simple shape is often modified under the influence of the context in which it appears. Fechner, in his study of proportion, spoke of *"kombinatorische Mitbestimmung."*[11] For instance, space value in architecture is affected, as Scott has pointed out, "by lighting and the position of shadows: the source of light attracts the eye and sets up an independent suggested movement of its own. It is affected by color: a dark floor and a light roof give a totally different space sensation to that created by a dark roof and a light floor. It is affected by our own expectancy: by the space we have immediately left. It is affected by the character of the predominating lines: an emphasis on verticals, as is well known, gives an illusion of greater height; an emphasis on horizontals gives a sense of greater breadth."[12] This means that in their search for rational shape investigators may have to concentrate more on potential simplicity than, as they have done so far, on actual simplicity. The tendency to simple shape is inherent in any one unit but often modified by the context, the way in which, say, an egg is a potential sphere modified by pressure while the shell hardens. A telling example can be found in Fechner's studies. When he asked observers to choose between rectangles of different shapes, he found a preference for proportions approaching that of the golden section. But when he measured the proportions of hundreds of museum paintings he discovered that on the average a considerably shorter rectangle was preferred: about 5 : 4 for upright pictures and about 4 : 3 for horizontally extended ones.[13] A moment's reflection shows why this should be so. In an empty rectangle the ratio between the two linear distances—roughly that of our postal card—is pleasant enough. But when it comes to a pictorial composition that is to be read not only in the directions of the two main dimensions but as a more closely knit whole, in which every point of the area is to be relatable to every other, the distances in the longer dimension would be relatively so large as to be unbridgeable for most purposes. Innumerable examples in which proportions are influenced by practical usage also come to mind.

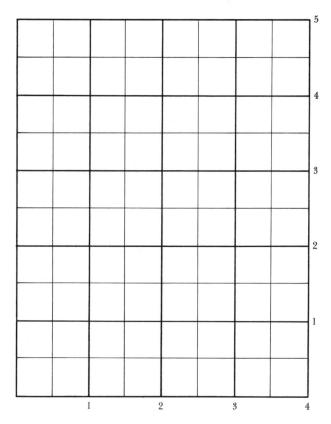

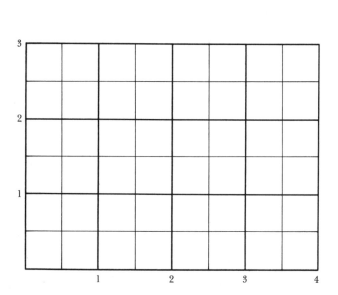

From what was said in the beginning it follows that shape preferences will not be determined solely by the degree of balance attained through the interplay of physiological forces in the visual apparatus. Often these purely perceptual aspects will be overlaid and modified by motivational needs at higher psychical levels. Examples can be drawn from what is generally treated under the headings of "taste" or "style." The rectangle of the golden section and the square may be equally balanced, but they carry different expression or meaning, the one showing directed tension, the other, massive symmetry. The expressive differences between slimness and thickness, straightness and curvedness, the relatively relaxed proportions deriving from the module and the tenser incommensurable ones—all these properties are well suited to reflect basic human attitudes. They have specific biological and cultural connotations, for instance, in the proportions of the human figure. When the title of "Miss Universe 1955" was given to a girl who measured 36" at the bust and hips and 24" at the waist, it is not enough to point out that her body satisfied the Pythagorean ratio 2 : 3 and probably looked harmonious for that reason and that her torso could be inscribed, perhaps, in the rectangle of the *Divina Proportione*. We must also see that these particular measurements make her the visual symbol of what a woman stands for here and today, and that the perhaps equally harmonious women of Rubens or the Pre-Raphaelites project different styles of life.

Preference for the particular degree of rationality to which a given pattern aspires is in itself the expression of a deep-seated attitude. The range from Mondrian, Nicholson, and Albers to, say, Rodin, reaches from an extreme need for safety, order, and reason to an equally radical enjoyment of lively complexity; and the demands of the Pythagorean adepts of the yardstick and the compass do not lead to absolute beauty but are only the manifestation of a particular style. As long as the analysis of rational shape remains a tool of the fully developed mind it can help to make perceived order explicit. When it replaces vision and stifles expression it becomes a game *in vacuo*.

1. Else Frenkel-Brunswik, "Intolerance of Ambiguity as an Emotional and Perceptual Personality Variable," in *Perception and Personality* (Jerome S. Bruner and David Krech, editors), Durham, N.C. (1949).
2. Le Corbusier, *The Modulor—A Harmonious Measure to the Human Scale Universally Applicable to Architecture and Mechanics,* Cambridge, Mass. (1954), p. 129.
3. Vitruvius, *The Ten Books on Architecture,* Book III, Chapter 1.
4. Le Corbusier, *op. cit.,* p. 107.
5. Geoffrey Scott, *The Architecture of Humanism,* Garden City (1954), p. 179.
6. *Ibid.,* p. 177.
7. Vitruvius, *loc. cit.*
8. D'Arcy Wentworth Thompson, *On Growth and Form,* New York (1945), p. 57.
9. C. H. Waddington, "The Character of Biological Form," in *Aspects of Form* (L. L. Whyte, editor), New York (1952), p. 45.
10. Alex B. Novikoff, "The Concept of Integrative Levels and Biology," in *Science* (1945), pp. 209–215.
11. Gustav Theodor Fechner, *Vorschule der Aesthetik,* Leipzig (1876), p. 187.
12. Scott, *op. cit.,* p. 170.
13. Fechner, *op. cit.,* p. 282.

Lawrence B. Anderson	Architect, teacher, administrator. Born Geneva, Minnesota, 1906. Studied at University of Minnesota and M.I.T., as well as in Paris. Joined M.I.T. faculty in 1933; became Head, Department of Architecture in 1947; Dean of the School of Architecture and Planning since 1965. In 1957 appointed Fulbright Lecturer, Danish Royal Academy of Fine Arts, Copenhagen; honorary member of Academy. Partner, architectural firm of Anderson, Beckwith and Haible. Consultant on campus planning: University of Minnesota, Rochester Institute of Technology, Boston University School of Medicine. Served on jury for Golden Gate Redevelopment Project, San Francisco, and as Advisor to Boston Government Center Commission. Presently on advisory committees: Office of Foreign Buildings, Dept. of State, and Boston Redevelopment Authority.
Rudolf Arnheim	Psychologist. Born Berlin. Studied at Berlin University: dissertation on the psychology of visual expression. 1933–38: Associate Editor of Publications, International Institute for Educational Film, League of Nations, Rome. In 1940 emigrated to the United States. 1941–42: Fellow, Guggenheim Foundation. Since 1943: teaching psychology and psychology of art, Sarah Lawrence College, Bronxville, N.Y.; Graduate Faculty, New School for Social Research, N.Y. 1959–60: Fulbright Lecturer, Ochanomizu University, Tokyo. Author: *Art and Visual Perception* (1954); *Film as Art* (1957); *Picasso's Guernica: The Genesis of a Painting* (1962); *Toward a Psychology of Art* (1966).
John Cage	Musical composer. Born Los Angeles, 1912. 1936–38: taught in Seattle, organizing percussion ensembles and presenting concerts for percussion instruments alone. 1943: New York, directed concert of percussion music sponsored by Museum of Modern Art and League of Composers. Devoted himself to works for "prepared piano," which he invented in 1938, receiving Guggenheim Fellowship and National Academy of Arts and Letters Award in 1949. 1951: organized group of musicians and engineers for making of music directly on magnetic tape. 1956–60: on faculty of the New School, New York. 1960: appointed Fellow of the Center for Advanced Studies, Wesleyan University. Teaches composition privately. Commissioned: 1947 by Ballet Society to write *The Seasons;* 1954 by Donaueschinger to write *34' 46.776" For Two Pianists;* 1961 by Montreal Festival Society to write a work for full orchestra, *Atlas Eclipticalis.* 1958: invited by Italian Radio to Studio di Fonologia where he made *Fontana Mix* for magnetic tape.
Ezra D. Ehrenkrantz	Architect. Bachelor of Architecture, M.I.T., 1954; Master of Architecture, University of Liverpool, 1956. Two Fulbright Fellowships at Building Research Station, Watford, England. Since 1958 faculty member, University of California. Partner, architectural firm of Leefe and Ehrenkrantz, San Francisco. Research grants: University of California for modular coordination and lighting; Ford Foundation for tropical architecture studies; Educational Facilities Laboratories Inc. for building product design and modular coordination; Housing and Home Finance Agency for migrant farm housing. Presently Project Architect for School Construction Systems Development, Stanford, California.

Gyorgy Kepes	Painter and designer. Born Selyp, Hungary, 1906. 1930–36: worked in Berlin and London on film, stage, and exhibition design. In 1937 came to the United States to head the Light and Color Department, Institute of Design, Chicago. Since 1946 Professor of Visual Design, M.I.T. Author: *Language of Vision; The New Landscape in Art and Science*. Editor of *The Visual Arts Today*. Most active as painter. His works are in the permanent collections of many museums, including: Albright Knox Art Gallery, Buffalo; Museum of Fine Arts, Boston; Museum of Fine Arts, Houston; Museum of Modern Art, New York; Museum of Art, San Francisco; Whitney Museum of American Art, New York.
Anthony Hill	Abstract artist. Born, London, 1930. 1950–54: abstract painting, collage and projects for limited serial production. Since 1955 has worked in constructive idiom (relief constructions). Has exhibited frequently in London and abroad. First one-man show of reliefs, Institute of Contemporary Art, London, 1958. Taught at the Regent Street Polytechnic Art School and presently at the Chelsea School of Art. Contributor to various art publications, in particular, the Dutch periodical *Structure*.
Ernö Lendvai	Musicologist. Born Hungary, 1925. Studied at the Budapest Academy of Music. From 1954 director of a conservatory and Professor at the Academy of Music. Since 1960, Music Director of Hungarian Radio and Television. Most important among his many publications are: *Bartók's Style* (1955) and *Bartók's Dramaturgy* (1964). In addition to his investigations of Bartók's composition, he is interested in Verdi's style and Toscanini's interpretation. He is at present preparing a book on Toscanini's interpretation of Beethoven.
Arthur L. Loeb	Chemical physicist and professional musician. Born Amsterdam, 1923. Scientific studies: University of Pennsylvania and Harvard. Musical education: New England Conservatory of Music and Amsterdam's Muzieklyceum. Formerly member of research staff, M.I.T. and Lincoln Laboratory; Guest Researcher, University of Utrecht; Associate Professor of Electrical Engineering, M.I.T. Presently Staff Scientist, Ledgemont Laboratory, Kennecott Copper Corporation. Author of many articles, and co-author: (with J. Th. G. Overbeek and P. H. Wiersema) *The Electrical Double Layer around Spherical Colloid Particles* (1961); (with Louis Harris) *Introduction to Wave Mechanics* (1963). Particular scientific fields of interest: mathematical crystallography; computers; the storage, retrieval, and communication of space patterns. Musical fields of interest: music for chamber and church choirs; music for dramatic productions; the consort of viols; harpsichord; contemporary music.
Richard P. Lohse	Painter. Born Zurich, 1902. 1917: first oil paintings, School of Arts and Crafts, Zurich. 1936: member of Schweizerischer Werkbund; since 1963 member of central board. 1937: co-founder of Allianz Vereinigung moderner Schweizer Künstler, Zurich. Travels and sojourns for studies in Great Britain, France, Italy, Holland, Germany, Greece. His art is principally concerned with the problems of series and groups. Has participated in innumerable exhibitions all over Europe, as well as in United States, Canada, Argentina, Brazil, and Japan, including many one-man shows. In addition to paintings in private collections in Switzerland and abroad, his works are represented in the permanent collections of the following museums: Kunsthaus, Zurich; Kunstmuseum, Basle; Museo do Arte moderna, São Paulo; Stedelijk Museum, Amsterdam.

François Molnar	Painter. Born Szentes, Hungary, 1922. Studied at the Academy of Fine Arts, Budapest, and Ecole des Beaux Arts, Paris. Also pursued studies in experimental psychology. Has lived in Paris since 1947. Worked in the Laboratory of Experimental Psychology of the Sorbonne on problems of aesthetics. Co-founder of Groupe de Recherche d'Art Visuel. Secretary General of the International Association of Experimental Esthetics. Presently carrying out research at the Institut d'Esthétique et des Sciences de l'Art of the University of Paris.
Philip Morrison	Physicist. Born New Jersey, 1915. Studied at Carnegie Institute of Technology and University of California at Berkeley. Ph.D. in theoretical physics, 1940. Faculty member in physics: San Francisco State College (1940–41); University of Illinois (1941–42); Cornell University (1946–65); and since 1965 at M.I.T. Wartime service, 1943–46, as physicist and group leader for Manhattan Project, Chicago, Los Alamos, Tinian, Japan. Participant in the development of secondary-school physics course of the Physical Science Study Committee (1956–); and in Elementary Science Study (1961–). Author of a number of papers and texts, both technical and popular, in physics, with applications to biology, geology, and astronomy.
Stanislaw Ulam	Mathematician. Born Poland. 1933: received doctorate, Polytechnic Institute, Lwow, Poland. 1936: to United States. Since 1944, Research Advisor, Los Alamos Scientific Laboratory and also presently Professor, University of Colorado. His basic ideas, along with those of Edward Teller, led to the development of the thermonuclear weapon. Has proposed extremely advanced methods of nuclear propulsion, leading to the organization of the Orion program. Initiator of so-called Monte Carlo Method, a procedure for finding solutions to mathematical and physical problems by random sampling. Keenly interested in the application of mathematics to biology; organized American Mathematical Society symposium on mathematical problems in the biological sciences. Author of many articles on set theory, topology, functional analysis, ergodic theory, theory of groups, and computational mathematics. His book, *A Collection of Mathematical Problems* (1960), surveys his wide range of interests.
C. H. Waddington	Professor of Animal Genetics, University of Edinburgh. Head of one of the largest research laboratories in fundamental biology in Europe. Most active and honored member of innumerable scientific organizations. Has worked in a wide variety of fields of biology, all however relating to one central topic, namely the way in which hereditary factors control the development of animals into adult forms with a definite architecture made up by the arrangement of parts of particular kinds arranged in particular patterns. His more general texts on such matters include: *Introduction to Modern Genetics* (1940); *Principles of Embryology* (1956); *New Patterns in Genetics and Development* (1962). Author also of a number of books attempting to relate biology to culture in general: *The Scientific Attitude* (1941); *The Ethical Animal* (1960); *The Nature of Life* (1961). Presently preparing *Behind Appearance,* a full-scale treatment of the relations between painting and the natural sciences in this century.

Designed by the arts staff, George Braziller, Inc.
Printed in offset by Connecticut Printers, Inc., Hartford, Conn.